DIVIDED IMAGE

DIVIDED IMAGE

A STUDY OF
WILLIAM BLAKE AND W. B. YEATS

by

MARGARET RUDD

ROUTLEDGE & KEGAN PAUL LTD

Broadway House, 68–74 Carter Lane

London

First published in 1953
by Routledge & Kegan Paul Ltd
Broadway House, 68–74 Carter Lane
London, E.C.4
Made and printed in Great Britain
by William Clowes and Sons Limited
London and Beccles

Eternity shuddered when they saw
Man begetting his likeness
On his own divided image.

The First Book of Urizen, p. 696, BLAKE

ACKNOWLEDGEMENTS

I WOULD like to thank Mrs. Yeats who put much kindness and material at my disposal, and Dr. Oliver Edwards who introduced me to Mrs. Yeats and to Mr. Joseph Hone. I am grateful to Mr. Hone for his interest and for putting me in touch with Mr. T. R. Henn who very kindly sent me the first draft of his book on Yeats. Other critics of both Blake and Yeats have been most helpful commentators, although I do not know them personally.

Above all I would like to thank Professor H. A. Hodges who was unfailingly available with intellectual stimulus and moral support.

Mr. George Goyder's collection of Blake drawings and paintings has been invaluable as have been more public collections.

There are many other friends I would like to thank for taking an interest while I wrote this book, particularly Father Victor White, O.P., and W. W. Robson, both of whom read the M.S. and made valuable comments.

A very special debt of gratitude is to the American Association of University Women without whose two generous Fellowships I could not have done this study.

M. E. R.

CONTENTS

INTRODUCTION

IT is perhaps as well to start by saying what I have *not* attempted to do in this study. There have been many valuable books on Yeats published recently, all of them chiefly concerned with presenting the available biographical data. Although indebted to these authors and to the kindness of Mrs. Yeats, this study is not a rival to the biographies. Indeed, it lacks much of the human warmth of such material in the bulk, and can only assume the richness as a background. Nor have I been concerned very much with textual criticism, except in one or two instances. The lack of these two concrete themes, and the very—shall we say 'fantastic'?—nature of the inquiry, leaves one more than a little open to such mild criticism as,

> *I do like a room with a floor;*
> *I don't mind about walls and a door,*
> *But this walking around*
> *With both feet off the ground*
> *Is getting to be quite a bore.*

Nevertheless, the risk must be run in the belief that Yeats' extraordinary hero-worship of his 'master' Blake can shed much light on what is obscure in Yeats' own 'philosophy' and in his psychological make-up. Although I have tried not to use the jargon of psychology, of necessity the approach is as much psychological as literary or philosophical. It is frankly Christian, as was that of Yeats' authority, Blake, which is perhaps useful in providing a yard-stick. It is vision, mystical vision, that Yeats longed to win in imitating Blake, and it is vision that we are examining in this study. Too often this leaves me talking about what a poem *says* rather than what it *is*. I am well aware of this danger.

Since such a discussion verges on to the dangerous and slippery no-man's-land of complex intangible ideas and relations, it is necessary to have the firm ground of defined terms. In these realms, where contrasts become confusions and words slip and slide and shift in an effort to embrace too much, clarification is essential.

'Mysticism' is perhaps the most misunderstood and misused word of all those to be defined. In modern popular usage, mysticism is used as a term of reproach and disapproval by the practical man. If he does not identify it with the unthinkable 'queerness' of asceticism, it tends to signify to him something altogether too misty and vague, something uncomfortably mysterious and intangible: as Huxley punned, 'misty schism'. This misuse may result from the fact that 'mystical' has always been used loosely to indicate anything that has depth beyond a surface meaning, as emblematic of something not stated but suggested. Hence, too, all poetry—in fact, all art that embodies moments of profound insight—has been termed, in this widest and too vague sense of the word, mystical.

Another modern misconception is to confuse mysticism with ancient mysteries and secret rites which were pagan and semi-magical in character. As a result, mysticism becomes erroneously associated with magical practices in general. This is the most dangerous misunderstanding.

The dictionary rather cautiously defines mysticism as follows:

'The doctrine that ultimate reality is revealed through a special mode of knowledge, which is distinct from perceptual and ideational cognition and is superior to them. Popular usage—view that certain events are supernatural, i.e. that they occur in violation of the knowable principles of the working of nature.'

This is all right so far as it goes. It does not make clear, however, that what the mystic desires above all is to be united with God after a period of discipline that frees him as much as possible from the limitations of natural causation. 'God', 'unity', and 'discipline' are the key words in a definition of mysticism in its precise sense, and it should only be used in this strict sense, as there are other words to cover what people mean when they use 'mystic' loosely or incorrectly.

The factor of a personal God cannot be over-emphasized in this relation of man to ultimate reality which we call mysticism. Many writers have gone astray in thinking that discipline and the desire to be united with some invisible force—be it abstract Beauty, the Good, or the Soul of the World—constituted a fair definition of mysticism. But such a definition would cover alchemy or magic, and magic is antithetical to mysticism. Such a definition is still too wide.

INTRODUCTION

To underline the contrast between mysticism and magic, and at the same time to define mysticism correctly, we can do no better than to quote Nicolas Berdyaev:

'Above all we must make a radical distinction between mysticism and magic. These spheres are totally different but are easily confused, for while the nature of mysticism is spiritual that of magic is naturalistic. Mysticism is union with God, magic with the spirits of nature and its elemental forces. Mysticism is the sphere of liberty, magic of necessity. Mysticism is detached and contemplative, magic is active and militant; it reveals the secret forces of humanity and of the world without being able to reach the depths of their divine origin. Mystical experience constitutes precisely a spiritual deliverance from the magic of the natural world, for we are fettered to this magic without always recognizing it. Mysticism is compared to magic because of the existence of a pseudo-mysticism. There are two types of such false mysticism, one naturalistic, the other psychological. But neither of them are effective means of reaching the real depths of the world of nature and of the soul. The only true mysticism is that of the spirit, in which a false magic and a false psychologism are both avoided. It is only in the depths of spiritual experience that man attains to God and passes beyond the limits of the natural and physical world.'[1]

The nature of magic may be deduced from this quotation, but just to make sure, I quote the staid authority of Webster's:

'Magic—the art or body of arts which pretends, or is believed to produce effects by the assistance of supernatural beings or departed spirits, or by a mastery of secret forces in nature . . . magical practices depended on the discovery of and interpretation of . . . correspondences which were occult or hidden from the popular ken. By the exercise of the will, by the careful observation of minute ceremonial rules, by the solemn enunciation of formulas . . . by a host of similar performances, the sorcerer tries to interpret the past and influence the future to control the forces of nature. . . . Magic grows out of the theory of causation.'

The prophet is, more specifically, 'one inspired or instructed by God to speak in his name, announcing future events.' He differs from the mystic only in emphasis, and not in kind. He is in just as violent

[1] N. Berdyaev, *Freedom and the Spirit*, p. 241.

opposition to the magician. He, too, may follow the mystic discipline of the spirit, learning to fasten first his imagination, then his intellect, then his affections, and finally his will upon God—not so much to become one with God as to be a fit earthly vehicle for God's Word. The Word is revealed to him in apocalyptic vision. The Apocalyptic is the prophet writ large. After *The Book of Revelation* the Christian apocalyptic tradition lost its intensity, although it bursts out vividly like a flame in isolated spots throughout the centuries: it is a very highly specialized form of prophecy, having traditional machinery such as the angel commentator, the symbolic beasts and the four-square city of Jerusalem. As orthodoxy will not easily accept a mystic, so again it is at first hesitant to accept the prophet who, by the very nature of revelation, brings something new to challenge the established. And there are, indeed, false prophets.

Yeats uses the term 'saint' synonymously with the term 'mystic' —summing up, as it were, all the highest achievements of men who have dedicated their lives to God.

This is not as wrong as it might appear, and though quite aware of subtler distinctions, I will use it as such unless otherwise indicated. More specifically, the word 'saint' has grown, from its New Testament sense of meaning anyone baptized, the dedicated people, as it were, to denote the growth of holiness, and finally to mean those who are outstandingly holy.

'Saint' is then a wider term than 'mystic', since the essence of mysticism is the conscious cultivation of the inner life. Mysticism is the introverted way of being holy. The Hindu would say that the first implies the second. The Christian would not. There is an introverted and an extroverted way of holiness. 'Saint' covers both, while mystic is merely the former. Some saints are mystics, others are not. The introverted saint treads the mystical way.

Very often revealed truth comes to prophets, mystics and saints in the form of visions. Frequently these chosen men are of the psychological type known as 'visionary'. However, it must be understood that a visionary is merely a person who belongs to a special psychological type, and that the capacity to see visions does not make one a prophet or mystic. Nor is it absolutely necessary that all mystics and prophets be visionaries. In fact, the mystic who sees only in terms of strong visual images may be one who is only on the lowest rung of the mystical ladder, where images crowd the psyche and the would-be mystic has not yet learned to fasten his imagination on God. On the other hand, the disciplined mystic may at the end, like St. Teresa, receive the revelation of truth in the form of vivid images.

One who is a visionary is, then, no more than one whose psychological make-up causes him to think in terms of images which seem more clear than objective reality. With it usually goes the tendency to read symbolical meanings into these visions.

Before going on to the main discussion, it is well to note G. K. Chesterton's wise little remark:

'A poet may be vague, but a mystic hates vagueness. A poet is a man who mixes up heaven and earth unconsciously. A mystic is a man who separates heaven and earth even if he enjoys them both.'[1]

[1] G. K. Chesterton, *William Blake*, p. 4.

Chapter One

THE PROPHET AND THE ENCHANTER

~~~~~~~~~~~~~~~~~~~~~~~~~~~~~~~~~~~~~

> Grant me an old man's frenzy.
> Myself must I remake
> Til I am . . . William Blake
> Who beat upon the wall
> Til Truth obeyed his call.[1]

THESE lines written by a seventy-year-old 'smiling public man', the first poet of his time, are strangely revealing. Roughly forty-five years earlier this poet was collaborating with Edwin Ellis to bring out a new edition of Blake's poems and illustrations. The poems were accompanied by two thick volumes of interpretation. Yeats, the young Irish poet, acknowledged Blake his master.

In his personal copy of the three-volumed Blake edition Yeats has written a paragraph invaluable in showing how much of the interpretation is his:

'The writing of this book is mainly Ellis', the thinking is as much mine as his. The biography is by him. He rewrote and trebled in size a biography of mine. The greater part of the "symbolic system" is my writing, and the rest of the book was written by Ellis working over short accounts of the books by me except in the case of the "literary period", the account of the minor poems and the account of Blake's art theories which are all his own except insofar as we discussed everything together. W.B.Y. May 3, 1900.'

This interpretation, to all intents and purposes his own version of Blake, had such a profound influence on Yeats, that at the age of

[1] Yeats, *Last Poems and Plays*, NYC, 1940, p. 17.

seventy we find him still Blake's disciple and hoping to fashion himself in Blake's image. This is particularly interesting since Yeats throughout his long life, and even before formulating his theory of Self and Anti-Self, was continually adopting one pose or another in an effort to construct a Mask or anti-self 'in all things opposite to the natural self' which is vulnerable and secret. The devotion to the image of Blake and what Blake stands for is the one stable factor in this search for both the true self and the anti-self, and as such, the significance of the relationship hardly needs stressing.

In fact, it seems more than likely that Blake had as much to do with the hidden contained self as with the bravado of the Mask. It was necessary for Yeats the poet to believe that the secret self which saw or tried to see visions and imaginings and which lived in what Mallarmé called 'le passage intérieur', was superior to the self living in the external world of newspapers and mediocrity where one must play a role or be lost. And it is evident that in Blake Yeats found authority not only for the glorification of imagination rather than the world of action, but for seeking a poetically spectacular form of Christian mysticism which, in more orthodox and unpoetic forms, repelled as much as it attracted him. In Blake he found too the crusading artist brandishing a spiritual sword—Blake the poet and visionary, but also a fierce prophet and a pugnaciously solid man of action who, when necessary, could run mediocrity—symbolized by an abusive soldier—with firmness out of his garden, or could go for forty-mile walks when his visions had tired him. Blake more than any other—more than Swift or Lear, Donne or O'Leary—combined qualities that belonged to both the man of action and to the dreamer, the swordsman and the saint, the enchanter and the mystic, and as such seemed a fusion of the self and anti-self, the man and the mask. And Yeats wanted above all, to be like Blake.

To examine the relationship of Blake to Yeats is to throw new light on the apparent paradoxes of Yeats, but it is also to let oneself in for a number of subtle distinctions that may, in Yeats' case, be confusions. Such as—did Yeats really see the difference between magic and mysticism, or did he confuse the two? For indeed it does seem strange to speak of Blake beating like a magician 'upon the wall till Truth obeyed his call', Blake who pleaded:

> Trembling I sit day and night . . .
> I rest not from my great task
> To open the Eternal Worlds, to open the Immortal Eyes

Of Man inwards into the Worlds of Thought, into Eternity
Ever expanding in the Bosom of God, the Human Imagination.
O Saviour pour upon me thy spirit of meekness and love!
Annihilate the selfhood in me; be thou all my life!
Guide thou my hand, which trembles exceedingly.[1]

Nor is there 'beating upon the wall' in the following lines, but a rushing and joyous acceptance of the suffering that must dog the footsteps of God's prophet:

Eternals! I hear your call gladly.
Dictate swift winged words and fear not
To unfold your dark visions of torment.[2]

What, then, we may ask, is Yeats' interpretation of Blake, for he wished to resemble Blake as he himself saw him. Does it have anything to do with the Blake who speaks in the passage above? And was Yeats conscious of the distinctions involved, or does he base his whole interpretation on confusions? This is the sort of question to ask and try to answer. An interesting problem is thus presented by Yeats himself. We are invited to examine and compare him with Blake, to set the two artists side by side and measure the modern Irish poet against the poet, painter and visionary, William Blake.

And the first step, I should think, is to clarify how each of the two poets presented himself to the world—what 'Mask', as Yeats would say, he most frequently wore.

*　　*　　*　　*　　*

Hear the voice of the Bard!
Who Present, Past and Future, sees;
Whose ears have heard
The Holy Word
That walked among the ancient trees,

Calling the lapsed Soul
And weeping in the evening dew;
That might controll
The starry pole,
And fallen, fallen light renew![3]

[1] Blake, *The Complete Poetry of William Blake*, NYC, 1946, p. 896.
[2] *Ibid.*, p. 686   [3] *Ibid.*, p. 547

Hear again the voice of the Bard, the prophetic Blake!

> *In futurity*
> *I prophetic see*
> *That the earth from sleep*
> *(Grave the sentence deep)*
>
> *Shall arise and seek*
> *For her maker meek;*
> *And the desert wild*
> *Become a garden mild.*[1]

Time and again Blake insists that his work is 'a Bard's prophetic Song',[2] crying 'Mark well my words! They are of your eternal salvation . . . I am Inspired I know it is Truth! for I Sing According to the inspiration of the Poetic Genius who is the eternal all-protecting Divine Humanity.'[3] Nothing in this of beating upon the wall till Truth obey his call! Rather, Christ Himself is the Poetic Genius who dictates words of eternal salvation to Blake. And therefore, Poetic Genius or Imagination is also Eternity. Through Imagination, we, living in the land of 'unbelief and fear', can reach a state of mind that is Heaven-on-earth, earth transformed. Single vision is death-in-life, Fourfold vision is Eternity. Blake is the prophet of Eternity. He pleads for words to express his vision:

> *. . . I see the Saviour over me*
> *Spreading his beams of love and dictating the words of this mild song . . .*
> *'Awake! awake O sleeper of the land of shadows, wake, expand!*
> *I am in you and you in me, mutual in love divine.'*
> *. . . O Lord my saviour, open thou the Gates*
> *And I will lead forth thy Words.*[4]

A perfect expression of *agape*, and a conviction of mystical experience are strong in these lines. Yet the emphasis is as much on the prophetic element, on the fact that it is Blake himself who must reveal the words of his God to the sleepers of 'the land of shadows'. It is he who must proclaim God's will for the future, that 'fallen, fallen light renew'.

Blake is undoubtedly convinced that he is a true mystic and the Prophet of Christ who is the only God. But he is also the Bard, and

---

[1] Blake, *The Complete Poetry of William Blake*, NYC, 1946, p. 550.
[2] *Ibid.*, p. 839.   [3] *Ibid.*, p. 852.   [4] *Ibid.*, pp. 894, 988.

so must identify Poet and Prophet. There seems in his case little of
the feeling that poet and mystic are incompatible, the one plunging
himself into the world perhaps with the hope of tapping the great
mystery beyond, the other denying the world and passing through
a period of asceticism until he can affirm by Grace the vision of earth
transfigured. From the beginning Blake equates the two, and though
at times they are in a state of considerable tension, he does not deny
the one in favour of the other, but rather maintains a precarious
balance, perhaps because the tension is not so much in himself, as
focused outside himself upon the figure of Christ.

It is inevitable, then, that Blake should identify the highest
Imagination or Poetic Genius with Christ, and so can say that
'Christianity is Art'[1] and 'Imagination is Eternity'.[2] However, he
himself elaborates upon these gnomic and startling contractions:

'I know of no other Christianity, and of no other Gospel than the
liberty of both body and mind to exercise the Divine Arts of the
Imagination, Imagination, the real and eternal World of which this
Vegetable Universe is but a faint Shadow, and in which we shall live
in our Eternal or Imaginative Bodies when these Vegetable Mortal
Bodies are no more ... What are all the gifts of the Gospel, are they
not all Mental Gifts? Is God a Spirit who must be worshipped in
Spirit and in Truth, and are not the Gifts of the Spirit Every Thing
to Man? O ye Religious, discountenance every one among you who
shall pretend to despise Art and Science! I call upon you in the name
of Jesus! ... Let every Christian, as much as in him lies, engage himself openly and publicly before all the World in some Mental pursuit
for the Building up of Jerusalem.'[3]

Of course, by Mental, Blake means imaginative. He goes on:

'A Poet, a Painter, a Musician, an Architect: the Man or Woman
who is not one of these is not a Christian.
You must leave Fathers and Mothers and Houses and Lands if they
stand in the way of Art.
Prayer is the Study of Art.
Praise is the Practise of Art.
Fasting, etc., all relate to Art.
The outward Ceremony is Antichrist.

[1] Blake, *The Complete Poetry of William Blake*, NYC, 1946, p. 1024.
[2] *Ibid.*, p. 1026.   [3] *Ibid.*, p. 989.

The Eternal Body of Man is The Imagination, that is,
God himself 〕
The Divine Body 〕 Jesus; we are his Members.
It manifests itself in his Works of Art (In Eternity All is Vision).'[1]

These passages define briefly the core of Blake's teaching, religious
and æsthetic. They are the dogmatic statements of a prophet who is
preaching what he has received in mystical vision. No matter how
complex become Blake's myths concerning Man's fall from Grace,
his experience and error in this vegetable universe, and the slow road
back to eternity—these points are the skeleton or framework.
For the moment we will consider only passages which prove that
Blake thought of himself as the Prophet, the artist who is secretary
to the supernatural, who is their instrument to rouse the human race
from complacent torpor, that it may awaken to Eternity.
Blake's letters are particularly interesting in showing the difficulties which stood in the way of the Prophet, and how stead-
fast he was to his vocation when it seemed to deny him every
material advantage. In one letter to the Reverend J. Trusler who had
ordered several designs with directions concerning their subject
matter and execution, Blake apologizes for not carrying out the
instructions:

'Revd. Sir,
I find more and more that my style of designing is a species by
itself, and in this which I send you have been compelled by my
Genius or Angel to follow where he led; . . . I could not do otherwise; it was out of my power! . . . And though I call them (designs)
mine, I know that they are not Mine, being of the same opinion
with Milton when he says that the Muse visits his slumbers and
awakes and governs his song when the Morn purples the East,
and being also in the predicament of that prophet who says: "I
can not go beyond the command of the Lord, to speak good or
bad." '[2]

The Reverend Trusler rejected the design with a letter full of harsh
criticisms of Blake, pointing out disgustedly that Blake's fancy seems
to be in the 'other world, or the world of spirits, which accords not
with my intentions, which, whilst living in this world, wish to

[1] Blake, *The Complete Poetry of William Blake*, NYC, 1946, p. 1023.
[2] *The Letters of William Blake*, London, 1906, p. 57.

follow the nature of it.'[1] Blake relates this episode in a letter to George Cumberland, and adds drily: 'I could not help smiling at the difference between the doctrines of Dr. Trusler and those of Christ.'[2] And in his defence to the Reverend Trusler Blake writes his famous view of Nature as Imagination or Christ Himself for those who have eyes to see. But this view, which is a momentary plunge into four-fold vision, does not keep Blake at other times from falling into the dualism of regarding nature as evil and to be renounced.

'I see everything I paint in this world, but everybody does not see alike. To the eyes of a miser a guinea is far more beautiful than the sun, and a bag worn with the use of money has more beautiful proportions than a vine filled with grapes. The tree which moves some to tears of joy is in the eyes of others only a green thing which stands in the way. Some see Nature all ridicule and deformity, and by these I shall not regulate my proportions; and some scarce see Nature at all. But to the eyes of the man of imagination, Nature is Imagination itself. As a man is, so he sees.'[3]

This letter, reposing in the Reverend Trusler's desk, was found marked by a note in the vicar's hand—'Blake, dim'd with superstition.'

The Rev'd. Sir would most certainly have thrown up his hands in horror had he seen the letter of sympathy Blake wrote to Haley when his son was dead:

'Thirteen years ago I lost a brother and with his spirit I converse daily and hourly in the spirit, and see him in my remembrance, in the regions of my imagination. I hear his advice and even now write from his dictate. Forgive me for expressing to you my enthusiasm, which I wish all to partake of, since to me it is a source of immortal joy, even in this world. By it I am the companion of angels.'[4]

And Blake writes to Thomas Butts about the mental heights and depths of the prophet:

'If I myself omit one duty to my station as soldier of Christ, it gives me the greatest of torments. I am not ashamed, afraid, or adverse to tell you what ought to be told: that I am under the direction of messengers from heaven, daily and nightly. But the

---

[1] *The Letters of William Blake*, London, 1906, p. 65.
[2] *Ibid.*, p. 65. [3] *Ibid.*, p. 62. [4] *Ibid.*, p. 68.

nature of such things is not, as some suppose, without trouble or care. Temptations are on the right hand and on the left. Behind, the sea of time and space roars and follows swiftly. He who keeps not right onwards is lost; and if our footsteps slide in the clay, how can we do otherwise than fear and tremble? But I should not have troubled you . . . for I never obtrude such things on others unless questioned, and then I never disguise the truth. But if we fear to do the dictates of our angels and tremble at the tasks set before us; if we refuse to do spiritual acts because of natural fears and natural desires, who can describe the dismal torments of such a state? I too well remember the threats I heard!—"If you, who are organized by Divine Providence for spiritual communion, refuse, and bury your talent in the earth . . . sorrow and desperation pursue you through life, and after death shame and confusion to eternity" . . . and now let me finish with assuring you that, though I have been very unhappy, I am so no longer. I am again emerged into the light of day; I still and shall to eternity embrace Christianity and adore Him who is the express image of God; but I have travelled through perils and darkness not unlike a champion. I have conquered and shall go on conquering. Nothing can withstand the fury of my course among the stars of God and the abysses of the accuser. My enthusiasm is still what it was, only enlarged and confirmed.'[1]

This lest we think of Blake always as the happy visionary.

No one reading Blake's account of his Dark Night, I feel sure, could argue that he was not firmly convinced that, cost what it may, he was God's prophet. Nor could these passages be called obscure, or anything but a subtle and lucid statement of a difficult state of mind. And the last passage shows, contrary to the mental picture most people have of Blake the happy mystic, that Blake had to fight doubts and despairs of the most torturous kind, and often without apparent cause—'I begin to emerge from a deep pit of melancholy—melancholy without any real reason—a disease which God keep you from.'[2]

The literary and prophetic result of this Dark Night was the poem *Milton* which Blake wrote:

'entirely from immediate dictation, twelve or sometimes twenty or thirty lines at a time, without premeditation and even against my

---

[1] *The Letters of William Blake*, London, 1906, p. 101.   [2] *Ibid.*, p. 70.

will. The time it has taken in writing was thus rendered non-existent, and an immense poem exists which seems to be the labour of a long life, all produced without labour or study . . . my heart is full of futurity . . . I will go on in the strength of the Lord; through Hell will I sing forth his praises; that the dragons may praise Him, and that those who dwell in darkness and in the seacoasts may be gathered into His kingdom.'[1]

If, then, the poet and the prophet are one and the same, the moment of prophetic revelation must be one with the moment of poetic vision. Although Blake claimed to have written down the words exactly as they were dictated by the supernaturals, he knew very well the importance of the significant moment in which imagination is busy at its shaping, the moment when the poet's work is done:

> Then Eno, a daughter of Beulah, took a Moment of Time
> And drew it out to seven thousand years with much care and affliction
> And many tears, and in every year made windows into Eden.
> She also took an atom of space and open'd its centre
> Into Infinitude and ornamented it with wondrous art . . .
> Every Time less than a pulsation of the artery
> Is equal in its period and value to Six Thousand Years,
> For in this Period the Poet's Work is Done, and all the Great
> Events of Time start forth and are conceived in such a Period,
> Within a Moment, a Pulsation of the Artery.[2]

Exactly how much Blake did shape and select with his imagination is a question which is better left for a while. What is certain, however, is that in the earlier poems and in all his designs Blake shaped and reshaped his work to a considerable extent. 'Execution is the chariot of genius',[3] he maintained, and in theory believed that 'Every poem must necessarily be a perfect Unity'. Even in the long and confusing prophetic book of Jerusalem which shows little sign of an artistic unity and selection, there is at least an attempt to channel his vision into poetic form: 'When this Verse was first dictated to me, I considered a Monotonous Cadence . . .'[4] In the later writings Blake was first of all the prophet, secondarily, the poet and

---

[1] The Letters of William Blake, London, 1906, p. 116.
[2] The Complete Poetry of William Blake, pp. 723, 874.
[3] Ibid., p. 1025.   [4] Ibid., p. 894.

9

craftsman. His discipline was mainly that of the mystical way, not the creative labour of the artist. He recorded messages from the unseen, and made little attempt at communication as the years passed and more and more visions of complex truth flooded over him.

In painting, engraving, and design Blake was more consistently and consciously the craftsman whose work was the chariot of genius and prophecy. He was eager to learn and to experiment with new techniques and to perfect them by practice. This is probably because in psychological type he was a visionary. To keep his sanity, he may have found it necessary *actively* to distance or externalize the vivid looming images inside his brain, so much more intense than outside life. It may have been imperative to distance those truths which came by looking 'with, not through the Eye'.

Thus we find Blake in his letters speaking frequently in the most practical terms about the merits, costs, and labour involved in the various tools of his art. The following passage—Blake's instructions for transferring a drawing to a metal plate for engraving—shows how very much in touch with practical matters he could be:

'As to laying on the wax, it is as follows:
Take a cake of virgin wax (I don't know what animal produces it), and stroke it regularly over the surface of a warm plate (the plate must be warm enough to melt the wax as it passes over), then immediately draw a feather over it, and you will get an even surface which, when cold will receive any impression minutely.

Note—The danger is in not covering the plate *all over*. . . . The pressure necessary to roll off the lines is the same as when you print, or not quite so great. I have not been able to send a proof of the bath, though I have done the corrections, my paper not being in order.'[1]

Until he is perfect enough to record the highest spiritual truths Blake says, 'I will leave no stone unturned and no path unexplored that leads to improvement in my beloved arts.'[2] He is pleased about his return from the country to London not only because 'I can alone carry on my visionary studies in London unannoyed, and that I may converse with my friends in eternity, see visions, dream dreams, and prophesy and speak parables unobserved and at liberty from the doubts of other mortals'[3] but because too 'I ought not to be away

[1] *The Letters of William Blake*, p. 54.   [2] *Ibid.*, p. 88.   [3] *Ibid.*, p. 114.

from the opportunities London affords of seeing fine pictures, and the various improvements in works of art going on in London.'[1] There is something touching about these mild wants, and certainly no hint of the seeker of spectacular effects.

Blake had definite opinions about various styles in painting. How he hated the fuzzy technique and chiaroscuro of the Venetians! And because of the same psychological characteristic that causes him to be called mad, Blake developed a unique artistic style of his own. This style depended upon what he calls the 'wirey bounding line', the precision of outline which defined the shapes he saw in vision and made them more clear than natural objects. For the sake of this clarity he insists not only upon the wirey bounding line but upon Minute Particulars:

'Art and Science cannot exist but in minutely organized Particulars and not in generalizing Demonstrations of the Rational Power. The Infinite alone resides in Definite and Determinate Identity.'[2]

And because he was called mad for this theory of art, Blake writes an ironical little poem:

> All pictures that's Painted with Sense and with Thought
> Are painted by Madmen as sure as a Groat;
> For the Greater the Fool in the Pencil more blest,
> And when they are drunk they always paint best.
> They never can Rafael it, Fuseli it, nor Blake it;
> If they can't see an outline, pray how can they make it?
> When Men will draw outlines begin you to jaw them;
> Madmen see outlines and therefore they draw them.[3]

Blake the artist has suffered much from the belief that Blake the prophet was mad. As a curiosity Blake attracts many, but his message is often as not dismissed with a shrug and a laugh. On the other hand, many find Blake's words uncomfortable, and question Blake's honesty in saying that he received his truths in mystical vision. These critics, oddly enough, attack him on the practical grounds of style and technique.

[1] *The Letters of William Blake*, p. 115.
[2] *The Complete Poetry of William Blake*, p. 961.
[3] *Ibid*, p. 1038.

II

G. K. Chesterton answers the question of the first group—'Was Blake mad?'—with practical good sense:

'It is easy enough to say, of course, in the non-committal modern manner that it all depends on how you define madness. If you mean it in its practical or legal sense (which is perhaps the most really useful sense of all), if you mean was William Blake unfit to look after himself, unable to exercise civic functions or to administer property, then certainly the answer is "No". Blake was a citizen, and capable of being a very good citizen. Blake, so far from being incapable of managing property, was capable (in so far as he chose) of collecting a great deal of it. His conduct was generally business-like; and when it was unbusiness-like it was not through any sub-human imbecility or superhuman abstraction, but generally through an unmixed exhibition of very human bad temper. Again, if when we say "Was Blake mad?" we mean was he fundamentally morbid, was his soul cut off from the universe and merely feeding on itself, then again the answer is emphatically "No". There was nothing defective about Blake; he was in contact with all the songs and smells of the universe, and he was entirely guiltless of that one evil element which is almost universal in the character of the morbidly insane—I mean secrecy. Yet again, if we mean by madness anything inconsistent or unreasonable, then Blake was not mad. Blake was one of the most consistent men that ever lived . . . on the basis of his own theory of things. . . . In all these aspects we can say with confidence that the man was not at least obviously mad or completely mad. *But* if we ask whether there was not some madness about him, whether his naturally just mind was not subject to some kind of disturbing influence which was not essential to itself, then we ask a very different question, and require, unless I am mistaken, a very different answer.'[1]

And Chesterton makes another point in favour of Blake's sanity:

'There was nothing of the obviously fervid and futile about Blake's supernaturalism. It is not his frenzy but his coolness that was startling. From his first meeting with Ezekiel under the tree he always talked of such spirits in an everyday intonation. There was plenty of pompous supernaturalism in the eighteenth century; but Blake's was the only natural supernaturalism. Many reputable persons reported miracles; he only mentioned them. He spoke of having

[1] G. K. Chesterton, *Wiillam Blake*, London, p. 71.

met Isaiah or Queen Elizabeth, not so much even as if the fact were indisputable, but rather as if so simple a thing were not worth disputing. Kings and prophets came from heaven or hell to sit to him, and he complained of them quite casually, as if they were troublesome professional models. . . . His private life, as he laid its foundations in his youth, had the same indescribable element; it was a sort of abrupt innocence.'[1]

And it was a sort of fierce and practical humour as well that helped him to keep his balance as he walked the thin tightrope between genius and madness. Blake is the only man who had enough common sense to insist that Tom Paine flee the country. But Blake himself wandered through the London streets wearing the red cap of freedom. It was Blake who taught his wife how to see visions, and Blake who spent time and labour perfecting new techniques of printing. And he is the man who, quite unlike the uncontrolled madman, could give vent to quite justified anger at his dull-witted patron, often humorously and in his private notebook:

> Thy Friendship oft has made my heart to ake:
> Do be my Enemy for Friendship's sake.[2]

or:

> I write the Rascal Thanks till he and I
> With Thanks and Compliments are quite drawn dry.[3]

And perhaps Blake's own epigrammatic verses on the question of whether he was mad should be allowed to give evidence for once, especially as they reveal the dull misunderstanding he had to put up with, and the sane humour with which he could retaliate. Surely it is the fate of any mystical genius who is also an innovator in art to be accused of madness. But how many could have borne direct attack by the bourgeois in mind, and even exploitation, as patiently as did Blake. A cry from the depths are the two lines:

> I found them blind: I taught them how to see;
> And now they know neither themselves nor me.[4]

[1] G. K. Chesterton, William Blake, London, p. 7.
[2] The Complete Poetry of William Blake, p. 1035.
[3] Ibid., p. 1038.   [4] Ibid., p. 1033.

And to Flaxman he writes:

> *You call me Mad: 'tis Folly to do so—*
> *To seek to turn a Madman to a Foe.*
> *If you think as you speak, you are an Ass.*
> *If you do not, you are but what you was.*[1]

Ungrammatical, but telling. He manages always to fling the joke back at the accusers:

> *When Men will draw outlines begin you to jaw them;*
> *Madmen see outlines and therefore they draw them.*

But there are bitter moments of anger, nevertheless spiced with rueful humour:

> *You see him spend his Soul in Prophecy.*
> *Do you believe it a confounded lie*
> *Till some Bookseller and the Public Fame*
> *Proves there is truth in his extravagant claim.*
>
> *For 'tis atrocious in a Friend you love*
> *To tell you any thing that he can't prove,*
> *And 'tis most wicked in a Christian Nation*
> *For any Man to pretend to Inspiration.*[2]

Continually stung by the small faith of those he thought his friends, Blake can at times only call them fools for mocking inspiration:

> *'Madman' I have been call'd: 'Fool' they call thee.*
> *I wonder which they Envy, Thee or Me?*[3]

or:

> *I mock thee not, tho' I by thee am Mocked.*
> *Thou call'st me Madman, but I call thee Blockhead.*[4]

Lonelier even than most artists, he had to retreat to his mountain-top, not to receive revelation which came to him at almost any time and in any place, but to escape the condemnation and insults of his fellow men:

> *Great things are done when Men and Mountains meet;*
> *This is not done by Jostling in the Street.*[5]

And so, whatever one thinks of Blake's sanity, the fact remains that

---

1 *The Complete Poetry of William Blake*, p. 1034. 2 *Ibid.*, p. 1040.
3 *Ibid.*, p. 1031. 4 *Ibid.*, p. 1031. 5 *Ibid.*, p. 1039.

Blake did indeed do great things on his mountain-top while his detractors, present and past, remain part of the undistinguished crowd 'Jostling in the Street'.

There are those, on the other hand, who do not level a charge of insanity against Blake, but rather deny him his mountain-top. The point of this game is to reduce Blake's visions to a set of dubious truths dressed up in a harlequin garb pieced together from the Old Masters by an artistic charlatan. Sceptical critics such as Anthony Blunt, not wishing to be disturbed by Blake's uncomfortably sincere mysticism, point out the similarity of some of Blake's drawings to old masters he may have known. Such critics make much of the fact that revisions and rough drafts of Blake's early poems are to be found, using this as proof that Blake did not write from 'dictation' or draw from visions. Mr. Blunt writes:

'curious is the case of Blake's most celebrated drawing, from his series of Visionary Heads. . . . Blake's mind was so soaked in works of art which he had studied, that these visions often took on forms reminiscent of existing works of art . . . when Blake was impressed by a figure in any work of art he seems to have absorbed it into his stock of visual images.'[1]

The implication is, of course, that Blake was not so much of a mystic and visionary as he would have us believe, but deliberately or as a pawn of his unconscious memory, took what was useful from other painters' work and presented it as spontaneous vision, a gift from the supernatural.

It might be noted in passing that however one draws the human figure, the attitude might be 'reminiscent' of a figure in some other painting without conscious or unconscious connection. And Mr. Blunt's argument must be carried one step further into the realm of psychology before so readily destroying Blake's claim to vision. A question must be asked of the psychologist about the relation of past influences to what the imagination 'sees'—in average people and in 'visionaries'. Is it a conscious relation, and does the fact that the vision may be presented in traditional terms lessen its authenticity?

The psychologist answers with a fact: the fact that most 'normal' people find that thoughts and images they believed to be spontaneous and original have, in truth, some ground in their forgotten

[1] A. Blunt, 'Blake's Pictorial Imagination', *Jnl. of Warburg and Courtauld Inst.*, vol. 6, 1943, p. 203.

past. The imagination must, of necessity, have past influences to build with as material, for the stock images of dream and fantasy soon prove a barren and familiar field. This is especially true of abnormally sensitive people whose imaginations are all the busier.

It follows that we must allow Blake—without criticism as we would allow any man—to use influences from his past in the creations of his imagination. In his case the influences were mostly artistic ones as art was more real to him than nature. And as he plainly says over and over again 'my world is imagination' he is also entitled to treat his visionary figures as real and original beings as undoubtedly they were to him. If one does not accept these visions as supernatural, they may be called hallucinations, but the important fact is that to Blake they were so real that he believed in them implicitly. Whether or not he modified them unconsciously or clothed them in traditional forms for the sake of communication is almost beside the point. There was nothing bogus about Blake's belief in his visions, although Mr. Blunt is right in believing that images from the past may have contributed something to their shape.

Blake was too much of an artist not to control his material to some extent. Hence the revisions and rough drafts and sketches. Probably the fact that he was an artist and could actively distance his visions by working out their expression saved him from insanity. For he seems often on the edge of the abyss, managing, through craftsmanship alone, to keep control of life. What psychology cannot explain is what makes such genius as his a genius in sum total adding up to much more than its past sensory experiences.

Leaving the question of Blake's sanity to return to Blake's interest in technique: Blake did painstakingly make copies of the Old Masters with whom he felt in sympathy—Michelangelo, Rafael, anything Gothic. 'For without Unceasing Practice nothing can be done. Practice is Art. If you leave off you are lost.'[1] He hated with energy the paintings of Sir Joshua Reynolds, Rubens, Rembrandt, and all classical forms, because of their dead ratios and lack of spiritual insight. Grecian is Mathematic Form: Gothic is Living Form. Mathematic Form is Eternal in the Reasoning Memory. Living Form is Eternal Existence.'[2] Although Blake could not abide

[1] *The Complete Poetry of William Blake*, p. 1024.
[2] *Ibid*, p. 1025

16

[handwritten margin notes: only spiritual art interested him — he found others dull]

the fuzzy style of the artists who are only concerned with nature, most of all he detested the earthbinding ratios and dogmas of Reason and the Natural Memory, both of which belong to Nature and not to Eternity. The apparent solidity of the natural world works as an illusion to fool people into thinking it reality, whereas they are in truth standing above an abyss and looking at what is a mere shadow of eternity.

The indefiniteness and the pantheistic mystery of Nature which these despised artists glorify has nothing to do with God but only with the false gods of witchcraft, magic, and Natural Religion:

> *The Ashes of Mystery began to animate: they called it Deism*
> *And Natural Religion; as of old, so anew began*
> *Babylon again in Infancy, call'd Natural Religion. . . .*
> *Denying in private, mocking God and Eternal Life, and in Public*
> *Collusion calling themselves Deists, Worshipping the Maternal*
> *Humanity, calling it Nature and Natural Religion.*
> *But still the thunder of Los peals aloud, and thus the thunders cry:*
> *'These beautiful Witchcrafts of Albion are gratified by Cruelty.'*[1]

The cruelty of witchcraft and the power-seeking quality of reasoning magic hold sway only where the worship of Nature and natural spirits takes the place of God; where people try to discover the hidden laws within the shifting dissolving boundaries of Nature, for the sake of gratifying their own love of power. Against this kind of magic Blake the prophet fights unceasingly whenever he opposes reason and misty indefiniteness in favour of the world of clearly defined spirit and imagination. The world of imagination does not shift and slide with the whims of the tyrant Reason, but is defined by the living and eternal 'wirey bounding line'. Blake clarifies this important distinction when he cries:

> 'What dost thou here, Elijah? Can a poet doubt the visions of Jehovah? Nature has no outline, but Imagination has. Nature has no tune, but Imagination has. Nature has no Supernatural and dissolves: Imagination is Eternity.'[2]

To fix once and for all this point that, contrary to popular belief, the true mystic, unlike the magician, insists on great precision and

---

[1] *The Complete Poetry of William Blake*, pp. 811, 1010.   [2] *Ibid.*, p. 1026.

clarity, it would be fitting to quote G. K. Chesterton's long but admirable comments:

'A verbal accident has confused the mystical with the mysterious. Mysticism is generally felt vaguely to be itself vague—a thing of clouds and curtains of darkness or concealing vapours, of bewildering conspiracies or impenetrable symbols. Some quacks have indeed dealt in such things: but no true mystic ever loved darkness rather than light. No pure mystic ever loved mere mystery. The mystic does not bring doubts and riddles: the doubts and riddles exist already. We all feel the riddle of the earth without anyone to point it out. The mystery of life is the plainest part of it. The clouds and curtains of darkness, the confounding vapours, these are the daily weather of this world. Whatever else we are accustomed to, we have grown accustomed to the unaccountable. Every stone or flower is a hieroglyphic of which we have lost the key; with every step of our lives we enter into the middle of some story which we are certain to misunderstand. The mystic is not the man who makes mysteries but the man who destroys them. The mystic is one who offers an explanation which may be true or false, but which is *always* comprehensible—by which I mean, not that it is always comprehended, but that it always can be comprehended, because there is always something to comprehend. The man whose meaning remains mysterious fails, I think, as a mystic: and Blake, as we shall see, did for certain peculiar reasons of his own, often fail in this way. But even when he was himself hard to be understood, it was never through himself not understanding: it was never because he was vague or mystified or groping, that he was unintelligible. While his utterance was not only dim but dense, his opinion was not only clear, but even cocksure. You and I may be a little vague about the relations of Albion to Jerusalem, but Blake is as certain about them as Mr. Chamberlain about the relations of Birmingham to the British Empire. And this can be said for his singular literary style even at his worst, that we always feel that he is saying something very plain and emphatic, even when we have not the wildest notion of what it is.

There is one element always to be remarked in the true mystic, however disputed his symbolism, and that is its brightness of colour and clearness of shape. I mean that we may be doubtful about the significance of a triangle or the precise lesson conveyed by a crimson

cow. But in the work of a real mystic the triangle is a hard mathematical triangle not to be mistaken for a cone or a polygon. The
cow is in colour a rich incurable crimson, and its shape is unques-
tionably a cow, not to be mistaken for any of its evolutionary rela-
tives, such as the buffalo or the bison. This can be seen very clearly,
for instance, in the Christian art of illumination as practised at
its best in the thirteenth and fourteenth centuries. The Christian
decorators being true mystics, were chiefly concerned to maintain
the reality of objects. For the highest dogma of the spiritual is to
affirm the material. By plain outline and positive colour these pious
artists strove chiefly to assert that a cat was truly in the eyes of God
a cat and that a dog was pre-eminently doggish. This decision
of tint and outline belongs not only to Blake's pictures, but
even to his poetry. Even in his description there is no darkness,
and practically, in the modern sense, no distance. All his animals
are as absolute as the animals on a shield of heraldry. His lambs
are of unsullied silver, his lions are of flaming gold. His lion
may lie down with his lamb, but he will never really mix with
him.'[1]

* * * * *

Blake by his own words is both Poet and Prophet, and thus
identifies poetry and mystical vision. This is clear enough from his
writings, and we would expect to find the young Yeats trying to
follow in his footsteps as closely as possible, for, as he says in his
autobiography: 'I had an unshakable conviction, arising how or
whence I cannot tell, that the invisible gates would open as they
had opened for Blake.'[2]

But to our surprise we find Yeats setting himself up as the magician, identifying poet and magician. This is in direct antithesis to
Blake's mysticism. Magic has to do with nature and nature spirits
and is what Blake condemned as Natural Religion, 'beautiful witch-
crafts', full of the allure of shifting dissolving outlines.

Nevertheless Yeats writes: 'Now as to Magic. It is a study which
I decided deliberately to make next to my poetry.'[3] Not only this,
but the claim that: 'If I had not made magic my constant study, I
could not have written a single word of my Blake book.' This is
very odd indeed: Yeats claiming to be Blake's disciple, yet also a

1 Chesterton, *William Blake*, p. 131.
2 Yeats, *Autobiography*, NYC, 1940, p. 218.
3 R. Ellman, *The Man and the Masks*, NYC, 1948, p. 94.

19

student of magic which he implies is necessary to the understanding of Blake. Magic is antithetical to mysticism. Blake was undoubtedly a mystic and Yeats knew it. This raises a host of questions.

Yeats not only is a student of magic, but identifies the enchanter with the poet. He draws up a magical creed:

'I believe in the practice and philosophy of what we have agreed to call magic, in what I must call the evocation of spirits, though I do not know what they are, in the power of creating magical illusions . . . and I believe in the doctrines, which have, as I think, been handed down from early times, and been the foundation of nearly all magical practices. These doctrines are—

(1) That the borders of our minds are ever shifting, and that many minds can flow into one another, as it were, and create or reveal a single mind, a single energy.

(2) That the borders of our memories are as shifting, and that our memories are a part of one great memory, the memory of Nature herself.

(3) That this great mind and great memory can be evoked by symbols.'[1]

Yeats adds:

'Why should not that medieval enchanter have made summer and all its blossoms seem to break forth in middle winter? May we not learn some day to rewrite our histories, when they touch upon these things? Men who are imaginative writers today may well have preferred to influence the imaginations of others more directly in past times. Instead of learning their craft with paper and a pen they may have sat for hours imagining themselves to be sticks and stones and beasts of the wood, till the images were so vivid that passers-by became but a part of the imagination of the dreamer, and wept or laughed or ran away as he would have them. Have not poetry and music arisen, as it seems, out of the sounds the enchanters made to help their imaginations to enchant, to charm, to bind with a spell themselves and the passers-by?'[2]

and elaborates:

'I cannot now think symbols less than the greatest of all powers,

---

[1] Yeats, *Essays*, London, 1924, p. 33.   [2] *Ibid.*, p. 52.

when they are used consciously by the masters of magic, or half-unconsciously by their successors, the poet, the musician, and the artist. . . . Whatever the passions of great men have gathered about becomes a symbol in the great memory, and in the hands of him who has the secret, it is a worker of wonders, a caller up of angels or of devils.'[1]

It is interesting to remember, in contrast, Blake's words about 'a Poet, a Painter, a Musician . . . the Man or Woman who is not one of these is not a Christian.'

It is significant that during the years Yeats was at work on his Blake book, he was also consciously developing his doctrine of magic and poetry, and his writings show the beginning of his theory of self and anti-self. On January 30, 1889, Yeats met Maud Gonne, and love became one of the themes weaving in and out of his books and his life, not sure to which it belonged. Much of the close association of these ideas in his mind must stem from this time factor. Ellman says of these crowded confusing years:

'Of all periods of Yeats' life the years from 1889 to 1903 are the most difficult to follow. He has so many interests and activities during this time, with so little obvious relation between them, that a strictly chronological account would give the impression of a man in a frenzy, beating on every door in the hotel in an attempt to find his own room. But while he was somewhat confused, the maze was not without a plan, a clue to which can be found in his increasing self-consciousness. His inclination, which had begun much earlier, to pose before the world as something different from what he was, to hide his secret self, had come to a point where he saw himself divided into two parts.'[2]

This frenzied search plus Yeats' pose as the magician raises another question: What did Yeats want from magic?

To accept the doctrine of magic, as Yeats does, implies the desire for an infinite power of mind to wield over nature. But Yeats showed no signs during his life of wishing to exercise such a power in any practical way as did the alchemists, Faust, and all true sorcerers. He seemed to want nothing more than an affirmation of the invisible by some sort of manifestation, some kind of vision. Still

[1] Yeats, *Essays*, London, 1924, p. 60.
[2] Ellman, *The Man and the Masks*, p. 70.

another question comes to mind—if Yeats wanted not practical power but spiritual knowledge, why did he not turn to religion instead of to magic, which would bring him much closer to his master, Blake?

This last question is in part answered by the following argument, which he puts forth in *Per Amica Silentia Lunæ*:

'All souls have a vehicle or body, and when one has said that, with More and the Platonists one has escaped from the abstract schools who seek always the Power of some Church or Institution, and found oneself with great poetry, and superstition which is but popular poetry, in a pleasant dangerous world. Beauty is indeed but bodily life in some ideal condition.'[1]

In other words, Yeats finds the solution of the Church too abstract, turning too much away from the world whose natural beauty the poet must love as much as spiritual beauty. He is always hoping to find—perhaps through magic—nature and spirit welded together and possessing 'bodily life in some ideal condition'. Yeats obviously thinks that Blake as a poet and as a rebel from Institution if not from the true Church, was on the side of the magician and natural beauty. He cannot see the problem in Chesterton's terms—that the highest doctrine of the spiritual is to affirm the material.

Both questions are answered further in the strange poem, *Ego, Dominus Tuus*. 'Hic', symbolizing the attitude of the religious man, cries reproachfully to 'Ille', the magician:

> On the grey sand beside the shallow stream,
> Under your old wind-beaten tower . . .
> You walk in the moon,
> And although you have passed the best of life, still trace,
> Enthralled by the unconquerable delusion,
> Magical shapes.

'Hic' is Yeats talking to his magical self who answers:

> By the help of an image,
> I call to my own opposite, summon all
> That I have handled least, least looked upon.

'Hic' replies:

> And I would find myself, and not an image

[1] Yeats, *Per Amica Silentia Lunæ*, London, 1938, p. 56.

22

recalling Dante, who

> *so utterly found himself*
> *That he made that hollow face of his*
> *More plain to the mind's eye than any face*
> *But that of Christ.*

And the magical 'Ille' answers with a further question:

> *And did he find himself,*
> *Or was it hunger that made it hollow*
> *A hunger for the apple on the bough*
> *Most out of reach?*

Yeats contends here that Dante's Beatrice was no more than the unattainable lady of the troubadours, presented in a highly exalted and religious form which blinds us to the worldly nature of the problem. Yeats feels that the abstraction of the human into the religious is a mistake, and by so doing:

> *We are but critics, or but half create,*
> *Timid, entangled, empty, and abashed.*

To Yeats the heresy of the troubadours was, of course, no heresy, but reality, caught as he was in the net of his own unrequited love for Maud Gonne. There are ladies, who, like the apple most out of reach, are unattainable, and Yeats would have liked Dante better if he had said so instead of making Beatrice attainable in a religious sense. It is obvious that the question of love is becoming tied up with that of poet-magician versus religious man.

Dependence upon the realm of spirit alone is evasion and half-truth, just as it is a half-truth for the man of the world to scorn the spirit and serve the world only 'in action, grow rich, popular, and full of influence'. Yeats was attracted to both, for him improbable, extremes: the saint and the man of action.

In one sense the answer to the question—what did Yeats want from magic?—is this. To Yeats, for a while mistaking the invisible for the spiritual, magic seemed a sort of reconciliation of spirit and the world of nature. It was neither crude action, nor dealing with abstraction. It seemed a way to force dream and reality to come together, and it seemed, perhaps, a technique of shaking loose an even greater vision.

All his life Yeats was troubled by the great discrepancy between his dreams and the actuality around him of Paudeens and Biddys and newspaper thrills. He longed to bring dream and reality together, to 'cry the Ineffable Name' that would shake down from among the stars a vision of ultimate truth. The way of the saint seemed too abstract and full of denial for him. But perhaps by the power of magical poetry he might evoke in a different way more and more powerful symbols that would lead him ever nearer to perfection. The pose of magician seems sometimes itself no more than a symbol—the myth of his own search for truth.

Despite his rejection of religion as a way for the poet who must sing of beautiful natural things, and despite his magical manifesto, Yeats does not deny that he seriously considered turning to religion. In a passage about Paris he says:

'Nothing remained the same but the preoccupation with religion. . . . It was no longer the soul, self-moving and self-teaching—the magical soul—but . . . Mother Church. Have not my thoughts run a like round, though I have not found my tradition in the Church, which was not the Church of my childhood, but where the tradition is, as I believe more universal and more ancient.'[1]

And so, when 'Hic' asks his final question of the magician:

> Why should you leave the lamp
> Burning alone beside an open book,
> And trace these characters upon the sand?

'Ille' answers:

> Because I seek an image . . .
> I call to the mysterious one who yet
> Shall walk the wet sand by the water's edge,
> And look most like me, being indeed my double,
> And prove of all imaginable things
> The most unlike, being my anti-self,
> And, standing by these characters, disclose
> All that I seek.

This is where Yeats' doctrine of self and anti-self ties in with his magical beliefs. Both urge the reconciliation of the ideal and the

[1] Yeats, *Per Amica Silentia Lunæ*, London, 1938, p. 94.

concrete, the natural and the invisible. Supreme magical unity would also seem to be that of self and anti-self.

The anti-self is the Mask—'a being in all things opposite to the natural state', 'an image of desire', 'an image . . . symbolical or evocative of that state of mind which is of all states of mind not impossible, the most difficult . . . because only the greatest obstacle that can be contemplated without despair, rouses the will to full intensity.'[1] It is in part an armour to defend the secret or dream self, in part a solid façade that is the social self, and in part an heroic pose to live up to in order to convince oneself of a certain value in the world of action as well as in that of dreams. The Mask belongs largely to the world of action, of concrete externality, while the natural self belongs to the inner, not the outer, landscape.

It is interesting to note Yeats' attitude to external nature. Although posing as the magician who is in theory highly interested in manipulating nature through its own secret keys or symbols, Yeats is, in actual fact, hardly interested in nature at all. He seems to see only general aspects of it and can use these with telling effect as external equivalents of the interior mood as in the Galway poems about the tower. From all reports he could not have been less interested in natural detail or in the beauty of nature. Partly, this was due to his poor eyesight which often made him see a double image, and partly, Mrs. Yeats thinks, due to his extremely poor visualizing powers which made him unable to remember details about places he had visited. Dorothy Wellesley makes some interesting notes on this subject:

'This matter of Yeats' visual life is deeply interesting. To an English poet it appears at times incredible. George Moore noted this characteristic; indeed he was more than malicious about it, as readers of his books concerning Yeats will well know.

I have come to the conclusion that this lack of "visualness", this lack of interest in natural beauty for its own sake, may originate in the fact that most of the Celtic poets are not concerned with nature at all. Yeats did not himself draw much inspiration from Nature, certainly from no details; only sometimes massed effects, such as a painter sees, influenced his verse. Referring to a poem of mine Yeats once said to me in an outburst of irritability: "Why can't you English poets keep flowers out of your poetry?" . . . I quote this to show

[1] Yeats, *Autobiography*, p. 170.

how strongly Yeats disliked flowers, and how his lack of observation concerning natural beauty was almost an active obsession, and how it does in my opinion dim most poems of his concerned with Nature. Not so with his thought.

But there is more to say in this connexion about Yeats. I said that Celtic poetry has shown no close love or observation of Nature. But of Yeats I think it is possible that to this racial characteristic must be added his extremely poor sight. His small dark eyes turned outwards, appear like those of a lizard and as though at times they were hidden by a film. His perspective therefore is perhaps abnormal. Perhaps he cannot see very much out of doors. Certainly it is that he sees nothing, when we sit together in my walled garden, in the beauty of any flower. The blossoming trees, however, interest him a little. But this is perhaps because blossoming trees play so large a part in Chinese poetry and Oriental philosophies. But he sees the beauty of the general effect and between his periods of fantastic prose will look up and say: "You have made a very beautiful garden," forgetting that he constantly says: "Why do you waste your time making your hands dirty just for the sake of a garden?" [1]

And of course there is the story of Yeats silently consuming some parsnips for dinner, and then remarking dreamily to Mrs. Yeats— 'That wasn't a very nice pudding.' No, the 'natural self' for Yeats was not that which was a child of nature and dealt with external things but something quite different and infinitely more vulnerable. There is a great discrepancy between it and the mask that one presents to the world, and which hardens through experience. 'I think that all happiness depends upon the energy to assume the mask of some other self; that all joyous or creative life is a rebirth as something not oneself.'[2] The true self is so hesitant, so delicately unsure about its own discoveries that it needs to have them objectified, altered even, by a stronger self, one who might say:

'I know that you were timid about your own thoughts, and nothing seems true that we find out for ourselves. Only the most delicate mind can discover the truth, and that mind is always hesitating. The truth comes to us like the morning lost in clouds hesitating. . . . We are only confident about the ideas of others. But there must be people like me to take up your thoughts, to believe

[1] Yeats, *Letters on Poetry*, p. 190.
[2] Unpublished diary.

in them because they are not your own, to put them on our faces like a mask . . . let me become all your dreams.'[1]

In other words, if the dreams of the secret self can be transmuted and expressed in apparently antithetical terms by the Mask, this distancing would make them less vulnerable. The mask of magician became, as it were, his most unchanging 'public philosophy', while Yeats himself was still trying to form the 'private philosophy'[2] of his natural self, much more elusive and hidden, much more difficult to express. A great deal has been written on the various Masks that Yeats assumed, but nothing at all has been said about the real and secret self, the self which is not the poet because the poet is identified with the magical Mask. This is perhaps because Yeats himself said that he did not understand it—'I know very little about myself.' I believe that consciously or in the realm of feeling, he understood what this secret self wished to be only too well and never expressed it through fear of seeming ridiculous. I think that the discovery of what this natural self was is the key to Yeats' devotion to Blake and to his interpretation of Blake. What *is* the secret self hidden behind the Mask of the magical poet? This is the next question to ask about Yeats.

It is perhaps what Yeats hints at in the story he tells of himself:

'The dull man . . . suddenly said to the whole room . . . "Yeats believes in magic; what nonsense." Henley said, "No, it may not be nonsense; black magic is all the go in Paris now." And then, turning towards me with a changed sound in his voice, "It is just a game, isn't it?" I replied . . . "One has had a vision: one wants to have another, that is all." '[3]

We are not, like the dull man, to take Yeats' magic at face value, nor are we to consider it merely a pointless game. This magic has a purpose behind itself. It must shake loose another kind of vision to appease the thirsting of the hidden self.

To return to the machinery of Yeats' magic: the book *A Vision*, revised several times, was its bible. In the first version of 1925, Yeats writes about friends who had turned to magic:

'Some were looking for spiritual happiness or for some form of unknown power, but I had a practical object. I wished for a system

---

[1] Ellman, *The Man and the Masks*, p. 173.   [2] *Ibid.*, p. 284.
[3] Yeats, *Autobiography*, p. 254.

of thought that would leave my imagination free to create as it chose and yet make all that it created, or could create, part of the one history, and that the soul's . . . what I have found is indeed nothing new, for I will show presently that Swedenborg and Blake and many before them knew that all things had their gyres; but Swedenborg and Blake preferred to explain them figuratively, and so I am the first to substitute for Biblical or mythological figures, historical movements and actual men and women.'[1]

A Vision is indeed an attempt to incorporate the whole of human history, and of human psychological types within the deterministic system of the Great Wheel. This Great Wheel is the pattern of Nature and is diagrammed as the Phases of the Moon. There are many subdivisions of the twenty-eight phases and so many possible combinations that there is much opportunity for magical geometry. The only possible escape from the wheel of nature is a dubious one in Phase 15 where 'chance and choice have become interchangeable without losing their identity'. He places Blake in the next phase, 16, where 'intellect . . . finds the soul's most radiant expression . . . and therefore self-knowledge and self-mastery.' He himself, along with Dante, Shelley, and Landor, is but one step lower than Blake in Phase 17, where there is 'creative imagination through antithetical emotion.' In this phase each person 'has for its supreme aim . . . to hide from himself and others this separation and disorder, and it conceals them under the emotional Image.'[2]

' When true to phase, the intellect must turn all its synthetic power to this task. It finds, not the impassioned myth that Phase 16 found, but a Mask of simplicity that is also intensity . . . This Mask may seem some Ahasuerus or Athanase . . . it may even dream of escaping from ill-luck by possessing the impersonal Body of Fate of its opposite phase.'

Unity of Being is most possible at this phase.

It is important to note that while the Mask of this his own Phase 17 is one of physical control and balance (such as Yeats' own Mask of magician, an 'Ahasuerus')—what Yeats calls the Body of Fate and which is imposed by the train of external events on to the inner self, is that of the saint from Phase 27.[3] This is to say that while Yeats'

---

[1] Yeats, *A Vision*, London, 1925, xi.   [2] *Ibid.*, p. 75.
[3] *Ibid.*, 1937 edition, see pp. 141, 180.

28

Mask is the magician, his natural self has more to do with the Saint! The connecting link seems to be romantic love, for the poet 'selects some object of desire for a representation of the Mask as Image, some woman perhaps, and the Body of Fate snatches away the object'[1]—that is, the poet-magician projects a romantic image or ideal on to some woman ('Shelley's Venus Urania, Dante's Beatrice, or even the Great Yellow Rose of the *Paradiso*'[2]) and then the Body of Fate or Saint snatches away this worldly eros. And how typical it is of Yeats the magician to describe the saint as the man who 'has a secret that makes him better than other men.'[3]

From the evidence of *A Vision*, which, at best, is somewhat woolly, though set forth in magnificent prose, it would seem that while Yeats' mask is the magician (or at times some other strongly physical and extrovert mask) his hidden natural self has the potentialities of the saint. It would seem, too, that the experience of unhappy romantic love would have a vital importance in joining the two selves. This sounds so fantastic, especially coming from the doubtful logic of *A Vision*, that it is necessary to turn elsewhere for verification.

Meanwhile let us pass on from the complex geometry of *A Vision*—most of which says no more than that balance arises from the tension of opposites—to the rest of Yeats' magical structure.

Yeats tries to embrace as a basic pantheism to back-drop his magic, the theory of Anima Mundi. Although throughout the ages many magicians have used the terms of pantheism—particularly that of 'Unity of Being'—pantheism and magic are nevertheless mutually contradictory. The point of confusion is that both are concerned with the secret laws of nature. The neo-Platonic devotees of the world soul, such as More, kept it subsidiary to a Christian belief. This is perhaps why Yeats' belief in Anima Mundi seems always somewhat separate from his magic and theory of self and Mask, being, as it were, a loose thread that fits in nowhere.

Such a pantheism, as differentiated from mysticism, is interested in the unity of all that *is*. Mysticism, on the other hand, goes one step further, crying with Blake: 'All that lives is *Holy*.' In sharp contrast to both, magic is not really concerned with unity at all, but with the separation of the controlled nature and the magician with his superior mental force. It is over-againstness, not togetherness.

[1] Yeats, *A Vision*, 1937 edition, p. 141. [2] *Ibid.*, p. 141. [3] *Ibid.*, p. 180.

The magician wishes neither to be absorbed into a pantheist unity, nor to unite anything except the cause and effect of a particular situation. He glories in the supposed split between matter and mind and as such is dualistic and always involved in conflict.

It is rather difficult to say what Yeats meant by his magical use of the term, Anima Mundi. Sometimes he seems almost to be talking in terms of Jungian psychology of that great world of unconscious magery which emerges in folklore, psychic phenomena and automatic art. At others, he seems to be talking Henry More platonism which has close associations with Christian supernatural beliefs. In his prose writings there are but hints and partial explanations of what he meant. Again and again, he writes, he found himself

'face to face with the Anima Mundi described by Platonic philosophers, and more especially in modern times by Henry More, which has a memory independent of embodied individual memories, though they constantly enrich it with their images and thought.'[1]

And, he adds,

'I know now that revelation is from the self, but from that age-long memoried self that shapes the elaborate shell of the mollusc and the child in the womb, that teaches the birds to make their nest; and that genius is the crisis which joins our buried self for certain moments to our trivial daily mind.'

'Automatic script may well have been but a process of remembering. I think that Plato symbolized by the word "memory" a relation to the timeless.'

'I came to believe in a great memory passing on from generation to generation. But that was not enough, for these images showed intention and choice. They had a relation to what one knew and yet were an extension of one's knowledge. If no mind was there, why should I suddenly come upon salt and antimony, upon the liquefaction of gold, as they were understood by the alchemists, or upon some detail of a cabalistic system verified at last by a learned scholar from his never-published manuscript, and who can have put together so ingeniously working by some law of association and yet with clear intention and personal application, certain mythological images. . . . The thought was again and again before me that this study had created a contact or mingling with minds who had

[1] Yeats, *Autobiography*, p. 225.

followed a like study in some other age, and that these minds still saw and thought and chose. Our daily thought was certainly but the line of foam at the shallow edge of a vast luminous sea; Henry More's Anima Mundi, Wordsworth's "immortal sea which brought us hither . . . and near whose edge the children sport", in that sea there were some who swam or sailed, explorers who perhaps knew all its shores.'

One could even sail to Byzantium on this sea.

Edwin Ellis, Yeats' collaborator on the Blake volumes, throws a little light on what Yeats meant by the Anima Mundi, and on its connection with magic:

'In an article on Magic published in a volume of meditations, called by the Blakean title *Ideas of Good and Evil*, by the former collaborator of the present writer, Mr. W. B. Yeats, all who are interested in it may find an account of certain experiences that caused Mr. Yeats to form a belief in the objective existence of a general memory, which is not that of any individual, which exists as it were in the air, and on which by means of magical invocations or symbols, we can draw by will. Events are recorded in the air, not the respirable air, the astral, and magic gives us ingress to that reservoir of unspoken history.'[1]

Yeats tells about the souls of the living and of the dead in Anima Mundi:

'All souls have a vehicle or body, and when one has said that, with More and the Platonists one has escaped from the abstract schools who seek always the power of some church or institution. . . . Beauty is indeed but bodily life in some ideal condition. The vehicle of the soul is what used to be called the animal spirits. . . . The soul has a plastic power, and can after death or during life, should the vehicle leave the body for a while, mould it to any shape it will by an act of imagination. . . . The vehicle once separated from the living man or woman may be moulded by the souls of others as readily as by its own soul, and even it seems by the soul of the living. It becomes a part for a while of that stream of images which I have compared to reflections upon water . . . if all our mental images no less than apparitions (and I see no reason to distinguish) are forms existing in the general vehicle of Anima Mundi, and mirrored in

[1] Edwin Ellis, *The Real Blake*, London, 1907, p. 27.

our particular vehicle, many crooked things are made straight. I am persuaded that a logical process, or a series of related images, has body and period, and I think of Anima Mundi as a great pool or garden where it moves through its allotted growth like a great water plant or fragrantly branches in the air. . . . The soul by changes of "vital congruity", More says, draws to it a certain thought, and this thought draws by its association the sequence of many thoughts, endowing them with a life in the vehicle meted out according to the intensity of the first perception. A seed is set growing, and this growth may go on apart from the power, apart even from the knowledge of the soul. . . . We carry to Anima Mundi our memory, and that memory is for a time our external world; and all passionate moments recur again and again, for all passion desires its own recurrence more than any event. . . . When all sequence comes to an end, time comes to an end, and the soul puts on a rhythmic or spiritual body or luminous body and contemplates all the events of its memory and every possible impulse in an eternal possession of itself in one single moment. That condition is alone animate, all the rest is phantasy . . . communication in the Anima Mundi is through the association of thoughts or images or objects; and the famous dead and those of whom but a faint memory lingers, can still . . . tread the corridor and take the empty chair.'[1]

This brings to mind in passing the little poem in which Yeats uses Blake's image of beholding eternity in one throb of the artery:

> For one throb of the artery,
> While on that old grey stone I sat,
> Under the old wind-broken tree,
> I knew that One is animate,
> Mankind inanimate phantasy.[2]

In other words, Yeats believes that the poet-magician may throw his poetic symbol into the pool of the great memory and according to its power this stone will send out circles that reach ever nearer the width of the pool: and the sound of the stone dropping into the deeps will awaken a like experience in every mind that hears, and we will have come a little nearer the truth both about the visible surface and the hidden depths. The symbol, by the links of association

---

[1] Yeats, *Per Amica Silentia Lunæ*, p. 56.
[2] Yeats, *Collected Poems*, p. 218.

it sets into motion, comes ever nearer the core of truth, which seems to consist of memory architypes or perhaps of modified Platonic Ideas.

It is a sense of tapping invisible depths that interests Yeats much more than the unity of life. And in this it ties up with his magic. But in another way such a theory is but an effort on Yeats' part to prove to himself that spirits can be evoked and the invisible forced to materialize. As such, it stems perhaps from wishful thinking.

The confusion that the theory of Anima Mundi introduces into Yeats' 'system' may lie, in part, in the fact that Yeats swallowed a good deal of Henry More's philosophy wholesale without apparent reference to More's central theology. Yeats was an intellectual magpie in this sense and would have no hesitation, says Mrs. Yeats, 'in stealing the wings from an Angel, had he the opportunity and thought it would benefit his poetry.'

In the writings of Henry More, the Anima Mundi is mixed up with magic. But magic, in turn, is indissolubly connected with theology. In the *Anthroposophia Theomagica*, one 'questioner' of More complains:

'There's no body now but would laugh to hear that a particular Angell turns upon every Orb, as so many dogs in wheels turn the spit at the fire. So that it seems far below such a grand Theomagician as you are, to tell us such incredible fopperies as these to be false.'[1]

The fun-poking critic of *Observations upon Anthroposophia Theomagica*, commenting on More's statement: 'Next to God I owe all I have to Agrippa,' cries horrified: 'What? more than to the Prophets and Apostles, Anthroposophus? The business is for your fame-sake, you have more desire to be thought a Conjurer than a Christian.'[2] Like More, Yeats too claims concern with the ghost of Cornelius Agrippa and, again like More, uses Plotinus as authority that, in More's words, the 'World is . . . the grand Magus or Enchanter'; and again, that 'Anima Mundi . . . passes through all the Matter of the World, and is present in every place to doe all feats that there are to be done.' All this is added impetus to Yeats' wish to ally magic and mysticism not only in Blake but in himself. But the way that he assimilates More into his 'philosophy' is highly confusing.

A fitting comment, perhaps, is the nonsense of More's critic who

---

[1] Henry More, *Observations upon Anthroposophia Theomagica*, London, 1650, p. 50.   [2] *Ibid.*, p. 37.

cries: *'Fulgineous spawn of Nature.* A rare expression! This Magician has turned Nature into a Fish by his Art. Surely such dreams float in his swimmering brains, as in the Prophets, who tels us so Authentick stories of his delicious Albebut.'[1]

For it is evident that there is nothing supernatural or truly mystical about Yeats' theory. Yet he claims that 'the mystical life is the centre of all that I do and all that I think and all that I write,'[2] and we have seen how in *A Vision* his mask of magician is allied with the saint, and how his interest in Henry More presents the idea of the Theomagus.

As it actually stands, Yeats' theory is merely one of natural magic with Oriental and neo-Platonic overtones plus a good deal of wishful thinking and hocus-pocus, most of which cannot be taken seriously. As such, it is completely incompatible with Blake's final mystical affirmation in Christ, for Yeats' doctrine dispenses with Christ altogether. Whereas Blake expresses what he has been given in a moment of Grace and revelation, Yeats uses his tools of expression in a magical way in order to force a moment of vision. To see whether the hints about the saints' connexion with his secret self are arbitrary or whether they really have bearing in Yeats' own life and on his very personal interpretation of Blake, we must turn to autobiographical material.

[1] Henry More, *Observations upon Anthroposophia Theomagica*, London, 1650, p. 18.
[2] Ellman, *The Man and the Masks*, p. 94.

Chapter Two

'THE QUARREL WITH OURSELVES'

~~~~~~

'Indeed I remember little of childhood but its pain. I have grown happier with every year of life as though gradually conquering something in myself, for certainly my miseries were not made by others, but were a part of my own mind.'[1]

A FRAGILE, dreaming child, Yeats remembers himself when at fifty he wrote *Reveries Over Childhood*. He was a difficult child to teach because 'I found it hard to attend to anything less interesting than my thoughts.'[2] By his opinionated and strong-bodied family of Middletons, Pollexfens, and Yeats, he was considered mentally and physically deficient. Only much later did Yeats' father pay him the one compliment which turned his head, that by marriage with a Pollexfen he had given a tongue to the sea-cliffs. Even this early misunderstanding Yeats later turned into a link with Blake:

'The man or boy of genius is very generally hated or scorned by the average man or boy until the day come for him to charm them into unwilling homage. Until that day he has often to cry with Blake, "Why was I born with a different face?" For his abstracted ways and his strange interests arouse the hatred of the uncommon which lies deep in the common heart.'[3]

Moreover, although he admired his atheist father, the artist

---

[1] Yeats, *Autobiography*, p. 12.   [2] *Ibid.*, p. 23.
[3] Yeats, *William Blake* edition, London, 1893, p. xx.

J. B. Yeats, above all others, he was terribly afraid of him and of his maternal grandfather, William Pollexfen.

'Some of my misery was loneliness and some of it fear of old William Pollexfen my grandfather. . . . I think I confused my grandfather with God, for I remember in one of my attacks of melancholy praying that he might punish me for my sins. . . . I was often devout, my eyes filling with tears at the thought of God and for my own sins, but I hated church.'[1]

Although his father was himself an atheist and never went to church—probably in reaction against his own clerical father—he threw a book at the head of the small boy who one day announced that he would not go to church. And Yeats remembers—

'the only lessons I ever learned were those my father taught me, for he terrified me by descriptions of my moral degradation and he humiliated me by my likeness to disagreeable people.[2]

'Once my father came with me riding too, and was very exacting. He was indignant and threatening because he did not think I rode well. "You must do everything well," he said, "that the Pollexfens respect, though you must do other things also." He used to say the same about my lessons, and tell me to be good at mathematics. I can see now that he had a sense of inferiority among these energetic successful people.'[3]

Yet Yeats was very much affected by his father's unbelief, and out of fear and a desire for his favour, wished to please and be like him:

'my father's unbelief had set me thinking about the evidence of religion and I weighed the matter perpetually with great anxiety for I did not think I could live without religion. All my religious emotions were, I think, connected with clouds and cloudy glimpses of luminous sky, perhaps because of some Bible picture of God's speaking to Abraham or the like. At least I can remember the sight moving me to tears. One day I got a decisive argument for belief,' the fifty-year-old Yeats says with rueful humour. 'A cow was about to calve, and I went to the field where the cow was with some farm-hands who carried a lantern, and next day I heard that the cow had calved in the early morning. I asked everybody how calves were

---

[1] Yeats, *Autobiography*, pp. 8, 23.   [2] *Ibid.*, p. 23.   [3] *Ibid.*, p. 48.

born, and because nobody would tell me, made up my mind that nobody knew. They were the gift of God, that much was certain.'[1]

The fearful, sensitive child, all of his dreams on the side of the spirit, was so influenced by his father's impatience with religion, that even his gentle mother's piety could not give him faith in what he longed to believe. Instead he listened to his father on poetic belief as a substitute for religion:

'There are two kinds of belief: the poetical and the religious. That of the poet comes when the man within has found some method or manner of thinking or arrangement of fact (such as is only possible in dreams) by which to express and embody an absolute freedom, such that his whole inner and outer self can expand in a full satisfaction. In religious belief there is absent the consciousness of liberty. Religion is the denial of liberty. An enforced peace is set up among the warring feelings. By the help of something quite external, as for instance the fear of hell, some feelings are chained up and thrust into dungeons that some other feelings may hold sway and all the ethical systems yet invented are a similar denial of liberty, that is why the true poet is neither moral nor religious.'[2]

What could Yeats do in his childhood about his great need for religion which fought against the equally pressing influence of his father? Most critics believe that he denied religion altogether in favour of an esoteric occultism. Obviously he was not strong enough to rebel and openly enrol himself on the side of religion, for, 'held by my father's scepticism',[3] Yeats had not 'a talent for conviction'. He could only 'face authority with the timidity born of excuse and evasion. Evasion and excuse were in the event as wise as the housebuilding instinct of the beaver,'[4] he added, implying that he had learned to hide his true self in a sort of shell.

He had convinced himself that he wanted to be a scientist, thinking that this perhaps would give him prestige with his literal and doubting father, who nevertheless believed in science, in the human personality, and in the arts. Yeats spent nights in secret wooded places and in lonely caves 'on the excuse of catching moths',[5] but

---

[1] Yeats, *Autobiography*, p. 25.
[2] Ellman, *The Man and the Masks*, p. 19.
[3] Yeats, *Autobiography*, p. 81.   [4] *Ibid.*, p. 53.   [5] *Ibid.*, p. 57.

really for the magical adventure of it. Soon he admitted this to himself and says in his autobiography:

'My interest in science began to fade, and presently I said to myself, "It has all been a misunderstanding." I remember how soon I tired of my specimens, and how little I knew after all my years of collecting . . . . I still carried my green net, but I began to play at being a sage, a magician, or a poet.'[1]

It is easy to see how Yeats made the step from science to magic as a cover for religion that might please his father. For it was one of the current popular doctrines (introduced by such anthropologists as Frazer, whose work J. B. Yeats almost surely knew and whose books W. B. Yeats later possessed) that magic is the ancestor of science: that science is, as it were, skilled magic. Whether or not J. B. Yeats knew Frazer, he would have known and approved of this view. And to Yeats both the means for pleasing his father by assuming a strong and pseudo-scientific personality, and the opportunities magic afforded for concerning himself with the invisible— would have made the pose of magician a brilliant idea. Magic, allied to science, was agreeable to a materialist father who wanted his children to have strong personalities into the bargain. And it seemed not too alien to the poetic boy whose dreams were much more misty and unfactual than science, and who had given up the God who lived beyond the 'luminous' cloud.

At this time 'my father's influence upon my thoughts was at its height'.[2] And J. B. Yeats, although an artist, had a pragmatic mind, sceptical, factual, and hating the abstract: 'he did not care even for a fine lyric passion unless he felt some actual man behind its elaboration of beauty . . . he thought Keats a greater poet than Shelley because less abstract.'[3] This influence of his father probably accounts for a great deal of the brilliant concrete and personal quality of Yeats' finest poems; instead of going off into a haze of abstraction as in his philosophy, in his most esoteric poems he still cultivated the particular. This is what makes the love poems such as *Her Praise* and *The Folly of Being Comforted* so very moving. However, in his youth, the main motive was to cover up his religious leanings by an attitude which was naturalistic, non-abstract, and had the force of personal power. An interest in magic was the more than adequate solution, particularly as there were psychic qualities in the family, indeed

[1] Yeats, *Autobiography*, p. 57. [2] *Ibid.*, p. 59. [3] *Ibid.*, p. 59.

between Yeats and his father to such an extent that the grown-up poet in Dublin or London would write to his old father (who spent his last years in New York) recounting a dream or mood that would be astonishingly echoed in the letter posted by his father the same day.

More deliberately Yeats began to toy with the idea of an assumed self or pose to disguise and channel into safe waters his religious yearnings. He had already left the art school where he had been sent, and announced that poetry would be his career. He began to think that all good poets had or must assume masks:

'If a man is to write lyric poetry he must be shaped by nature and art to some one out of half a dozen traditional poses, and be lover or saint, sage or sensualist, or mere mocker of all life; and that none but that stroke of luckless luck can open before him the accumulated expression of the world. And this thought before it could be knowledge was instinct.'[1]

Because of his father the pose of saint was out of the question, and anyhow ridiculous in one considered by his family to be so undistinguished. Speaking of the saint's abstraction and consequent eschewal by the poet, Yeats nevertheless offers him high praise and in a somewhat wistful manner:

'The poet finds and makes his mask in disappointment, the hero in defeat. The desire that is satisfied is not a great desire, nor has the shoulder used all its might that an unbreakable gate had never strained. The saint alone is not deceived, neither thrusting with his shoulder, nor holding out unsatisfied hands. He would climb without wandering to the antithetical self of the world, the Indian narrowing his thought in meditation or driving it away in contemplation, the Christian copying Christ, the antithetical self of the classical world. For a hero loves the world till it breaks him, and the poet till it has broken faith; but while the world was debonair, the saint has turned away and because he renounced Experience itself, he will wear his mask as he finds it.'[2]

It is a moving passage in which Yeats, seeing clearly the transcendence of the saint, condemns the poet to the heart-breaking search for the dream that seems better than reality, the romantic ideal that stays beautiful only while it is not actual. And of course he follows the

[1] Yeats, *Autobiography*, p. 77.　　[2] Yeats, *Per Amica Silentia Lunæ*, p. 33.

popular view of the saint as necessarily the ascetic renouncing the world.

The only other way of escaping the poet's fate of chasing will-o'-the-wisps was to become a solid and what seemed to Yeats unimaginative man of action. This of course was unthinkable, though there were times in Yeats' life when he longed to be just this.

Magic seemed to make the best alliance with poetry, and this was reinforced by the tone of the arts in the 'nineties. It was a period where the young æsthetes, reclining on yellow satin sofas, metaphorically when not actually, preached art for art's sake. Yeats' particular slant was that of the Celtic twilight, and he was nearly lost in that glimmering faery world, lured on by his own Belle Dame sans Merci. However, his own life made him more and more conscious of human problems and the split within himself, and soon the magician emerged from the land of forgetfulness and irresponsibility wielding his sword labelled 'Words alone are certain good'.

Groping nearer to the substance of the pose, Yeats became interested in theosophy and many branches of cabalistic occultism, more in search of an authoritative substitute religion than as a poetic gesture. He was a founding member of the Dublin Hermetic Society:

'I had, when we first made our society, proposed for our consideration, that whatever the great poets had affirmed in their finest moments was the nearest we could come to an authoritative religion, and that their mythology, their spirits of water and wind were but literal truths. . . . I was soon to vex my father by defining truth as "the dramatically appropriate utterance of the highest man". And had I been asked to define the "highest man", I would have said perhaps, "We can but find him as Homer found Odysseus when he was looking for a theme." '[1]

And yet his father was all for 'personal utterance', and was probably the power behind the scene when Yeats wrote that if good luck or bad luck made his life interesting he would become a great poet.

Even his Blake studies were started with an aura of supernaturalism:

'We took it almost as a sign of Blake's personal help when we discovered that the spring of 1889, when we first joined our know-

[1] Yeats, *Autobiography*, p. 80

40

ledge, was one hundred years from the publication of *The Book of Thel*, the first published of the Prophetic Books, as though it were firmly established that the dead delight in anniversaries.'[1]

Yeats can be very engaging when he pokes gentle fun at himself wearing a Mask: it is Yeats who tells us of the young man in the Byronic tie and the assumed Hamlet stalk, pausing to gaze at his reflection in glass windows. It is Yeats who admits with a grin his magpie thirst for knowledge and the rather ridiculous air of an age-ing man poking around inquisitively for scraps of intellectual experi-ence: 'It was no business of mine, and that was precisely why I could not keep out of it.'[2] We are too apt to smile condescendingly on the white-haired poet who, having once learned a phrase in Hebrew, says with an air of solemnity—'I have forgotten my Hebrew.' Yeats was no fool, but something of the Fool was put on for our benefit and delight. And 'the Saint and Fool are close of kin'.

Between 1887 and 1891 Yeats recognizes his problem and its tentative solution more clearly:

'I was unlike others of my generation in one thing only. I am very religious, and deprived by Huxley and Tyndall, whom I detested, of the simple-minded religion of my childhood, I had made a new religion, almost an infallible church of poetic tradition, of a fardel of stories, and of personages, and of emotions, inseparable from their first expression, passed on from generation to generation by poets and painters with some help from philosophers and theologians. I wished for a world where I could discover this tradition perpetually, and not in pictures and in poems only, but in tiles round the chimney-piece and in the hangings that kept out the draught. I had even created a dogma: "Because those imaginary people are created out of the deepest instinct of man to be his measure and his norm, what-ever I can imagine those mouths speaking may be the nearest I can go to truth." When I listened they seemed always to speak of one thing only: they, their loves, every incident of their lives, were steeped in the supernatural.'[3]

But elsewhere Yeats says: 'I was vexed and bewildered, and I am still bewildered and still vexed, finding it a poor and crazy thing that we who have imagined so many noble persons cannot bring our flesh to heel.'[4]

---

[1] Yeats, *Autobiography*, p. 171.　[2] *Ibid.*, p. 300.　[3] *Ibid.*, p. 101.　[4] *Ibid.*, p. 37.

Later Yeats justifies his turning away from the Christianity of his childhood to a religion of poetry:

'To seek God too soon is not less sinful than to seek God too late. We must love man, woman, or child, we must exhaust ambition, intellect, desire, dedicating all things as they pass or we come to God with empty hands.'[1]

He justifies, too, that this move was originally based on the fear of his father's disapproval with this thought:

'I think profound philosophy must come from terror, an abyss opens under our feet; inherited convictions, the presuppositions of our thoughts, those Fathers of the Church Lionel Johnson expounded, drop into the abyss. Whether we will or no we must ask the ancient questions: Is there reality anywhere? Is there a God? Is there a soul? We cry with the Indian Sacred Books: "They have put a golden stopper into the neck of the bottle: pull it! Let out reality!" '[2]

During these crowded years Yeats was writing his Blake book with Edwin Ellis, experimenting with magic and occultism, and elaborating his search for a pose into the doctrine of self and anti-self. He defines the anti-self or Mask as that 'image—always opposite to the natural self' which he must wear for safety's sake,

'playing a game like that of a child where one loses the infinite pain of self-realization in a grotesque or solemn painted face put on that one may hide from the terror of judgment. . . . Perhaps all the sins and energies of the world are . . . but the world's flight from an infinite blinding beam.'[3]

And of himself Yeats says: 'It is perhaps because nature has made me a gregarious man, going hither and thither looking for conversation, and ready to deny from fear or favour his dearest conviction, that I love proud and lonely things.'[4] *Ready to deny from fear or favour his dearest conviction!* And elsewhere he says:

'I began occasionally telling people that one should believe whatever had been believed in all countries and periods, and only reject any part of it after much evidence, instead of starting all over afresh

---

[1] Yeats, *Essays*, 31-36, *Cuala*, p. 129.   [2] *Ibid.*
[3] Yeats, *Essays*, p. 497.   [4] Yeats, *Autobiography*, p. 149.

and only believing what one could prove. *But I was always ready to deny or turn into a joke what was for all that my secret fanaticism.*'[1]

However, Yeats could and did talk freely about his search for a Mask to *hide* his secret fanaticism. It was Wilde who said that a man is not able to speak the truth until he wears a mask, and Yeats, who had learned from his father that he must hide his secret self and, paradoxically, make poetry rich in personal utterance, welcomed this thought.

He tells of the image he has in mind for the Mask:

'my mind gave itself to gregarious Shelley's dream of a young man, his hair blanched with sorrow, studying philosophy in some lonely tower, or of his old man, master of all human knowledge, hidden from human sight in some shell-strewn cavern on the Mediterranean shore. One passage above all rang perpetually in my ears:

> *Some feign he is Enoch: others dream*
> *He was pre-Adamite, and has survived*
> *Cycles of generation and of ruin.*
> *The sage, in truth, by dreadful abstinence,*
> *And conquering penance of the mutinous flesh,*
> *Deep contemplation and unwearied study,*
> *In years outstretched beyond the date of man,*
> *May have attained to sovereignty and science*
> *Over those strong and secret things and thoughts*
> *Which others fear and know not.*
> MAHMUD: *I would talk*
> *With this old Jew.*
> HASSAN: *Thy will is even now*
> *Made known to him where he dwells in a sea-cavern*
> *'Mid the Demonesi, less accessible*
> *Than thou or God! He who would question him*
> *Must sail alone at sunset where the stream*
> *Of ocean sleeps around those foamless isles,*
> *When the young moon is westering as now,*
> *And evening airs wander upon the wave.*
> *And, when the pines of that bee-pasturing isle,*
> *Green Erebinthus, quench the fiery shadow*
> *Of his gilt prow within the sapphire water,*

[1] Yeats, *Autobiography*, p. 70.

Then must the lonely helmsman cry aloud
"Ahasuerus!" and the caverns round
Will answer "Ahasuerus!" If his prayer
Be granted, a faint meteor will arise,
Lighting him over Marmora; and a wind
Will rush out of the sighing pine-forest,
And with the wind a storm of harmony
Unutterably sweet, and pilot him
Through the soft twilight to the Bosphorus.
Thence, at the hour and place and circumstance
Fit for the matter of their conference,
The Jew appears. Few dare, and few who dare
Win the desired communion.'[1]

Yeats emphasizes the strange personal significance that this passage from Shelley's poem had for him:

'Already in Dublin, I had been attracted to the Theosophists because they had affirmed the real existence of the Jew, or of his life, and, apart from whatever might have been imagined by Huxley, Tyndall, Carolus Duran, and Bastien-Lepage, I saw nothing against his reality. Presently having heard that Madame Blavatsky had arrived from France or from India I thought it time to look the matter up. Certainly if wisdom existed anywhere in the world it must be in some lonely mind admitting no duty to us, communing with God only, conceding nothing from fear or favour. Have not all people, while bound together in a single mind or task, believed that such men existed and paid them that honour, or paid it to their mere shadow, which they have refused to philanthropists and to men of learning?'[2]

It is easy to see that the Mask of Enchanter is in part a compensation for the fact that Yeats was not officially a 'man of learning'. Yeats often thinks wishfully about what might have happened 'if I had gone to a university, and learned all the classical foundations of English literature and English culture, all that great erudition which once accepted frees the mind from restlessness. . . . Lacking sufficient recognized precedent I must needs find out some reason for all I did.'[3]

It is a curious conception, this old magician Jew of Yeats who has more than a touch of the ascetic about him and is, paradoxically, in

---

[1] Yeats, *Autobiography*, p. 150. [2] *Ibid.*, p. 151. [3] *Ibid.*, p. 145.

direct communion with God. Except for the fact that Yeats has shown us how clearly he knew the distinction between enchanter and mystic (or 'Saint' as he sums up all the highest religious activities of man)—we would think that it was a confusion. And we are still a little baffled as to which traditional pose he has chosen for his mask, although it had seemed to be the enchanter, Theomagus, in fact.

The fact is, that Yeats is at the crucial turning point. He sounds rather as if he might make the great break with his father's scientific beliefs and become whole-heartedly religious and perhaps even pursue the mystical way. For whatever he had chosen, Yeats was incapable of pursuing a middle way. In fact, he had said that when he took up the study of theosophy he began to escape from his father's influence. Might he not escape altogether and turn from the mask of magician to the attitude of a saint, which, when openly believed, overcomes dichotomy and has no need of a Mask. On the other hand, we fear that he may slip and plunge too deeply into the magical studies he had begun, making magic his substitute for religion in order to attain 'sovereignty and science' over secret things.

Yeats chose magic. Deliberately he adjusted the Mask of the Enchanter.

The deciding factor in this choice was his love for Maud Gonne. He loved her as the troubadours loved their ladies, and she seemed as unattainable. He was twenty-three when he first met this beautiful, vibrant woman, violent in her political fanaticism and breath-taking in her heroic loveliness. Yeats fell desperately in love.

Before he met Maud Gonne, the shy and awkward poet had been completely inexperienced in the ways of women—despite two sisters—and was always making 'blunders when I paid calls or visits.' But he dreamed of beautiful ideal women, who 'were modelled on those in my favourite poets and loved in brief tragedy, or like the girl in *The Revolt of Islam*, accompanied their lovers through all manner of wild places, lawless women without homes and without children.'[1]

He had an ideal of celibacy close to the asceticism of the religious man: 'I thought that having conquered bodily desire and the inclination of mind towards women and love, I should live as Thoreau lived, seeking wisdom.'[2] But there was the physical side as well:

'Sometimes I told myself very adventurous love-stories with myself for hero, and at other times I planned out a life of lonely

---

[1] Yeats, *Autobiography*, pp. 58, 60.   [2] *Ibid.*, p. 64.

austerity, and at other times mixed the ideals and planned a life of lonely austerity mitigated by periodical lapses. . . . I was a Romantic, my head full of the mysterious women of Rossetti, and those hesitating faces in the art of Burne-Jones seemed always awaiting.'[1]

Indeed this is the exact state of romantic schizophrenia into which medieval troubadours got themselves. If de Rougemont is right that courtly love is related to a dualism in Western culture which can be traced not only to the Kathars but also to the Druid worship of the Celts, Yeats may have come to it by a more or less direct route down the ages, although it is an attitude common to sensitive men. Later he reached the solution of the troubadours which was to love the unattainable woman in an idealistic way, serve her with spiritual acts, but to find physical satisfaction elsewhere. The poems about his search for physical satisfaction are as poignant as the more idealistic and plaintive longings for Maud Gonne. Usually he puts the former into the mouth of a woman:

> What lively lad most pleasured me
> Of all that with me lay?
> I answer that I gave my soul
> And loved in misery,
> But had great pleasure with a lad
> That I loved bodily.[2]

Maud Gonne was a fanatic in Irish politics. Yeats turned his poetic mind to politics and succeeded in becoming a statesman. Maud Gonne was interested in the Irish theatre. Yeats wrote a play for her and started a theatre and made her into Kathleen ni Houlihan, Ireland herself. 'I thought her supernatural,' he said.

But the important fact for our purposes is that Maud Gonne was highly interested in the occult, and it was not until much later that she became a Roman Catholic. The pose of the enigmatic, powerful magician would have appealed very much to her at the time Yeats fell in love with her, and it should have given the shy dreamer a certain worldly confidence. As it worked out, despite Yeats' pose of magician-poet she married a soldier, a man of action, and Yeats, in true troubadour fashion, was poetically forlorn. There is truth in Maud Gonne's saying that the world should thank her for not

---

[1] Yeats, *Autobiography*, p. 134.   [2] Yeats, *Collected Poems*, p. 315.

marrying 'Willie', although she is shockingly smug about her conquest. Yeats, too, at the age of fifty-two, gave up his modified asceticism and married, and from then on we hear little about woman as a romantic ideal, and more of the actuality of love.

My point is that his romantic love for Maud Gonne was the deciding factor in Yeats' battle between religion and magic. Because of her, Yeats put on the Mask of Enchanter, but the battle underneath grew, if anything, worse. The drama of the inner life was just beginning. This checks with Yeats' description of his own type in *A Vision*, Phase 17.

It was soon after this that we find him formulating his magical creed, identifying the sorcerer and the poet, elevating Ahasuerus into the archetypal Enchanter. He made himself believe that to have turned religious might have harmed his poetry, for

'such men do not assume wisdom or beauty as Shelley did, when he masked himself as Ahasuerus, or as Prince Athanais, nor do they pursue an Image through a world that had else seemed an uninhabitable wilderness till amid the privations of that pursuit, the Image is no more Pandemos, but Urania; for such men must cast all Masks and fly the Image, till that Image, transfigured because of their cruelties of self-abasement, becomes itself some Image or epitome of the whole natural or supernatural world, and itself pursues.'[1]

We must remember that the Image which the masked poet pursues is an ideal woman of some sort whether Beatrice, Sophia, or a transmuted Maud Gonne. The saint has neither need of a Mask nor of an Image and has transcended conflict. The Mask, the Image, and the conflict are precisely what Yeats could not give up. But even here he hints that by wielding a powerful Image he can perhaps reach through to some vision of the supernatural world. The symbol or Image of Maud Gonne becomes in a way the most powerful arrow in the magical poet's quiver, and he may yet shoot down the moon.

'What we call romance, poetry, intellectual beauty is the only signal that the supreme Enchanter, or someone in His councils, is speaking of what has been, and shall be again, in the consummation of time.'[2]

The surface identification with magic rather than with religion is complete. But in fact the question is not settled at all in Yeats'

[1] Yeats, *Autobiography*, p. 212.   [2] Yeats, *Essays*, p. 59.

'private philosophy'. In the words of his story, *The Wisdom of the King*:

"The years passed and the child grew from childhood into boyhood, and from boyhood into manhood, and from being curious about all things he became busy with strange and subtle thoughts which came to him in dreams, and with distinctions between things long held the same, and with the resemblance of things long held different.'[1]

Having, as a boy, reached for magic to hide his religious nature from his father, and having, as a young man in love with a beautiful woman, deliberately made the pose his own, Yeats, more mature, is now trying to put together again the opposites within him. He wishes to show his two selves as the two sides of a penny, the two halves of the 'apple out of reach' that make his own 'Unity of Being'. Yet more and more fully he realizes the antithesis between magic and religion. In his play, *The Unicorn from the Stars*, he has the priest say to the boy:

'I had almost got back to my own place when I thought of it. I have run part of the way. It is very important; it is about the trance you have been in. When one is inspired from above, either in trance or in contemplation, one remembers afterwards all that one has seen and read. I think there must be something about it in St. Thomas. . . . But Martin, there is another kind of inspiration, or rather an obsession or possession. A diabolical power comes into one's body or overshadows it. Those whose bodies are taken hold of in this way, jugglers, and witches, and the like, can often tell what is happening in distant places, or what is going to happen, but when they come out of that state they remember nothing. . . . Nature is a great sleep; there are dangerous and evil spirits in her dreams, but God is above Nature. She is a darkness, but He makes everything clear; He is light.'[2]

Ireland is a country where magic and religion have existed side by side quite comfortably through the long ages. Yeats went into Irish politics because of Maud Gonne, but he was very much concerned with the heroic past of Ireland long before he met her. Again, it is the same poignant recognition by the romantic of the

---

[1] Yeats, *The Secret Rose*, p. 17.   [2] Yeats, *Collected Plays*, p. 348.

dichotomy between actual and ideal. This theme of Ireland weaves in and out of his complicated system of contraries. It is the Mask of Magician which can also help Ireland.

The ideal Ireland, full of ancient meaning and heroic mythology, must join with the drab mediocrity of modern Ireland, the land of 'Paudeens and Biddys'. Yeats wishes to 'set before Irishmen for special manual an Irish literature which, though made by many minds, would seem the work of a single mind, and turn our places of beauty or legendary association into holy symbols.'[1] Just as the union of self and Mask would create 'Unity of Being', so the joining of the two Irelands would become 'Unity of Culture'. If the Irish will 'but tell these stories to our children the Land will begin again to be a Holy Land.'[2] Myth, and especially Irish myth, is a way to divine truth, a way running parallel with Christianity:

'Myth is not, as Vico perhaps thought, a rudimentary form super-seded by reflection. Belief is the spring of all action; we assent to the conclusions of reflection but believe what myth presents; belief is love, and the concrete alone is loved; nor is it true that myth has no purpose but to bring round some discovery of a principle or a fact. The saint may touch through myth the utmost reach of human faculty and pass not to reflection but to unity with the source of his being.'[3]

And,

'the Irish stories make us understand why some Greek writers called myths the activities of the dæmons. The great virtues, the great joys, the great privations, come in myths, and, as it were, take man-kind between their naked arms and without putting off their divinity ... and when one thinks imagination can do no more (it) ... suddenly lifts romance into prophecy. ... The Church when it was the most powerful taught learned and unlearned to climb, as it were, to the great moral realities. ... The story-tellers of Ireland ... imagined as fine a fellowship, only it was to the æsthetic realities they would have us climb. ... The Irish poets had also, it may be, what seemed a supernatural sanction, for a chief poet had to understand not only innumerable kinds of poetry, but how to keep himself for nine days in a trance. Surely they believed or half believed in the historical

[1] Yeats, *Autobiography*, p. 218. [2] Yeats, *The Cutting of an Agate*, p. 11.
[3] Yeats, *Wheels and Butterflies*, p. 135.

reality of even their wildest imaginations. And so as soon as Christianity made their hearers desire a chronology that would run side by side with that of the Bible, they delighted in arranging their Kings and Queens, the shadows of forgotten mythology, in long lines that ascended to Adam and his Garden.'[1]

In his preface to Lady Gregory's book on Cuchalain, Yeats speaks of the Irish poets: 'They created for learned and unlearned alike, a communion of heroes, a cloud of stalwart witnesses; but because they were as much excited as a monk over his prayers, they did not think sufficiently about the shape of the poem and the story. . . . The wood-carver who first put a sword into St. Michael's hand would as soon have claimed as his own a thought which was perhaps put into his mind by St. Michael himself. . . . The Church when it was most powerful created an imaginative unity, for it taught learned and unlearned to climb, as it were, to the great moral realities through hierarchies of Cherubim and Seraphim, through clouds of saints and angels who had all their precise duties and privileges. The story-tellers of Ireland, perhaps of every primitive country, created a like unity, only it was to the great æsthetic realities that they taught the people to climb.' Yeats has here the implicit suggestion that the Church was most powerful when it did not distrust images as a legitimate part of the ladder to truth. But instead of elaborating this, he goes off into his usual parallelism, spiced with characteristic expressions like 'as it were', 'perhaps', 'it may be', that succeed only in pressing the button that releases a fine spray of mist to obscure everything!

And Yeats thinks that his self-indulged, magic-loving countrymen come as near to authoritative vision as the ascetics:

'They have no asceticism, but they are more visionary than any ascetic, and their invisible life is but the life about them made more perfect and more lasting, and the invisible people are their own images in the water.'[2]

What Yeats is perhaps trying to express is the feeling that more up-to-date peoples and civilizations have separated what was once and should be, a unity: that is—they have turned religion into a thin abstraction and separated it wholly from that great realm of irrational forces which manifests itself in folklore, myth, magic,

[1] Yeats, *The Cutting of an Agate*, pp. 7, 1, 3.   [2] *Ibid.*, p. 25.

superstition, the findings of psychology, and the less sophisticated ancestry of science.

Such ramifications of Yeats' main theory are sometimes difficult to follow and tenuous to comprehend. Yet it is wholly characteristic of Yeats to seek the intricate and esoteric, the unusual and the extreme. The association removed several steps from the common source is all the more fascinating to him because he felt at a disadvantage without a university training. 'Busy with strange and subtle thoughts', he could never respect 'a vision-seeking man' who made 'a choice of an almost easy kind of skill instead of the kind which is, of all those not impossible, the most difficult. Is it not certain that the Creator yawns in earthquake and thunder and other popular displays, but toils in rounding the delicate spiral of a shell?'[1] And it is in this spirit of 'the fascination of what's difficult' that Yeats' theories grew,—the spirit in which he pursued the task of seeking to become his own opposite, in order to transcend his own warring selves.

And yet,

'even in my most perfect moment, I would be two selves, the one watching with heavy eyes the other's moment of content. I had heaped about me the gold born in the crucibles of others; but the supreme moment of the alchemist, the transmutation of the weary heart into a weariless spirit, was as far from me as, I doubted not, it had been from him also.'[2]

Yeats still finds himself divided into two selves, and neither of them content. He must choose 'perfection of the life or of the work'. For although he *seems* to have chosen perfection of the work through his magical techniques, the desire for a noble life pulls him in the other direction still. And he plunges deeper into the dream of reconciliation.

'Every writer, even every small writer, who has belonged to the great tradition, has had his dream of an impossibly noble life, and the greater he is, the more does it seem to plunge him into some beautiful or bitter reverie. Some, and of these are all the earliest poets of the world, gave it direct expression; others mingle it so subtly with reality, that it is a day's work to untangle it; others bring it most near by showing one whatever is most its contrary . . . so

[1] Yeats, *Autobiography*, p. 213. [2] Yeats, *Stories of Red Hanrahan*, p. 194.

transformed by the dream that they would choose blindness rather than reality.'[1]

'Others bring it most near by showing one whatever is most its contrary.' This is, of course, Yeats' own way, the deliberate masking of his own 'secret fanaticism'. And the magician-poet says: 'the more I tried to make my art deliberately beautiful, the more did I follow the opposite of myself ... our deceit will give us style, mastery, that dignity, that lofty and severe quality Verlaine spoke of.'[2]

Yeats was not able to admit this until his boyhood was long past. While he was under his father's influence he pretended that the Mask was the whole truth. And even now when he can tell us that the mask is but a pose to hide the inner self that is totally different, he finds it impossible to expose the 'secret fanaticism' to ridicule and mockery. Besides, Yeats likes secrets. But he cannot resist giving solemn and mysterious hints.

The first hints come with the first admissions that magic is no more than a mask. In 1914 Yeats writes once more of Michael Robartes who, in Yeats' earlier stories, had always symbolized the magical self. Robartes appears 'looking something between a debauchee, a saint, and a peasant', and reminiscing of their student days in Paris, tries to lure the poet into further magical adventures. Yeats consents, but finds that:

'when we had started and Michael Robartes had fallen asleep, as he soon did, his sleeping face, in which there was no sign of all that had so shaken me and now kept me wakeful, was to my excited mind more like a mask than a face. The fancy possessed me that the man behind it had dissolved away like salt in water, and that it had laughed, sighed, appealed and denounced at the bidding of beings greater or less than man. "This is not Michael Robartes at all; Michael Robartes is dead; dead for ten or twenty years perhaps," I kept repeating to myself.'[3]

The mask, for perhaps twenty years, has been but a Mask, not an attitude which out of fear he must impose on the world as the truth of his nature. The Mask, paradoxically, was assumed to please his father, and yet helped him to break away: 'it was only when I began to study psychical research that I broke away from my father's

[1] Yeats, *The Cutting of an Agate*, p. 45. [2] *Ibid.*, p. 68.
[3] Yeats, *Rosa Alchemicha*, p. 210.

influence.'[1] It was now no more or less than a deliberate poetic pose.

The interior division which troubled Yeats' childhood on a very primitive emotional level, is now a complexly sophisticated and almost flaunted theory, after having been submerged for years in the murky machinery of his occultism. At last Yeats seems to have emerged from pseudo-mysticism and obscure, certainly suspect, dabbling in esoteric lore. And he emerges bringing with him some highly interesting ideas concerning dream and reality and the self. These ideas were implicit in his earlier beliefs, but are only crystallized after much mental struggle and experiment. From his statements it is quite evident that the anti-self or mask is for him that of the magician. But, although we have seen that the religious side of himself was what he was trying to hide, Yeats is very cautious about admitting that his secret dream of an impossibly noble life is the aspiration towards sainthood, that is, towards mysticism, since Yeats summed up all the highest religious activities of man in the one word, the 'Saint'.

As usual he proceeds to his admission by 'excuse and evasion'— hints rather than statements, and quite rightly so for it is indeed amusing to think of the 'sixty-year-old public man' with a halo. Dazzling us by words and delicate distinctions, and impersonal comparisons between the saint and the magical poet, he almost succeeds in keeping us from recognizing a personal issue. In *The Two Kinds of Asceticism* he writes that:

'the imaginative writer differs from the saint in that he identifies himself—to the neglect of his own soul, alas!—with the soul of the world, and frees himself from all that is impermanent in that soul, an ascetic not of wine and women, but of the newspapers.'[2]

The undertone is, of course, that Yeats is trying to justify his own identification with Anima Mundi, while knowing better. He goes on comparing poet and saint, making subtle distinctions that really serve to bring them closer together and emphasize common ground:

'That which is permanent in the soul of the world upon the other hand, the great passions that trouble all and have but a brief recurring life of flower and seed in any man, is the renunciation of the Saint who seeks not an eternal art, but his own eternity. The

[1] Yeats, *Autobiography*, p. 79.   [2] Yeats, *The Cutting of an Agate*, p. 94.

artist stands between the saint and the world of impermanent things.
. . . The end for art is the ecstasy awakened by the presence before
an ever-changing mind of what is permanent in the world, or by
the arousing of that mind itself into the very delicate and fastidious
mood habitual with it when it is seeking those permanent and recurring things. There is a little bit of both ecstasies at all times, but at
this time we have a small measure of the creative impulse itself, of
the divine vision, a great one of "the lost traveller's dream under the
hill".'[1]

The Saint and the poet are over all, Yeats goes on to say: they are
complementary halves. Together they find the truth.

'There is an old saying that God is a circle whose centre is everywhere. If this is true the saint goes to the centre, the poet and artist
to the ring where everything comes round again. The poet must
not seek for what is still and fixed, for that has no life for him. . . .
Is it that all things are made by the struggle of the individual and the
world of the unchanging and the returning, and that the Saint and
the poet are over all, and that the poet has made his home in the
serpent's mouth? . . . Instinct creates the recurring and the beautiful,
all the winding of the serpent . . . sanctity has its straight also, darting
from the centre, and with these arrows the many-coloured serpent,
theme of all our poetry, is maimed and hunted. He who finds the
white arrow shall have wisdom older than the serpent, but what of
the black arrow? How much knowledge, how heavy a quiver of the
crow-feathered ebony rods can the soul endure?'[2]

In other words, how far can Yeats go in magical knowledge for the
sake of his art without jeopardizing his soul, without disturbing the
delicate balance?

'Only when we are saint or sage, and renounce Experience itself,
can we, in imagery of the Christian Caballa, leave the sudden
lightening and the path of the serpent and become the bowman
who aims his arrow at the centre of the sun.'[3]

Aldous Huxley says that most poets and 'men of genius take such
infinite pains not to become saints'[4] because if they climbed high
enough in the mystical Way, the labour of composition would be

[1] Yeats, *The Cutting of an Agate*, p. 94.   [2] *Ibid.*, p. 97.
[3] Yeats, *Essays*, p. 504.   [4] Aldous Huxley, *Time Must Have a Stop*, p. 247.

a hindrance. And so out of self-preservation they do not climb to where their great insight might and should take them. And Yeats says:

'When I think of any great poetical writer of the past ... I comprehend if I know the lineaments of his life, that the work is the man's flight from his entire horoscope, his blind struggle in the network of the stars.'[1]

or

'I understand why there is a deep enmity between a man and his destiny, and why a man loves nothing but his destiny.'[2]

We are still not absolutely sure what Yeats thinks his destiny is, destiny being the hidden and fleed-from self which lies beyond the mask of enchanter. We suspect from Yeats' hints that it is the man of religion who treads the mystical way and sees visions—all that he sums up in the figure of the Saint. And the following lines confirm this as nothing else short of a direct statement could. Keeping in mind the figure of the magician, Ahasuerus, and Yeats' adoption of the tower symbol as his own as well as of 'cold windy lights', let us read Yeats' description:

'The other day I was walking towards Urbino ... I was alone amid a visionary, fantastic, impossible scenery ... away south upon another mountain a medieval tower, with no buildings near or any sign of life, rose into the clouds. I saw suddenly in the mind's eye an old man, erect, and a little gaunt, standing in the door of the tower, while about him broke a windy light. He was the poet who had at last, because he had done so much for the word's sake, come to share in the dignity of the Saint. ... And though he had but sought it for the word's sake, ... it had come at last into his body and mind. Certainly as he stood there he knew how from behind that laborious mood, that pose, that genius, no flower of himself but all himself, looked out as from behind a mask that other Who alone of all men, the country people say, is not a hair's breadth more nor less than six feet high.'[3]

And Sturge Moore 'had occasion to remark that Yeats' ... sole object was to break through the so-called real world ... to some eternal world.'[4] It is the technique, the 'laborious mood' of the poet

[1] Yeats, *Essays*, p. 489.   [2] *Ibid.*, p. 499.   [3] *Ibid.*, p. 360.
[4] L. MacNeice, *The Poetry of W. B. Y.*, p. 20.

magician which will 'beat upon the wall till Truth obey his call' and the vision of the true self, the saint be won.

But alas, this final, austere picture of the saint and enchanter united is only in Yeats' imagination, the goal towards which he must climb. He is still 'two selves, the one watching with heavy eyes the other's moment of content.' 'Out of the quarrel with ourselves we make poetry . . . no mind can engender till divided in two.'[1] For although 'in all great poetical styles there is saint or hero' Yeats thinks it useless to argue 'as if any poet or painter or musician could be other than an enchanter calling with a persuasive or compelling ritual, creatures, noble or ignoble, divine or dæmonic . . . that he never imagined, out of the bottomless depths of imaginations he never foresaw; as if the noblest achievement of art was not when the artist enfolds himself in darkness, while he casts over his readers a light as of a wild and terrible dawn.'[2]

[1] Yeats, *Essays*, p. 495.   [2] *Ibid.*, p. 174.

Chapter Three

'TIL I AM WILLIAM BLAKE'

~~~~~~

I T is not surprising that the Saint and the Enchanter can live together as well as battle within the mind of a poet, particularly
in a country like Ireland where the two traditions have lived side
by side for so many centuries, and indeed are sometimes mingled.
But Yeats reached his conclusion by devious ways, and in combination with his varied theories, the conviction that his true self is the
saint seems a little fantastic. 'For years,' he writes in the introduction
to *Resurrection*,

'I have been preoccupied with a certain myth that was itself a reply
to a myth.'

And yet, sometimes the myths are not opposed, but muddled, and
as Ellman says, he

'read mystical writers because they saw symbols in everything, and
with the same general purpose he sought out those who said they
could manipulate external nature by magic.'[1]

But what, we may ask, does Yeats' belief that he is divided into
two selves have to do with Yeats' interpretation of Blake? Does it
shed any light on the strange phraseology of the lines quoted at
the start—

> *Myself must I remake*
> *Til I am ... William Blake*
> *Who beat upon the wall*
> *Til Truth obeyed his call.*

[1] Ellman, *The Man and the Masks*, p. 55.

This is Yeats the magician speaking of Blake as if he, too, were a magician, using shock tactics to shake loose a greater truth than Yeats has yet found. And yet it is evident that Yeats realized the antithesis between magic and mysticism, and indeed he often makes it quite clear that he realizes the mystical nature of Blake's work.

Actually, both sides of Yeats wanted to claim Blake as authority for their existence: the side which is the public self and is the 'laborious mood' of poet and enchanter, and the secret self which is summed up in the inclusive name of Saint. This causes great confusion. Over and over we find what are apparently contradictory statements about Blake, or ambiguous ones. For instance, Yeats writes: 'If I had not made magic my constant study I could not have written a single word of my Blake book.'[1] His next sentence proclaims that

'the mystical life is the centre of all that I do and all that I think and all that I write. . . . I have always considered myself a voice of what I consider to be a greater renaissance—the revolt of the soul against the intellect—now beginning in the world.'

This would sound very much as if Yeats were confusing or identifying magic and mysticism, had we not seen how painfully well he understood the difference. Consequently we can only judge that he is speaking first in the voice of the magician, and then in the voice of the 'saint'. Thus he says one moment that the poet cannot 'be other than an enchanter', and the next compares Blake's 'anger against causes and purposes he but half understood' to 'that veritable madness an Eastern scripture thinks permissible among the saints; for he who half lives in eternity endures a rending of the structure of the mind, a crucifixion of the intellectual body,'[2] and 'solitary men in moments of contemplation receive, as I think, the creative impulse from the lowest of the Nine Hierarchies.'[3]

Sometimes without actually saying it (his old trick of evasion) Yeats strongly implies that Blake was in sympathy with magic. For instance, he writes:

'I could tell of strange images of strange enchantments . . . after all, one can but bear witness less to convince him who won't believe than to protect him who does, as Blake puts it, enduring "unbelief

[1] Ellman, *The Man and the Masks*, p. 94.
[2] Yeats, *Essays*, p. 156.   [3] *Ibid.*, p. 195.

58

and misbelief and ridicule as best one may".... All men, certainly all imaginative men, must be forever casting forth enchantments, glamours, illusions, and all men, especially tranquil men who have no powerful egotistic life, must be continually passing under their power.'[1]

Yeats suggests that Blake and indeed all mystics believe in his pantheistic great memory of nature:

'Blake had not such mastery over figure and drapery as had Botticelli, but he could sympathize with the persons and delight in the scenery of the "Inferno" and the "Purgatorio" as Botticelli could not and fill them with a mysterious and spiritual significance born perhaps of mystical pantheism.... Mystics of many countries and many centuries, have spoken of this memory; and the honest men and charlatans who keep the magical traditions which will some day be studied as a part of folk-lore, base most that is of importance in their claims upon this memory.... I have found it in the prophetic books of William Blake, who calls its images "the bright sculpture of Los's Halls".... At whatever risk we must cry out that imagination is always seeking to remake the world according to the impulses and the patterns in that great Memory. Can there be anything so important as to cry out what we call romance, poetry, and intellectual beauty is the only signal that the supreme Enchanter, or some one in His Councils, is speaking.'[2]

Or, telling about magically evoked visions, Yeats implies that Blake is the authority: 'it may be, as Blake said of one of his poems, that the author was in eternity.'[3]

It is interesting to note that, so concerned was he with his own sense of dualism between spiritual and natural things, Yeats in one paragraph reverses Blake's meaning completely to coincide with his own view. Blake cries over and over that there is no dualism between body and soul, but Yeats interprets:

'All such solutions (as Natural Religion) according to him arise from the belief that natural and spiritual things do not differ in kind; for if they do so differ, no mere analysis of nature as it exists outside our minds can solve the problems of mental life. This absolute difference may be described as the first postulate of all mystics.'[4]

---

[1] Yeats, *Essays*, p. 46.   [2] *Ibid.*, pp. 59, 224.   [3] *Ibid.*, p. 42.
[4] Yeats and Ellis, *William Blake*, Vol. I, p. 236.

Yeats speaks from a slightly different slant in the following passage, but is equally conscientious in trying to make Blake as much like himself as possible:

'When one reads Blake it is as though the spray of an inexhaustible fountain of beauty was blown into our faces, and not merely when one reads the *Songs of Innocence*, or the lyrics he wished to call *The Ideas of Good and Evil*, but when one reads those "Prophetic Works" in which he spoke confusedly and obscurely because he spoke of things for whose speaking he could find no models in the world about him. He was a symbolist who had to invent his symbols; and his counties of England with their correspondence to tribes of Israel, and his mountains and rivers, with their correspondence to parts of a man's body, are arbitrary as some of the symbolism in the *Axel* of symbolist Villiers de L'Isle Adam is arbitrary, while they mix incongruous things as *Axel* does not. He was a man crying out for a mythology, and trying to make one because he did not find one to his hand. Had he been a Catholic of Dante's time he would have been content with Mary and the Angels; or had he been a scholar of our time he would have taken his symbols where Wagner took his from Norse mythology, or have followed with the help of Professor Rhys, that pathway into Welsh mythology which he found in "Jerusalem"; or have gone to Ireland—and he was probably an Irishman—and chosen for his symbols the sacred mountains, along whose sides the peasant still sees enchanted fires, and the divinities which had not faded from the belief, if they have faded from the prayers of simple hearts; and have spoken without mixing incongruous things because he spoke of things that have long been steeped in emotion; and have been less obscure because a traditional mythology stood on the margin of his sacred darkness. If "Enitharmon" had been named Freia, or Gwydeon, or Danu, and made live in Ancient Norway or Ancient Wales, or Ancient Ireland, we would have forgotten that her maker was a mystic.'[1]

'We would have forgotten that her maker was a mystic'! Surely this is both curious and significant. Yeats seems to feel that Blake the poet should have, like himself, carefully hidden all mystical leanings, have not allowed himself to be swept away as in the later prophetic writings. Yet Blake the seeker and finder of truth was almost envied by Yeats. Yeats wanted the vision of the 'Saint' that

[1] Yeats, *Essays*, p. 140.

Blake had, but while creating would prefer to forget it in favour of the enchanter's technique, for

'the systematic mystic is not the greatest of artists because his imagination is too great to be bounded by a picture or song, and because only imperfection in a mirror of perfection, or perfection in a mirror of imperfection delight our frailty. There is indeed a systematic mystic in every poet or painter who, like Rossetti, delights in a traditional symbolism, or, like Wagner, delights in a personal symbolism; and such men often fall into trances, or have waking dreams.'[1]

And so he scolds Blake a little for being too frankly the mystic, and is convinced that Blake, given the opportunity, would have gone eagerly to the 'enchanted fires' of Ireland, and like himself become one of the company of sorcerers.

To emphasize the fact that the mystic does not suffer by masking as the enchanter, Yeats adds the comfortable thought that 'there is indeed a systematic mystic in every poet or painter who . . . delights in symbolism.' Convinced that his own painfully evolved method of reaching the vision of the saint through its own opposite—and, paradoxically, its own mask—of the magician-poet, was the only way for the artist, most of his ambiguous and unorthodox interpretation of Blake stems from the fact that he is convincing himself that Blake, too, arrived at his vision by this method. For, he asks—is it not true that

'all Art, that is not mere story-telling or mere portraiture, is symbolic, and has the purpose of those symbolic talismans which medieval magicians made with complex colours and forms, and bade their patients ponder over daily, and guard with holy secrecy; for it entangles, in complex colours and forms, a part of the Divine Essence . . . our dreams make all things perfect . . . symbols are the only things free enough from all bonds to speak of perfection.

'Wagner's dramas, Keats' odes, Blake's pictures and poems, Calvert's pictures . . . but differ from the religious art of Giotto and his disciples in having accepted all symbolisms, and the symbolism of the ancient shepherds and star-gazers, the symbolism of bodily beauty which seemed a wicked thing to Fra Angelico, the symbolism in day and night, and winter, spring, and autumn, once so great a

[1] Yeats, *Essays*, p. 185.

part of an older religion than Christianity . . . Blake represented the shapes of beauty haunting our moments of inspiration: shapes held by most for the frailest of ephemera, but by him for a people older than the world, citizens of eternity . . . purifying one's mind, as with a flame, in study of the works of the great masters, who were great because they had been granted by divine favour a vision of the unfallen world from which others have been kept apart by the flaming sword which turns every way.'[1]

Remembering Yeats' lines about the 'old saying that God is a circle whose centre is everywhere', and that 'the saint goes to the centre, the poet and artist to the ring where everything comes round again . . . instinct creates the recurring and the beautiful, all the winding of the serpent', the following lines from the Blake book are in significant relation:

'With the finality of the sectary and reformer Swedenborg believed that his new revelation was to last forever and not to be merely a new turn of the wheel. Blake's mind was infinitely more subtle. Not only did it widen the whole doctrine of the Three Churches by tracing its relation to Nature, and all bodily and mental growth, but it deepened it by making it part of the inevitable rotation of all things. Blake dared to see that the serpent must always keep its tail in its mouth, and creed follow creed, no matter how bitter be our longing for finality. Into this ever-revolving circle Christ only can descend and draw man upward out of nature into supernature, out of the "wheel of birth" into the eternity of the uncreated.'[2]

Since this concept of Christ descending into the wheel of birth is an almost exact foretaste of Phase 15 of *A Vision*, we can conclude that even earlier than 1892 Yeats had the main structure of ideas for his magical system. These ideas were supposed to come from the 'unknown instructors', but they are so like this early view of Blake —from the wheel of nature to the one outlet in the 15th phase where, through the accident of freedom, man may ascend out of determinism—that we can have no doubt that Yeats' interpretation of Blake was behind *A Vision*. If Yeats had forgotten the source, we must at least identify the 'unknown instructors' with the unconscious.

[1] Yeats, *Essays*, pp. 178, 230. [2] Yeats and Ellis, *William Blake*, Vol. I, p. 293.

It is evident that, in his own mind at least, Yeats has established that Blake had a magical side, despite Samuel Palmer's insistence that Blake 'was a man without a mask'.[1] However, Yeats always keeps an eye on Blake the mystic, or, as he would say, the saint. 'Blake even desired, when his eyes were fixed on the ultimate, that his efforts and art might receive no reward on the immediate plane. It is the language of the saints.'[2] And, he adds:

'It must never be forgotten that whatever Blake borrowed from Swedenborg and Boehme, from mystic or Kabalist, he turned to his own purpose and transferred into a new system, growing like a flower from its own roots ... and he stands among the mystics of Europe, beside Jacob Boehme and the makers of the kabala as original as they are and as profound. He is one of those great artificers of God who uttered mysterious truths.'[3]

But in the next few pages, Yeats slips back into the magical interpretation of Blake's work:

'Merlin's book lies open before us, and if we cannot decipher its mystical symbols, then we may dream over the melody of evocations that are not for our conjuring, and over the strange colours and woven forms of the spread pages.'[4]

Finally, magic and religion are joined together in Yeats' interpretation of Blake, at the risk of distorting Blake's own meaning. Yeats says:

'The next (quotation) shows that theology and magic were receiving together a share of contemplation unusually penetrating even for Blake.

TO GOD

If you have formed a circle to go into,
Go into it yourself and see what you would do.

and

Since all the Riches of this world
May be gifts from the Devil, etc.'[5]

[1] Samuel Palmer, *Letters*, p. 170.
[2] Yeats and Ellis, *William Blake*, Vol. I, p. 293.
[3] Yeats, 1906 edition of *Blake*, intro., p. xxxi.   [4] *Ibid.*, p. xxxvi.
[5] Yeats and Ellis, *William Blake*, Vol. I, p. 226.

It is significant to note how Yeats paraphrases Blake's attitude to imagination:

'In Imagination only we find a Human Faculty that touches nature on one side and spirit on the other. Imagination may be described as that which is sent bringing spirit to nature, entering into nature and seemingly losing its spirit, that nature being revealed as symbol may lose the power to delude.'[1]

This is purely Yeatsian phraseology, and it turns Blake's idea of imagination into what almost looks like Yeats' theory of magical symbols which are the links between dream and reality.

Quite often Yeats went to almost wild extremes to make Blake seem like himself, or himself like Blake. He used the most charlatan of magical tricks in an effort to see visions. On the shakiest evidence[2] he 'proved' that Blake was Irish, and he was as pleased as a child in the similarity of their initials. And with all solemnity he wrote the following lines in the three-volume edition of Blake:

'It is possible that he (Blake) received initiation into an order of Christian kabalists then established in London and known as "The Hermetic Students of the Golden Dawn". Of course this conjecture is not susceptible of proof. He would have said nothing about such initiation even if he had received it. The "students" in question do not name themselves or each other and the subject of their study is nothing less than universal magic.'[3]

Needless to say, Yeats was a member of the 'Hermetic Students of the Golden Dawn'. Later in the Blake book, Yeats and Ellis say:

'The writers of this book may say with the famous Eliphas Levi Zahed: "I have evoked and I have seen", and in the vision produced by the evocations of symbolic magic they have learnt, what Blake knew so well, that the phantoms often appear in forms not inherent in themselves, but borrowed from the personality of the seer as a clothing for their impalpable essence. These palpable forms would have been classed by Blake as a portion of the "covering cherub" or mask of created form in which the uncreated spirit makes itself visible.'[4]

[1] Yeats and Ellis, *William Blake*, Vol. I, preface, p. xiii.
[2] See Appendix.
[3] Yeats and Ellis, *William Blake*, Vol. I, p. 24.   [4] *Ibid.*, p. 288.

This is but a highly ornate way of expressing Yeats' theory that the hidden spiritual self seeks a visible mask, although Yeats had not yet published his doctrine of self and mask. In many parts of the Blake book we find hints of coming Yeatsian doctrine as well as evidence that he thought of Blake as both mystic and enchanter.

Speaking of a line in Blake's *Marriage of Heaven and Hell*, Yeats gives some insight into his own problem:

'The next memorable fancy states the fundamental doctrine of transcendentalism in its positive forms—" a firm persuasion that a thing is so makes it so". This is the root of hypnotic suggestion and all magic. Incidentally, it refutes the negative side of transcendentalism which has got to deny nature any objectivity, for it is evident that objectivity can come into existence from its opposite by means of a firm persuasion.'[1]

In other words, if Yeats can believe hard enough in his dreams, he can project a nature as perfect—'our dreams make all things perfect,' and 'objectivity can come into existence from its opposite by means of a firm persuasion.' The Blake that seems magical as well as mystic, seems to provide a solution for Yeats' own battle of dream versus reality. That is, if one could only find the key of a firm enough persuasion. It is grand to cry—

> .... *declare my faith*
> *I mock Plotinus' thought*
> *And cry in Plato's teeth,*
> *Death and life were not*
> *Till man made up the whole,*
> *Made lock, stock and barrel*
> *Out of his bitter soul.*[2]

But Yeats, for all his declaration of faith in arrogant magical vision and in what he longed to believe, could never, like Blake, have absolute conviction that they were so:

> *And yet, and yet,*
> *Is this my dream,*
> *Or the truth?*[3]

It made him, perhaps, a more poignant poet. Yeats hoped that

---

1 Yeats and Ellis, *William Blake*, Vol. II, p. 69.
2 Yeats, *Collected Poems*, p. 229.   3 *Ibid.*, p. 155.

Blake had walked the same way. For if he had, there was Truth at the end of the walk.

Yeats had not even a 'firm persuasion' about his own interpretation of Blake. In May 1900 he wrote a paragraph in his personal copy of the 1893 Blake:

'This book is full of misprints. There is a good deal here and there in the biography, etc., with which I am not in agreement. I think that some of my own "constructive symbolism"—is put with too much confidence. It is mainly right but should be used rather as an interpretive hypothesis than as a certainty. The circulation by the Zoas, which seems to me unlike anything in traditional symbolism is the chief case of uncertainty, but most that I have written on the subject is at least part of Blake's plan. There is also uncertainty about the personages who are mentioned by him too seldom to make one know them perfectly; here and then elsewhere.'[1]

And a margin note in his own handwriting on page 265 states that in reference to the rotation of Luvah and Orc he now finds 'HPV[2] a doubtful authority—I would never quote him now.' And on the elaborate chart facing page 280 Yeats remarks: 'I feel rather uncertain about the alternations of the twelve tribes in this chart. May 1900.' And in March 1902, going over the books once again, he jots down on page 314: 'I am not convinced that Blake's colour scheme was founded on Boehme's.'

It is interesting to note that the studies of Blake by Denis Saurat, who is mostly concerned with Blake's so-called occultism, made a strong impression on Yeats. In his own copy of Saurat's *Blake and Modern Thought*, there are many marked passages. There are one or two marginal comments worth noting. On page 19 where Saurat interprets Blake's theory of contraries, Yeats adds: 'Hegel and Fichte's *dialectic* in the rough. I think there was no such thought known in England in Blake's day. It is fundamental in Blake.' Yeats made it fundamental in his own thought, no matter what we think of its magnitude in Blake's system. On page 31 there is a humorous note that speaks for itself: 'Blake is difficult and perhaps meant to be. Hayley was so clear.' When, on page 82, Saurat entitles Blake's theories 'a strange mystical imperialism', Yeats scratches impatiently:

---

[1] Note in Yeats' handwriting in his private copy of the Yeats and Ellis *Blake* volumes.

[2] Madame Blavatsky.

'Oh Saurat! When England awakens she becomes the whole world because "the flood of Time and Space" has disappeared—you cannot localize or imperialize eternity.' And on page 85:

'to sum—Blake did not think England the place of primitive humanity or of the original wisdom because these were before the flood of Time and Space. The historical Druids he thought degenerate man . . . He spoke of England and its past because he lived there . . . Blake seeks the near and particular always. Saurat, like Blake's other critics, never recognizes Blake's humour, his love of bewildering, his art-student tricks.'

Blake had humour, yes—the precise and observant sense of fun that can make sacred things endearing and concrete, was always ready. But as for 'his love of bewildering', and his 'art-student tricks', these seem more the property of the magician who cried: 'Myself must I remake, til I am William Blake.'

Chapter Four

'WITH ALL THE FURY OF A SPIRITUAL EXISTENCE'

Is there any evidence to justify Yeats' unorthodox interpretation of Blake—the view that Blake, like himself and as authority for himself, was both saint and enchanter? Could these two sides possibly be at war in the prophetic Blake, and did he perhaps shake down the vision of the mystic by the shock tactics of the enchanter? This thought seems almost unworthy of consideration when it is so apparent from the very surface of Blake's work that he was all prophet, or, as Yeats would say, all saint. But most interpretations of Blake are based on a surface view which is certainly confusing enough without burrowing any deeper. Could we, if we looked far enough, find the enchanter hidden behind the pose of prophet, just as we found the saint hiding somewhere, if not very near, behind Yeats' mask of magician?

To ascertain this, Blake's work must be examined on a deeper level. Evidence must be found for or against the conflict. At any rate, we must ask why Yeats could believe these two sides to be at war within Blake's mind.

The very fact that Yeats thought Blake a great poet might have been enough for him to call him a magician too, for Yeats equated poet and magician. But this reason alone is far too subjective even for Yeats, and we must at least give his view of Blake a chance. We must look for aspects of Blake's work that might be called magical, and see whether they are in conflict with his mysticism.

If there is a magical side to Blake, it must be a side which works through nature and is in conflict with it in so far as it seeks control. It is obvious that Blake did not scorn to take symbols from the realm of nature, no matter how he decries Nature at times. His paintings and his poems are full of such symbols. This Yeats would be able to use as an argument that Blake was magical, and used magical symbols from nature to break through to the saint's vision. For, were he mystic or saint alone, he would, according to Yeats, have 'renounced Experience' in order to climb 'to the antithetical self of the world'. Yeats could conceive of the saint expressing his vision in terms of light or nothingness, or in abstractions, but he could not grasp the mystic's vision of nature transformed. He would conclude that Blake's use of natural symbol was magical. Is he perhaps right? It is interesting to note that no less a person than G. K. Chesterton also hints that Blake had something of the magician about him: he may well be following Yeats and Ellis in this, however, as he also swallows their theory that Blake was an Irishman, an O'Neill.

'The revolt of the eighteenth century ... did not merely release naturalism, but a certain kind of supernaturalism also. And of this particular kind of supernaturalism Blake is particularly the heir. Its coarse embodiment is Cagliostro. Its noble embodiment is Swedenborg. But in both cases it can be remarked that the mysticism marks an effort to escape from or even forget the historic Christian, and especially the Catholic Church. Cagliostro being a man of mean spirituality, separated himself from Catholicism by rearing against it a blazing pageant of mystical paganism, of triangles, secret seals, Eleusinian initiation, and all the vulgar refinements of a secret society. Swedenborg being a man of large and noble spirituality, marked his separation from Catholicism by inventing out of his own innocence and genius all the old Catholic doctrines. ... There was in Blake a great deal of Swedenborg (as he would have been the first to admit), and there was, occasionally, a little of Cagliostro. Blake did not belong to a secret society: for, to tell the truth, he had some difficulty in belonging to any society. But Blake did talk a secret language. He had something of that haughty and oligarchic element in his mysticism which marked the old pagan secret societies and which marks the Theosophists and oriental initiates to this day. There was in him, besides the beneficent wealth of Swedenborg, some touch of Cagliostro and the Freemasons. These things Blake did inherit from that break up of belief that can be called the eighteenth century.'[1]

And many other critics hint that there is a side to Blake that is not only magical, but almost allied to diabolic powers. Instead of

[1] Chesterton, *William Blake*, p. 124.

hinting, let us examine Blake's attitude to Nature and to the powers behind it, and try to determine, more or less prosaically, whether there were in fact two sides at war in Blake—or whether the critics are too facile at sticking the label of occultism on what they do not understand in the mystical sphere.

Although in his fully developed philosophy Blake often decries Nature or the Mundane Shell as illusion, one would be inclined to think of Blake in his youth as much more interested in nature than in mysticism, judging by the poem titles in his first book, *Poetical Sketches:* 'To Spring', 'To Summer', 'To Autumn', 'To Winter', 'To The Evening Star', and 'To Morning'. Hazlitt numbered Blake among those 'whose ideas are like a stormy night, with the clouds driven rapidly across, and the blue sky gleaming between.'[1] The poems in *Poetical Sketches* (1783) are, for the most part, perfectly straightforward and rather derivative invocations to the seasons and events of each day, personified of course, and with much natural observation for adornment. There was, at least in Blake's youth, a side that was interested in natural phenomena. Yeats, in his own small edition of Blake's poetry, says of the *Poetical Sketches*:

'This was the only purely literary and purely artistic period of his life; for in a very short time he came to look upon poetry and art as a language for the utterance of conceptions, which, however beautiful, were none the less thought out more for their visionary truth than for their beauty. The change made him a greater poet and a greater artist.'[2]

This is the change Yeats hoped would happen to him if he made powerful enough symbols out of natural beauty. He goes on about *Poetical Sketches:*

'The poems mark an epoch in English literature, for they were the first opening of the long-sealed well of English poetry; they, and not the works of Cowper and Thompson and Chatterton, being the true heralds of our modern poetry of nature and enthusiasm. There is in them no trace of mysticism, but phrases and figures of speech which were soon to pass from the metaphorical to the symbolic stage, and put on mystical significance.'[3]

It is not until we reach the two lovely lyrics in this book called 'Song' and 'Mad Song' that we find Blake's interest in the events

[1] William Hazlitt.   [2] Yeats and Ellis, *William Blake*, Vol. I, p. xxviii.   [3] *Ibid.*

of nature becoming subservient to something else, and at the same time, the charming but stilted 'poetic' language and form giving way to simpler, more striking words and a subtle rhyming music.

SONG

How sweet I roam'd from field to field,
And tasted all the summer's pride,
Till I the prince of love beheld
Who in the sunny beams did glide!

He shew'd me lilies for my hair,
And blushing roses for my brow.
He led me through his gardens fair,
Where all his golden pleasures grow.

With sweet May dews my wings were wet,
And Phoebus fir'd my vocal rage;
He caught me in his silken net,
And shut me in his golden cage.

He loves to sit and hear me sing,
Then, laughing, sports and plays with me;
Then stretches out my golden wing,
And mocks my loss of liberty.

A startling precision of word and image has come to replace the rather laboured points of the preceding poems, as, for example:

My lord was like a flower upon the brows
Of lusty May! Ah, life is frail as flower!
Oh ghastly death! withdraw thy cruel hand,
Seek'st thou that flow'r to deck thy horrid temples?[1]

It is to be doubted if even the young Hayley could rival this!

More important in this 'Song' is the 'something else' by which the nature imagery is controlled and pared down to the bare bones. It is the beginning of Blake's mystical philosophy. Paradoxically, this mysticism which destroys much of the coherence of the later prophetic books, is the very thing whose addition to the early lyrics tautens and unifies image and thought.

It is quite obvious that 'Song' is no mere invocation to a season or star as are the preceding lyrics. Simpler in expression, it gains

[1] The Blake poems quoted are all from *The Complete Poetry of William Blake.*

complexity of thought. Relating the joy of wandering through nature with a free heart, Blake contrasts the heightened sensitivity to natural beauty that love brings, a sensitivity that becomes eventually a tyranny over the senses. We are not sure whether this love is eros or agape. The latter would, of course, make the end much more subtle. The image of the bird caught in a net foreshadows other poems, as does the hatred of restraining forces.

There are many words in this poem which, without being excessive, suggest natural images: 'field', 'summer', 'sunny beams', 'roses', 'lilies', 'gardens', 'May dews', 'golden wings', and 'fir'd'. It is not unlikely that the choice of some of these words is unconsciously symbolic. Roaming from field to field in the height of summer may well mean the freedom of wandering from one happy state of mind to another in innocence. The lilies and blushing roses are symbols that may have led towards Blake's later view of love as both innocent and passionate. 'Golden', repeated three times in this poem and suggested a fourth in 'sunny', has a special significance for Blake always.

In this same book of poems written between the ages of twelve and twenty, the 'Mad Song' is quite perfect of its kind, and also serves to illustrate the new depth and control given to the nature imagery by Blake's dawning mystical sense:

MAD SONG

The wild winds weep,
And the night is a-cold;
Come hither, Sleep,
And my griefs unfold:
But lo! the morning peeps
Over the eastern steeps,
And the rustling birds of dawn
The earth do scorn.

Lo! to the vault
Of paved heaven
With sorrow fraught
My notes are driven:
They strike the ear of night,
Make weep the eyes of day:
They make mad the roaring winds,
And with tempests play.

> *Like a fiend in a cloud,*
> *With howling woe,*
> *After night I do crowd,*
> *And with night will go;*
> *I turn my back to the east,*
> *From whence comforts have increas'd;*
> *For light does seize my brain*
> *With frantic pain.*

There is startling likeness in this to a Chinese love poem written in 718 B.C. from the Palace of Wei, which to my mind has a mystical tone infusing the erotic plaint:

> *The wind blows from the North.*
> *He looks and his eyes are cold.*
> *He looks and smiles and then goes forth,*
> *My grief grows old.*
>
> *The wind blows and the dust:*
> *Tomorrow he swears he will come.*
> *His words are kind, but he breaks his trust,*
> *My heart is numb.*
>
> *All day the wind blew strong,*
> *The sun was buried deep.*
> *I have thought of him so long, so long,*
> *I cannot sleep.*
>
> *The clouds are black with night,*
> *The thunder brings no rain.*
> *I wake and there is no light.*
> *I bear my pain.*[1]

The last four lines of Blake's poem may be what they appear to be, a description of dawn, and no more. Somehow they seem more intense, electric with a subtler significance. Could they not, perhaps, express the situation of the mystic turning both from the material comforts of the world and half from the fearful light of vision into the dark night of the soul, not trusting his capacity for truth. It is the situation of Perceval as portrayed in Julien Grecque's *The Fisher King*; the essentially dazzling, simple, and attainable truth made obscure and difficult, 'gloved' as it were by the facile doubts of the

---

[1] Helen Waddell, *Lyrics from the Chinese*, London, 1945, p. 11.

sick and impotent intellectual who is meant to guard it. It is a stage on the mystic Way which must be passed through or fester with excess of abnegation. The light and darkness are both in Blake's brain, and the light is as painful as only naked truth can be. The title takes on an ironic twist if this interpretation is true. 'Winds', 'night', 'heaven', 'morning', 'tempests', 'cloud', 'light', form the more cosmic natural images of this poem. How perfect in contrast is the particular observation of 'rustling birds of dawn'.

In the *Songs of Innocence and Experience* (1794), such a technique of natural image and metaphysical thought welded in powerful and vivid simplicity, is strengthened even further by another dimension. Words and music, image and thought are inseparable from mystical vision. And each poem is now set within a symbolic design, sometimes carrying out the thought and imagery of the poem, sometimes adding to it or contrasting with it significantly. The effect is as beautiful as a medieval illuminated manuscript, which was undoubtedly where Blake found inspiration.

The general title page presenting the two books is lettered: *Songs of Innocence and Experience, Shewing the Two Contrary States of the Human Soul*. The lettering is swept by birds and flames which roar over Adam and Eve who are crawling like beasts out of Eden. The position of Eve, on all fours, is striking in its likeness to the later picture of Nebuchadnezzar. Eve, the eternal female, symbolizing intuition and the senses, has become completely earthbound and bestial upon leaving Paradise, while Adam, the male who has become the spectre or misuse of reason, is still half upright, and is clutching his head in fear of his god, Urizen's wrath. This is reading much of Blake's later stated beliefs into the design, but the implications are all there.

The important thing about the *Songs* is that so vivid are the natural images and the surface concepts that the poems can be sensibly coherent and 'charming' even to those who do not understand Blake's mysticism which is far from mere charm. The compilers of children's anthologies who include *The Tyger* as a nice animal poem would be horrified if they read a little more Blake and discovered the true meaning of this poem. Mr. Binyon says: 'the verse seems spontaneously to flower into design and decoration, and as such it has charmed the world.'

There is much of this kind of enchantment in Blake's work at this time, and it is almost possible to argue with Yeats that in poetry of

this kind there is a magical union of nature and spirit in songs that
are powerfully beautiful. However, there seems little of the magical
purpose in Blake. Yet the audience is entranced more than awakened
by the voice of the prophet in these *Songs*, and is lured to the brink of
Truth rather than jarred by its clarion call. The means to Blake's
mystical end may very well be called magical in this period.

The poem which Blake calls the 'Introduction' to the *Songs of
Innocence* (1789) is one of his most famous:

> *Piping down the valleys wild,*
>   *Piping songs of pleasant glee,*
> *On a cloud I saw a child,*
>   *And he laughing said to me:*
>
> *'Pipe a song about a lamb!'*
>   *So I piped with merry cheer.*
> *'Piper, pipe that song again';*
>   *So I piped: he wept to hear.*
>
> *'Piper, sit thee down and write*
>   *In a book, that all may read.'*
> *So he vanished from my sight,*
>   *And I pluck'd a hollow reed,*
>
> *And I made a rural pen,*
>   *And I stain'd the water clear,*
> *And I wrote my happy songs*
>   *Every child may joy to hear.*

The pleasing freshness of the bard 'piping down the valleys wild';
the vision of the child on the low-hanging cloud, unheralded by
claps of thunder and gothic lightning; the poet plucking a hollow
reed for pen and staining the clear waters for ink—these images vary
from a quiet familiarity with the supernatural to a rural homeliness,
showing a feeling for country enchantment that rivals that of Yeats
in search of magical tales among the Irish peasants. Yet it is never
ostentatiously or deliberately a spell cast over the reader, as, for
instance, in Yeats' *Song of Wandering Aengus*:

> *I went out to the hazel wood*
> *Because a fire was in my head,*
> *And cut and peeled a hazel wand,*
> *And hooked a berry to a thread.*

And when white moths were on the wing,
And moth-like stars were flickering out,
I dropped the berry in the stream
And caught a little, silver trout, etc.

The twining, leafy margin illuminations of Blake's poem draws us into the Middle Ages, the time which to Yeats seemed mostly a time of legend and alchemy, and for Blake an age of imagination. There are many ingredients in even such a poem of child-like innocence that Yeats might, through a series of associations, or as he would say, 'correspondences', call part of the magician's brew.

It is interesting to note that Blake, in a letter to George Cumberland dated December 23, 1796, makes a *joke* about the relation between magic and art: 'I have likewise had by me all the summer six plates which you desired me to get made for you. They have laid on my shelf, without speaking to tell me whose they were, or what they were at all, and it was some time (when I found them) before I could divine whence they came or whither they were bound, or whether they were to lie there to eternity. I have now sent them to you to be transmuted, thou real alchymist!'

The 'Laughing Song' is a curious poem to have been written by the poet who later called external Nature more or less scornfully 'this Vegetable Universe', and who hated the Deists who worshipped 'the Maternal Humanity, calling it Nature and Natural Religion.'[1]

When the green woods laugh with the voice of joy,
And the dimpling stream runs laughing by,
When the air does laugh with our merry wit,
And the green hill laughs with the noise of it.

When the meadows laugh with lively green
And the grasshopper laughs in the merry scene,
When Mary and Susan and Emily
With their sweet round mouths sing Ha, Ha, He.

When the painted birds laugh in the shade
Where our table with cherries and nuts is spread,
Come love and be merry and join with me
To sing the sweet chorus of Ha, Ha, He.

[1] *The Complete Poetry of William Blake*, p. 1010.

A border of birds and tendrils surrounds the song, and above is a drawing of the shaded table and its laughing guests. The poem and its marginal design make as pleasant a picture of the creatures of nature responding to the human mood as one could find in literature. It is easy to see how Yeats with his belief in the Anima Mundi and in 'correspondences' could interpret this as a similar view, and take this poem as, in his sense, 'magical'.

The setting of Blake's poem, 'The Lamb', is one of the most charming pastoral pieces in the book. A child stands playing with a lamb, one of a large flock. Above them two delicate trees twine upwards until they meet in a high wind-swept arch. The poem itself is in two stanzas, the first a description of the lamb, and the second joining in a few words the child, the lamb, and Christ. The natural and the mystical are complementary here, and the unity is stated clearly enough to reach any child.

THE LAMB

Little Lamb, who made thee?
Dost thou know who made thee?
Gave thee life and bid thee feed
By the stream and o'er the mead;
Gave thee clothing of delight,
Softest clothing, woolly, bright,
Gave thee such a tender voice,
Making all the vales rejoice?
    Little Lamb, who made thee?
    Dost thou know who made thee?

Little Lamb, I'll tell thee,
Little Lamb, I'll tell thee:
He is called by thy name,
For he calls himself a Lamb.
He is meek, and he is mild;
He became a little child.
I a child, and thou a lamb,
We are called by his name.
    Little Lamb, God bless thee!
    Little Lamb, God bless thee!

The poem 'Night' is surrounded by graceful wind-tossed trees, moonlit angels ascending, and gliding earthly figures more heroic than life. It begins with lines full of poetically pleasing natural description:

> The sun descending in the west,
> The evening star does shine;
> The birds are silent in their nest,
> And I must seek for mine.
> The moon like a flower
> In heaven's high bower,
> With silent delight
> Sits and smiles on the night.

It tells of the angels' care of earthly creatures while the world sleeps: 'They look in every thoughtless nest', and 'Keep them all from care.' And

> When wolves and tigers howl for prey,
> They pitying stand and weep;
> Seeking to drive their thirst away,
> And keep them from the sheep;
> But if they rush dreadful,
> The angels, most heedful
> Receive each mild spirit
> New worlds to inherit.

> And there the Lion's ruddy eyes
> Shall flow with tears of gold,
> And pitying the tender cries,
> and walking round the fold,
> Saying ' wrath, by his meekness,
> And by his health, sickness
> Is driven away
> From our immortal day.'

In Blake there is the acute awareness of the gap between actual and ideal which is in Yeats. Yeats tried to bridge it by magical power. If he deduced that Blake had tried to do the same thing, he forgot that Blake was not seeking to break through to the ideal, leaving the actual behind—but to see the actual transformed by the incarnation of the ideal, the earth glorified by the coming of Christ. Where Blake *knows* he can join Nature and eternity through the vision of Christ, Yeats wants to find a vision of he knows not what

Truth by a magical synthesis of two worlds, a drawing together of dream and reality, a sucking up of reality into the dream.

Nevertheless, Yeats was right in thinking that Blake is enough interested in nature and natural symbols to use them with the intensity of the magical poet. Unlike the first period of *Poetical Sketches*, Blake's second period goes beyond a mere interest in describing nature. There is a growing perception of nature images as symbolizing a higher invisible world. There is new tension and vivid simplicity created by playing the image and its mystical counterpart against each other in a way that might be mistaken for a kind of magic were it not for the insistence on Christ the Redeemer.

The poem 'A Dream', quite different from the dreamy wavering effects Yeats wished to produce in his youth, reveals a great compassion for actual creatures, and a precise interpretation of their habits and small tragedies:

> Once a dream did weave a shade
> O'er my Angel-guarded bed,
> That an Emmet lost its way
> Where on grass methought I lay.
>
> Troubled, 'wildered, and forlorn,
> Dark, benighted, travel-worn,
> Over many a tangled spray,
> All heart-broke I heard her say:
>
> 'O my children! do they cry?
> Do they hear their father sigh?
> Do they look abroad to see,
> Now return and weep for me?'
>
> Pitying, I drop'd a tear;
> But I saw a glow-worm near,
> Who replied: 'What wailing wight
> Calls the watchman of the night?
>
> I am set to light the ground,
> While the beetle goes his round.
> Follow now the beetle's hum;
> Little wanderer, hie thee home!'

'A Cradle Song' does much the same kind of weaving together of appearance, dream, and eternal vision. The first stanza:

> Sweet dreams form a shade
> O'er my lovely infant's head;
> Sweet dreams of pleasant streams
> By happy, silent, moony beams.

foreshadows Blake's later description of Beulah, the moony realm of the poet's vision. It is interesting that Blake almost always speaks of dreams forming 'a shade' over the dreamer's head, like a hovering externalized vision.

Although Blake is certainly conscious of unredeemed Nature and Eternity as opposites, there is not, as yet, any evidence of a fierce personal battle raging within his own mind between these two sides. By the very nature of his theme in the songs, he seems equally interested in both worlds.

In the famous poem, 'The Divine Image', with its swirling flame of an illumination, Blake almost dogmatically welds physical humanity and divine spirit, the outer and the inner worlds.

And strangely enough, the poem about 'Holy Thursday' in London is full of nature similes and metaphors. The children walking in pairs, clean-faced and dressed in red and blue and green, 'into the high dome of Paul's they like Thames' waters flow'. 'These flowers of London town' sound like 'multitudes of lambs'. 'Like a mighty wind' is the hymn they sing to heaven, 'or like harmonious thunderings'. The top margin is decorated with a frieze of the children walking two by two behind the 'grey-headed beadles . . . with wands as white as snow', while the tall women walking in the opposite direction along the bottom margin have a single giant leader, bearded flowingly, like God.

In the companion poems about the little boy lost and found, there is an interesting transition, by means of natural images, from human to divine. The child follows a kind of will-o'-the-wisp through the dark forest, and suddenly instead of the human imperfect father who has allowed him to get lost, he finds God. The human father may well stand for the spectre. And again we may have a picture of the Dark Night of the Soul, the mystic in his 'lonely fen' led only by a 'wandering light' and crying in his despair, until, by the grace of God, the cloud or vapour lifts and he is led home.

The marginal designs for 'The Little Black Boy' are very striking.

At the beginning is a moonlit landscape surrounding the black mother and child, but at the end of the poem there is a sunlit scene in which Christ is seated with two small white boys at his knee. In the poem, the little black boy cries: 'I am black, but O! my soul is white!' His mother answers:

> 'Look on the rising sun: there God does live,
> And gives his light, and gives his heat away,
> And flowers and trees and beasts and men receive
> Comfort in morning, joy in the noonday.
>
> And we are put on earth a little space,
> That we may learn to bear the beams of love;
> And these black bodies and this sunburnt face
> Is but a cloud, and like a shady grove.'

God is the sun, his love the beams we must learn to bear, the black bodies a kindly shading cloud. Man cannot bear too much reality, there must be a cloud of unknowing for a while. The child's answer with the also symbolic images of cloud and lamb would, in the hands of another poet, dissolve into bathos. Blake escapes because the atmosphere of innocence he has created is so completely successful.

The 'Little Girl Lost' begins with the strangely moving lines:

> In futurity
> I prophetic see
> That the earth from sleep
> (Grave the sentence deep)
>
> Shall arise and seek
> For her maker meek;
> And the desert wild
> Become a garden mild.

Nature herself will *choose* God and so will be redeemed. It will become like the child Lyca who wandered far from home and lost herself. She fell asleep beneath a tree, and because of her innocence that thought no evil of wild creatures,

> The kingly lion stood
> And the virgin view'd
> Then he gamboll'd round
> O'er the hallowed ground.

> Leopards, tigers, play
> Round her as she lay,
> While the lion old
> Bow'd his mane of gold
>
> And her bosom lick
> And upon her neck
> From his eyes of flame
> Ruby tears there came.

The kingly animals take her off, still sleeping, to a safe cave. Meanwhile, her parents have been searching frantically and believe the worst has befallen their child. They meet the lion and are petrified with fright and fall to the ground, although the lion stands quietly beside them and 'their fears allay' by licking their hands.

> They look upon his eyes
> Fill'd with deep surprise,
> And wondering behold
> A spirit arm'd in gold.

The king of beasts takes them to his palace where they find Lyca, unharmed, and

> To this day they dwell
> In a lovely dell;
> Nor fear the wolvish howl
> Nor the lion's growl.

This is an important poem with its clear emphasis that nature's transformation depends on vision alone, on the eyes that can really *see*. The so-called lower creatures of nature are inferior and evil only because they are made so by man's arrogant and fearful state of soul. They are, in truth, as spiritually capable of self-transcendence as is man. When seen with innocent eyes they themselves become innocent. As Dr. Reinhold Niebuhr has written:

'The root of sin is in spirit and not in nature. The assertion of that fact distinguishes Christianity both from naturalism, which denies the reality of sin, and from various types of mysticism and dualism, which think that finiteness as such, or in other words, the body, is the basis of evil.'[1]

And we remember G. K. Chesterton's words about the highest doctrine of the spiritual being the affirmation of the material.

[1] Reinhold Niebuhr, *Beyond Tragedy*, p. 294.

A more definite proof of Blake's interest and sympathy for nature and all its creatures could not be wished for. If this is mysticism, Yeats is wrong in thinking that the mystic was divorced from nature and natural beauty. But if the mysticism is confined to the ascent of the individual human soul to union with God, what Blake is preaching is much wider and touches upon Yeats' enchanted ground.

The decoration surrounding the poem 'Blossom' is perhaps the loveliest in the book, and is a rich example of how Blake turns natural beauty into symbolic and mystical messages. A flame sweeps from the ground up the right margin and curves over the top of the poem to suggest a flaming blossoming tree to whose branches cling angels. Is it perhaps, and the poem itself, a memory of the time when Blake, a small boy who had said he saw shining angels sitting in the garden tree, was whipped for lying? The double image of tree and flame conjures up a host of spiritual meanings, chiefly those of the tree of life and the flame of divine love. The poem, in contrast, seems inexplicably simple on the surface, but the implication is that in nature, which has fallen from grace too, all is not so simple and joyful as it appears to us. Much the same idea as in those two wonderful lines:

> How do you know but ev'ry Bird that cuts the airy way
> Is an immense world of delight, clos'd by your senses five?

On a note of preparation for the disillusionment of experience, *The Songs of Innocence* ends:

> Folly is an endless maze
> Tangled roots perplex her ways.
> How many have fallen there!
> They stumble all night over bones of the dead,
> And feel they know not what but care,
> And wish to lead others, when they should be led.

People seem to prefer folly to truth. They stumble, as it were, over the roots of the tree of mystery, and through the dark night of illusion over the bones of past error. They ignore 'the opening morn, Image of truth reborn', and feel harassed with trouble, yet are dogmatic to their children about the way to ready truth.

In *Songs of Experience* (1794), the joyful surface harmony of the world breaks into fragments, and 'shades of the prison house' begin to close. Here, if anywhere, we should find evidence of a mental conflict in Blake, a feeling of being torn between spirit and nature, a suggestion as to whether the attitude of saint or enchanter will produce the best substitute for harmony.

The dream of innocence is shattered and the abyss gapes under what was apparently solid ground. Dream and actuality are wide apart, as is the vision of earth transformed by spring from the actual corruption of matter. What must this new awareness of conflict do to Blake's images and symbols? Can he possibly join the mystical idea and natural image as smoothly as before, or will there be a personal battle in which Blake will eventually be forced to choose sides—Nature or spirit? Is Blake sophisticated enough to keep both sides by affirming the conflict itself as most valuable, the vacillation higher than the choice?

The title-page presents two youthful figures weeping over the dead bodies of an old man and woman. Death has come to uproot the illusion of joy and harmony, not only the final physical death, but the incomprehensible dying of the spirit from day to day. And the voice of the prophet has a note of desperate pleading and ultimatum:

> Hear the voice of the Bard!
> Who Present, Past and Future sees;
> Whose ears have heard
> The Holy Word
> That walk'd among the ancient trees,
>
> Calling the lapsed Soul,
> And weeping in the evening dew;
> That might controll
> The starry pole,
> And fallen, fallen light renew!
>
> 'O Earth, O Earth, return!
> Arise from out the dewy grass;
> Night is worn,
> And the morn
> Rises from the slumberous mass.
>
> 'Turn away no more;
> Why wilt thou turn away?
> The starry floor,
> The wat'ry shore,
> Is giv'n thee till the break of day.'

Strangely, there is still the enchanter's delight in natural beauty, and in the soul's capacity to 'controll the starry pole'. It is the soul,

however, and not nature which has fallen. And nature turns away
from the soul which no longer sees her beauty: she grows ugly and full
of despair. Indeed, cries the bard, all that seems to be left from the old
harmony is the beauty of isolated natural images. But Earth answers:

> Earth rais'd up her head
> From the darkness dread and drear.
> Her light fled,
> Stony dread!
> And her locks cover'd with grey despair.
>
> 'Prison'd on wat'ry shore,
> Starry Jealousy does keep my den:
> Cold and hoar,
> Weeping o'er,
> I hear the father of the ancient men.
>
> Selfish father of men!
> Cruel, jealous, selfish fear!
> Can delight,
> Chain'd in night,
> The virgins of youth and morning bear?
>
> Does spring hide its joy
> When buds and blossoms grow?
> Does the sower
> Sow by night,
> Or the plowman in darkness plow?
>
> Break this heavy chain
> That does freeze my bones around.
> Selfish! vain!
> Eternal bane!
> That free Love with bondage bound.'

Earth herself is bound in the tyranny of man's unloving soul. It is
perhaps what Yeats meant when he said of Ireland—

> Hearts with one purpose alone
> Through summer and winter seem
> Enchanted to a stone
> To trouble the living stream.[1]

[1] Yeats, *Collected Poems*, p. 208.

and again, in his diary: 'the soul of Ireland has become a vapour and her body a stone.'[1] In Blake's poem the jealous father is Urizen, the god of abstract reason who has bewitched everything—both the free spirit and the once joyful earth. They have both fallen, but also grown antipodal. There is a gap between nature and spirit so great that they no longer understand one another. Each has become the other's tyrant, in that each berates and deludes and so chains the other to it. When such a state exists due to the false doctrines of Urizen, the search for truth is almost hopeless. Instead of the seeker who comes at last upon incarnate truth, you get the Idiot Questioner who will never know an answer when he finds one. In this kingdom of Urizen there is no truth but only doubt: it is a kingdom whose population increases at a great rate. There are only partial truths which masquerade as whole ones and so tyrannize over one another.

> The Questioner who sits so sly
> Shall never know how to Reply.
> He who replies to words of Doubt
> Doth put the light of knowledge out . . .
>
> He who Doubts from what he sees
> Will ne'er Believe, do what you Please.
> If the Sun and Moon should doubt,
> They'd immediately go out . . .
>
> A Riddle as the cricket's cry
> Is to Doubt a fit Reply.

In 'My Pretty Rose Tree' the mental state of jealousy tyrannizes over the beautiful natural image, just as 'The Lily' tells of the aggressive self-defence that even the mildest creatures must practise in a faithless world:

> The modest Rose puts forth a thorn:
> The humble Sheep a threatening horn.

This type of conflict between nature and mental states is, in a sense, sharply different from Yeats' awareness of conflict. Yeats felt that the actuality about him did not live up to his dream, a kind of romantic will-o'-the-wisp. His solution was to concentrate with such

[1] Unpublished diary.

86

mental power upon some natural imperfect image—say a rose—
that the very force of concentration would evoke the Truth of Roseness and suggest all its beauty. Blake, on the other hand, is insisting
that all the truth and beauty is actually before our eyes, only we
cannot see it. It once more reveals Blake's mind as essentially prophetic, that is, desiring correction of physical nature through
spiritual improvement. But the images do sometimes seem ambiguous in this second period, and it is fairly easy to see why Yeats might
think Blake magical in that he tries to join the dream and nature
transformed by powerful intermediate symbols. The very use of
symbols taken from nature would seem to Yeats magical rather than
mystical, for, rightly or wrongly, he identified the saint with the
ascetic who must 'renounce the world' and all its images.

'The Garden of Love' underlines the increasing awareness of
conflict:

> I went to the Garden of Love
> And saw what I ne'er had seen:
> A Chapel was built in the midst
> Where I used to play on the green.
>
> And the gates of this chapel were shut,
> And 'Thou shalt not' writ over the door:
> So I turn'd to the Garden of Love
> That so many sweet flowers bore.
>
> And I saw it was filled with graves
> And tomb-stones where flowers should be:
> And Priests in black gowns were walking their rounds,
> And binding with briars my joys and desires.

The poem is remarkable not only in its succinct statement of Blake's
later, more intricate philosophy—that of Urizen's priests binding
and calling wrong what is but the natural expression of divine love
—but in its imagery. Beautiful natural things have been replaced
by man-made artificiality, just as innocent harmony has been ousted
by abstract rule: the laughing green has become an unfriendly chapel
with 'Thou Shalt Not' written over the closed door; the flowers of
love have turned to tombstones, indicating the solid opacity of
spiritual death, instead of being 'the gateway to eternity'. The illustration shows two weeping children beseeching the frowning priest

who tends the tombs. Snake-like shapes curve around and through the poem, and brambles form a network below.

Wrath is a living tree; it is watered by fears and weeping; its sun is deceit and false smiles, and so it bears a poisoned apple. This is the theme of 'A Poison Tree' which shows how warped the values of innocence become in the world of experience. This is again stressed by the 'Nurse's Song'. The 'Nurse's Song' in the *Songs of Innocence* told of the children who laughingly plead for an extra hour of play-time, and the nurse who benevolently grants it. Quite different are the words of the nurse in *Songs of Experience*:

> *When the voices of children are heard on the green*
> *And whisperings are in the dale,*
> *The days of my youth rise fresh in my mind,*
> *My face turns green and pale.*
>
> *Then come home, my children, the sun is gone down,*
> *And the dews of night arise;*
> *Your spring and your day are wasted in play,*
> *And your winter and night in disguise.*

Oddly enough, the illustration for this poem is the loveliest in the book, showing the nurse's graceful figure in the doorway behind a slim little boy, while a small girl is crouched in thought against the grey wall twined with colourful grapes and tendrils and leaves.

The most remarkable thing about Blake's mysticism is his view on love. This is not to repeat what those who are shocked by Blake's doctrine of free love have said many times. Rather, it is to point out the astonishing fact that at one blow Blake eludes the poet's eternal problem of the romantic ideal, the mystic's bugbear of asceticism, and the philosopher's headache about distinctions between eros and agape. Blake does away with all these problems by movingly stating his case that the senses are the gateway to eternity. When the desire of eros or earthly love is made actual, incarnated as it were, instead of abstracted to a romantic ideal or ruled out by stern laws of purity—then, and only then, does it become agape or spiritual love. The dualism of body and spirit is overcome by incarnate love. The act of love is the surest way to spiritual vision. For, when they are separated, the male and female principles are at war and falsely self-sufficient, even falsely spiritual. But when they come together, their unity touches the source of all Unity and all love.

And so asceticism (of images in general as well as of the flesh) is a half-truth. When it stands as a whole truth it becomes evil and tyrannical. It is the tyrant god Urizen who dictates false virtue and false purity to bind and inhibit love, and seem evil. Rather, it is the very desire which is inhibited, which becomes stagnant and dangerous. Reason creates the dualism between body and spirit, and invents ingenuous theories and laws to drive them further apart. Love is vision: love is imagination: love is unity. Therefore, only with the eyes of love can we at last see the world transformed and even Urizen resurrected.

This is the crux of Blake's mysticism. It is also subject to gross misinterpretation by all types of Puritans and materialists, the former using it as a weapon against Blake's spirituality, and the latter seeing in Blake the forerunner of their own lowest-common-denominator philosophy of life. There are at least three poems in *Songs of Experience* which deal with this subject, a subject which recurs again and again.

The famous poem called 'The Tyger' is perhaps the most magical —in the true sense—lyric that Blake ever wrote. It is also one of the most beautiful of English poems:

THE TYGER

Tyger! Tyger! burning bright
In the forests of the night,
What immortal hand or eye
Could frame thy fearful symmetry?

In what distant deeps or skies
Burnt the fire of thine eyes?
On what wings dare he aspire?
What the hand dare seize the fire?

And what shoulder, and what art,
Could twist the sinews of thy heart?
And when thy heart began to beat,
What dread hand? and what dread feet?

What the hammer? what the chain?
In what furnace was thy brain?
What the anvil? what dread grasp
Dare its deadly terrors clasp?

When the stars threw down their spears,
And water'd heaven with their tears,
Did he smile his work to see?
Did he who made the Lamb make thee?

Tyger! Tyger! burning bright
In the forests of the night,
What immortal hand or eye
Dare frame thy fearful symmetry?

In the art of this poem there is magic such as Yeats meant. The almost conversational bareness of the words (rivalling the metaphysical poets in control), and the contrasting richness of the key words and images bursting out like the fire symbol which rules the poem—these show the enchanter's deliberate manipulations of technique for the purposes of evocation. Most of all, the chanting quality of the lyric, the constant repetition of phrases and slight variations upon a single line, betray the magician's technique. And there is evocative power in the controlled and inevitable repetition of the first stanza in the last, save one word which leaps out like a challenge.

There is dynamic restraint in the juxtaposition of natural images that are generally thought of as opposite. It is as if they are drawn together by a mighty power or spell, and they exist in close tension: 'burning bright' and 'forests of the night'; the visionary spiritual 'eye' and the active shaping 'hand'; 'deeps' of the sea and lofty 'skies'; 'wings' soaring from nature and the 'fire' consuming itself in dream upon nature's hearth; finally, the delicate living 'brain' and the inanimate 'hammer', 'chain', and 'anvil'. There is great contrast and synthesis, magical synthesis, in the very framework of the poem. The images and ideas that compose it seem almost too many and diverse when taken one by one. And yet the bare bones of the poem stand stark and powerful and final. Blake could well have said when he finished this poem: 'words obey my call'.

In a less technical sense, this poem is magical. To get inside the tiger, to master the essence of tigerness, and so to control the image or symbol of the Tyger, would be the magician's approach. And Blake has come very near to this. His tiger stands for that whole secret aspect of nature which men call evil, which burns with a terrible beauty in the forests of the night, and is the domain of magic. Like the enchanter, Blake is drawn into it, overwhelmed by its

magnificence and significance, by the choice between the Tyger and
the Lamb. He flings an unanswered question at the Creator who
dared to confront man with the Tyger as well as with the Lamb. The
daring of God almost intoxicates Blake, and he seems ready to take
up the challenge. Despite his firm stand on the side of the Lamb of
Christ, Blake is bewitched by the burning energy of evil and satanic
nature which is contained in the image of the tiger. And he is not
really sure that it is evil since God created it: perhaps it is only an
abstract law of Urizen which calls the Tyger, like sex, evil. On the
other hand, there is a conflict in Blake's mind which has not been
there before: the question arises whether the same Creator actually *did*
create the Lamb and the Tyger. This question contains the possibility
of a dualism which is the essence of magic. The attempt to answer
the question accounts for much of the upside-downness and glorification of energy in such works as the *Marriage of Heaven and Hell*
(1793). Until now there has been in Blake's poetry an interest in nature
and a desire for nature transformed. But only now is there any sign
of a conflict in Blake's mind as to whether some deity of darkness in-
habits nature, and whether there is not as much fascination in choosing
to follow this deity, as in following the Lamb to nature transformed.

It has been noted that men of great spirituality are capable of the
greatest evil.

Satan, seen in *Milton* as the archetypal Enchanter, has also to do
with Urizen, the god of this world. In fact, the two seem sometimes
one. Urizen's false rational materialism is satanic, a misuse and
forcing of created Nature in a magical way: 'What can be Created
can be Destroyed. Adam is only the Natural Man and not the Soul
or Imagination.' The poem called 'To the Accuser who is The God
of This World' also states this:

> Truly my Satan thou art but a Dunce
> And dost not know the Garment from the Man.
> Every Harlot was a Virgin once,
> Nor canst thou ever change Kate into Nan.
>
> Tho' thou art worship'd by the Names Divine
> Of Jesus and Jehovah thou art still
> The Son of Man in weary Night decline
> The Lost Traveller's Dream under the Hill.

That is, that the false god who is worshipped by most people as Jesus,
the true God, has, in fact, nothing to do with Incarnation, or with the

truth expressed in this book about the senses being the gateways to eternity. He has rather to do with natural religion, a kind of magical nightmare that repeats itself until the meaning of Incarnation is grasped.

The crude and murky *Tiriel* (1789) is also in this second period. It may well be an early attempt at creating the mythology of reason against imagination. The blind old man, once a tyrant, who 'darkling o'er the mountains sought his pathless way' is probably an early form of the false god Urizen who poses as reality. 'Tiriel' is a kind of anagram of 'reality'. His brother Ijim, who speaks against him in righteous wrath, may possibly be read as an anagram of 'image', that is, Imagination, who later becomes Los. Tiriel's five daughters may stand for the five senses, while Har and Heva are very difficult to identify, except that Har seems to be the false law that accompanies Tiriel's, or later Urizen's, false wisdom. The most interesting part of this book is, however, the deleted passage that throws light on the *Book of Thel*. The significant lines, with a few preceding lines for context, are as follows:

> *Thy laws, O Har, and Tiriel's wisdom end together in a curse.*
> *Why is one law given to the Lion and the patient Ox?*
> *Dost thou not see that men cannot be formed all alike,*
> *Some nostril'd wide, breathing out blood; some close shut up*
> *In silent deceit, poisons inhaling from the morning rose,*
> *With daggers hid beneath their lips and poison in their tongue*
> *Or eyed with little sparks of Hell and with infernal brands*
> *Flinging flames of discontent and plagues of dark despair;*
> *Or those whose mouths are graves, whose teeth the gates of eternal death.*
> *Can wisdom be put in a silver rod, or love in a golden bowl?*

Later, after both *Tiriel* and *Thel* were written, we find these lines in *The Vision of the Daughters of Albion*:

> *Does not the eagle scorn the earth and despise the treasures beneath?*
> *But the mole knoweth what is there, and the worm shall tell thee.*

The *Book of Thel* (1789) is Blake's only fairy tale. And it is the only one of Blake's books which deals with choice and the tragic vacillation between two possibilities. It is more magical poetry than is to be found except in isolated passages in the other prophetic books.

> *Does the Eagle know what is in the pit?*
> *Or wilt thou go ask the Mole?*
> *Can Wisdom be put in a silver rod?*
> *Or Love in a golden bowl?*

This is 'Thel's Motto'. Looking at it we would interpret that synthesis lies in the acceptance of opposites, in the acknowledgment of functional difference. If the eagle takes inspiration from the air, the mole finds a different knowledge burrowing underground. Neither Wisdom alone, nor Love alone, can fulfil the other's function. They must be somehow united. The rod and the bowl are obviously sexual symbols, and this gives a hint of Blake's later solution.

A summary of the poem's theme is in order here, before an attempt to relate 'Thel's Motto' to her story. The language of this shortest and most lyrical prophetic book is nearer to the magical simplicity and power of 'The Tyger' than to the verbosity of the other prophetic works. Yet its symbolism and meaning are not as simple and pleasant as many commentators have been led to believe by the gentle and lucid style.

> The daughters of the Seraphim led round their sunny flocks,
> All but the youngest: she in paleness sought the secret air, . . .
> . . . her gentle lamentation falls like morning dew.

Thel's lament is the question—'what is the purpose of human life?' The humble Lily of the Valley answers her first, saying that 'he who smiles on all' smiles on the lowly flower as upon every creature. But Thel is not satisfied: she has all the dreamy longing of youth, and she replies that the Lily, unlike herself, has a function, and can give 'to those who cannot crave' perfume and beauty. But Man who craves and feels and aspires alone seems to have no purpose and seems to live and die, a solitary misfit:

> . . . Thel is like a faint cloud kindled at the rising sun:
> I vanish from my pearly throne, and who shall find my place?
> . . . I pass away: yet I complain and no one hears my voice.

Next Thel questions a golden cloud who answers in terms that seem but an argument for the conservation of matter. Thel replies that she is different,

> . . . because I fade away;
> And all shall say, 'Without a use this shining woman lived,
> Or did she only live to be at death the food of worms?'

When, in despair, Thel questions the worm, she has a kind of double vision, and cries astonished:

> Art thou a Worm? Image of weakness, art thou but a Worm?
> I see thee like an infant wrapped in the Lily's leaf.

The clod of clay hears Thel and tries to help her by saying that she too has pondered the mystery of life, and found that she must accept it without knowing the answer. The matron Clay asks Thel to enter her house, saying that it is given her 'to enter and return'. Through calling up the symbol of the Clay, Thel reaches through to the unknown and finds the desired knowledge. In fact, Yeats is not so wrong in describing Thel's whole procedure as if it were a series of magical evocations:

'The cloud having fulfilled its purpose and called up the Worm, as it had been itself called up by the Lily, sails on,'[1]
and 'The power who guards the realm of clay lifts the bar.'[2]

> Thel enter'd in and saw the secrets of the land unknown.
> She saw the couches of the dead, and where the fibrous roots
> Of every heart on earth infixes deep its restless twists:
> A land of sorrowes and of tears where never smile was seen. . . .
> To her own grave plot she came and there she sat down
> And heard this voice of sorrow breathed from the hollow pit.
>
> 'Why cannot the Ear be closed to its own destruction?
> Or the glist'ning Eye to the poison of a smile?
> Why are Eyelids stor'd with arrows ready drawn,
> Where a thousand fighting men in ambush lie?
> Or an Eye of gifts and graces show'ring fruits and coined gold?
> Why a Tongue impress'd with honey from every wind?
> Why an Ear, a whirlpool fierce to draw creations in?
> Why a Nostril wide inhaling terror, trembling, and affright?
> Why a tender curb upon the youthful burning boy?
> Why a little curtain of flesh on the bed of our desire?'
> The Virgin started from her seat, and with a shriek
> Fled back unhinder'd till she came into the vales of Har.

How powerful and harsh an ending this is after the gentle lyrical presentation of the first three sections. The wistful luminous state of innocence which was Thel's in the values of Har now seems dragged in the mud by the overwhelming clamour of the senses. It is the senses Thel has discovered, and they seem to her the gate into death, not to eternity, because they are the victims of a corrupted spiritual vision. Thel's gentle longing for an answer to life, and the complacent answers she had already found, had not prepared her for

---

[1] Yeats and Ellis, *William Blake*, Vol. II, p. 93.   [2] *Ibid.*, p. 94.

this harshness. She is not equal to it. This final answer is itself a question and presents her with a violent choice. And she flees from it back to the vales of Har, the False puritanism of Urizen's Law. Her own question was—why should men, who are earth's highest creatures, alone live and die without a purpose. And the reply is the query—why is there always danger and evil attached to the sensory life of man as to no other creature's.

The implied solution is plain. Man's purpose in life is to choose to incarnate. He alone is not determined by natural function: neither like the mole must he burrow underground, nor like the eagle, soar to the heights. He can choose the heights or the depths: he alone can choose to transcend mere vegetable life, but he must choose to incarnate first. And thus, he alone finds temptation and danger in sensory life which, to animals and plants, does not seem evil. His function is spiritual: it is freedom, not the necessity of material compulsion. Man can choose the spiritual path, or he can choose the life of the animals, but he cannot remain innocent in the life of the senses as animals do, because by his very nature he can see beyond his passions, which therefore seem evil. 'Unorganized Innocence: An Impossibility: Innocence dwells with Wisdom, but never with Ignorance.'[1] True innocence is achieved only when man has made the initial choice to enter into experience and gone far beyond to see that Nature is not evil, but can be transfigured by his own way of seeing it: then, and only then, the senses are seen as gateways to eternity.

Man's purpose in living is to face the choice inherent in experience. The choice is individual and solitary and different for each man. He may wander restlessly through life, not sure that he has made the right choice—perhaps yearn for the invisible things he has denied himself, or feel that he is missing the pleasures of a life guided by the senses. There is tragedy possible in the reversibility of man's choice as well as in the fact that he is free to make the wrong choice. But man alone is capable of tragedy or of ecstasy. The way of death, of purposelessness, is only when he shirks the responsibility of deliberate choice. And it is a frightening thing to choose in solitariness a goal that is beyond oneself and beyond visibility, a goal that one can never wholly comprehend.

Thel takes the way of death: she flees from the responsibility of choice back to the vales of illusion. It is not that she chooses the way

[1] *The Complete Poetry of William Blake*, p. 834.

of spirit in fleeing from the passions, because she has never yet lived
in the world of experience where the choice is necessary. And there
is falsity in renouncing the world without knowing it. She only
sees the situation which demands choice, and she runs shrieking from
it. This is perhaps why Blake named her Thel, which read forwards,
it has been suggested, may mean 'θελω'—'I will' or 'desire', but
which backwards becomes Lethe or forgetfulness.

In this way has Blake justified the state of experience or conflict.
It becomes, in fact, the most important phase of man's spiritual
voyage, the phase in which he chooses either nature or to go beyond
nature to invisible things, accepting meanwhile the necessity of both.
Working through visible things to get to the mystery beyond may,
by its very nature, seem a magical process, even if its goal is not:

What is the price of Experience? do men buy it for a song?
Or Wisdom for a dance in the street? No, it is bought with the price
Of all that a man hath, his house, his wife, his children.
Wisdom is sold in the desolate market where none come to buy,
And in the wither'd field where the farmer ploughs for bread in vain.
It is an easy thing to triumph in the summer sun . . .
Thus I could sing and thus rejoice: but it is not so with me.[1]

Nor are the illustrations to the *Book of Thel* as simple and orthodox
as many commentators think. If anything they are more direct than
the text. Some critics believe that the last section of the poem, and
Thel's motto, are of a much later date than the rest. But the title-
page illustration as well as the deleted lines from *Tiriel* show that
the theme of the last section was in Blake's mind when he drew it
at the beginning of the poem. The picture shows Thel looking
horrified at the sight of pollinating flowers which represent the
passions as the flowers are personified in two embracing human
figures. And the picture heading the first page of text represents in
different terms the thought of Thel's motto: a lonely male figure
soars in ecstasy after an eagle's flight, while down on earth is a scene
of ordinary family life. A figure with a sword and shield floats on
the level separating the two realms. Both of these pictures are done
with deceptive grace in gentle pastel shades, so that one tends to
overlook the vigorous and unorthodox messages. The plates showing
Thel with the Lily, the Cloud, and the Worm are more famous
for their tender beauty. The final plate showing the children of

[1] *The Complete Poetry of William Blake*, p. 744.

innocence astride and driving the serpent of evil is a metaphorical statement of what Thel, in fact, has done.

In a sense Thel, written in 1789, is Blake's most dualistic and ambiguous work. It is as if Blake himself is half-fleeing from the senses which he later extols: certainly he is trying to convince *himself* that there should be no division between the senses and the spiritual realm since each contributes something that the other cannot. All this repressed energy that we feel at the end of Thel bursts forth in the *Marriage of Heaven and Hell* (1793) in a kind of perverted way that is no solution at all. There is evidence in the poetry written in his private notebooks at exactly this same time, 1793, when Blake was convincing himself of the value of an almost diabolic energy of the senses, that he found that his wife, Catherine, was the victim of a Thel-like ambiguity and sought to escape the intensity of physical love by withdrawing into what seems to Blake a false religious purity. Middleton Murry, who first points out that this ambiguity must have existed in Catherine, thinks that it was precipitated by her jealousy when Blake told her he had loved another woman. Mr. Murry bases this on the lovely poem:

> Never seek to tell thy love
>   Love that never told can be;
> For the gentle wind doth move
>   Silently, invisibly.

> I told my love, I told my love,
>   I told her all my heart,
> Trembling, cold, in ghastly fears—
>   Ah, she doth depart.

> Soon as she was gone from me
>   A traveller came by
> Silently, invisibly—
>   O, was no deny. (*He took her with a sigh.*) [variant]

I can find no evidence that Blake did actually love another woman after his marriage, and Catherine certainly knew all about his unhappy love for 'Polly' before his marriage. I would think rather that Blake in his 30's and after about ten years of marriage suddenly lost all his own Thel-like inhibitions, told his wife of this new passion

for her and frightened her into retreat. And no wonder, if his passion
suddenly took on the rather diabolic tone of liberation that rings in
the *Marriage of Heaven and Hell*, that she, a comparatively simple
woman of a naïvely religious cast, retreated altogether. The interesting thing is that *she*, not Blake, seems to have turned in her distress
to some other man or image of a man more 'pure' in his love perhaps, one who would not use her as an instrument. The figure of
the 'traveller' indicates this and is, I am sure, the same person as the
'angel' in the bitter little poem written at the same time (1793):

> *I asked a thief to steal me a peach:*
> *He turned up his eyes.*
> *I ask'd a lithe lady to lie her down:*
> *Holy and meek she cries.*
>
> *As soon as I went an angel came:*
> *He wink'd at the thief*
> *And smil'd at the dame,*
> *And without one word (spoke) (said)*
> *Had a peach from the tree,*
> *(And 'twixt earnest and joke) (And still as a maid)*
> *Enjoy'd the Lady.*

'Soon as she was gone from me a traveller came by' . . . 'As soon as
I went an angel came' . . . it is clear that Catherine Blake took
refuge from her ardent husband in a nun-like purity and possibly
allied herself with some cleric which was enough to seem to Blake
basest treachery, spiritual fornication in fact. This domestic crisis
began about 1793, but went on it seemed for many years, for between 1800 and 1803 Blake wrote the poem beginning 'My Spectre
around me night and day' which has puzzled so many commentators,
and which, I think, has the same theme of Catherine's desertion into
a miserable and woebegone chastity.

> *My Spectre around me night and day*
> *Like a Wild beast guards my way;*
> *My Emanation, far within,*
> *Weeps incessantly for my Sin.*
>
> *A fathomless and boundless Deep*
> *There we wander, there we weep;*
> *On the hungry craving wind*
> *My Sceptre follows thee behind.*

> *He scents thy footsteps in the snow*
> *Wheresoever thou dost go*
> *Thro' the wintry hail and rain:*
> *When wilt thou return again?*
>
> *When wilt thou return and view*
> *My loves, and them to life renew?*
> *When wilt thou return and live?*
> *When wilt thou pity, as I forgive? . . .*

The Spectre here is undoubtedly Blake's old puritanism giving in to that of his wife's despite his higher vision. There is a pathetic note in the image of the Spectre following her footsteps in the snow like a dumb and faithful dog. His emanation—which means his sexual nature and his female projection—weeps because it has come to believe that passion is wrong and a sin. The note of despair in the second stanza is summed up particularly in the image of the 'hungry craving wind'. It is interesting to note that in 'Never seek to tell thy love' the passing of love is indicated by the change of the 'gentle wind' that moved 'silently, invisibly' to a cold wind that made his wife tremble. Then the traveller came 'silently, invisibly'. It brings to mind Blake's early 'Mad Song' where in the forsaken night of the mystic,

> *The wild winds weep*
> *And the night is a-cold . . .*

'When wilt thou return?' Blake asks, and the woman answers:

> *Never, Never, I return!*
> *Still for victory I burn . . .*
> *I will fly and thou pursue*
> *Night and Morn the Flight renew.*

Blake says ironically:

> *Till I turn from Female Love*
> *And root up the Infernal Grove,*
> *I shall never worthy be*
> *To step into Eternity . . .*
>
> *Let us agree to give up Love*
> *And root up the Infernal Grove;*
> *Then we shall return and see*
> *The worlds of happy Eternity.*

And yet the touching and half rueful tenderness with which Blake bore with his wife's difficulties remains in the pity of the unplaced stanza:

> *Poor, pale, pitiable form*
> *That I follow in a storm;*
> *Iron tears and groans of lead*
> *Bind about my aching head.*

That everything came right in the end is more or less proved in the final union of Jerusalem and Albion, who, as Middleton Murry points out, are Catherine and William as well as mythological symbols.

This view of Blake's troubles is borne out by a letter of his dated October 23, 1804, where he speaks of the bestializing power of the rational Spectre: 'O Glory! and O Delight! I have entirely reduced that spectrous fiend to his station, whose annoyance has been the ruin of my labours for the last passed twenty years of my life. He is the enemy of conjugal love ... Thank God I was not altogether a beast as he was; but I was a slave bound in a mill among beasts and devils. These beasts and these devils are now, together with myself, become children of light and liberty, and my feet and my wife's feet are free from fetters.'

Between 1795 and 1804 Blake learned enough about this long period of despair to tell of it in the *Four Zoas or Vala*. This prophetic book is chaotic precisely because it is the mythology of breakdown written at a point when the way out—later seen as the love of male and female grounded in the incarnate godhead—was seen but not clearly apprehended. Relationship between male and female has been broken, and each tries to be falsely self-sufficient or seeks the wrong mate. Vala is perhaps Catherine in her false state, become, in fact, a harlot in 'the Cruelties of Holiness'. The lines in the MS. poem quoted above are startlingly echoed in 'O when will you return, Vala the Wanderer?' Enitharmon, the beautiful female who lures the male to destruction yet refuses to open her gates to Paradise, is possibly another aspect of Catherine. It is significant that Blake goes exhaustingly into the family history of each of his gigantic figures: breakdown has a history that includes the parents. I do not intend to labour any further the psychological approach to Blake's work, but it does seem important to make this guess about his relationship to his wife, which, if true, throws so much light on what is obscure in the prophetic books, and could be followed through at great length.

In the following quotation from *Vala*, Blake repeats significantly the fact that his emanation—his sexual nature—weeps before the closed gates to eternity, the womb.

> *The Daughters of Beulah beheld the Emanation; they pitied,*
> *They wept before the Inner gates of Enitharmon's bosom,*
> *And of her fine wrought brain, and of her bowels within her loins.*
> *These gates within, Glorious and bright, open into Beulah*
> *From Enitharmon's inward parts; but the bright female terror*
> *Refus'd to open the bright gates; she clos'd and barr'd them fast*
> *Lest Los should enter into Beulah thro' her beautiful gates.*
>
> *The Emanation stood before the Gates of Enitharmon,*
> *Weeping; the Daughters of Beulah silent in the porches*
> *Spread her a couch unknown to Enitharmon . . .*

In the *Visions of the Daughters of Albion* (1793), Blake gives us one more fable of the state of experience, showing the negative side or choice. Just as in *Thel* he showed the unsatisfactory effects of running from a necessary choice, so in this fable he shows us the unhappy results of choosing weakly, or rather, of acting without having the enduring courage and 'firm persuasion' of the implied choice. *Thel* shows that unorganized innocence will not do, and the *Visions of the Daughters of Albion* claims that uncourageous experience is equally bad. Both tales warn against taking the negative side of choice—whether the choice be innocence or experience—for only a positive choice will lead to any truth.

The way of the eagle will lead no more surely to its own portion of truth than will the pursuit of the mole underground. It follows from this sort of argument that the magician, working positively within the limited realm of experience, may discover some truths as valid as the saint finds, he who is working through organized innocence in the realm of supernatural. Soon Blake must reveal his own choice. For he has not yet made it. He is still undergoing the disillusioning process of experience and trying to make some sense of it. The gap between spirit and nature troubles him as it troubles Yeats, and like Yeats he seems to advocate the magical working through natural symbol in the realm of nature as freely as he stresses the innocence of supernature. He does not see the ideal, as he did in his own state of innocence, as nature transformed by spirit, so much as he sees the two opposed and equally valid realms between which we must make a choice.

> Father, O father! what do we here
> In this land of unbelief and fear?
> The Land of Dreams is better far,
> Above the light of the Morning Star.

This is a form of romantic idealism, the preference for the far-off, the dream rather than actuality after the apparent surface harmony of actuality breaks up into conflict. The strange illustration in the *Gates of Paradise* labelled 'I want! I want!' and portraying a small human figure trying to climb to the moon, is another indication of Blake's full knowledge of this state of mind.

In the *Visions of the Daughters of Albion*, Oothoon is a Thel who has made the plunge into the world of experience, that is, of the senses. Her spiritual search has been for beauty, even more beauty, and it leads her to the passions. Yeats and Ellis say of this idea, stressing its importance in an attempt to vindicate the magical poet:

'Oothoon's beauty being spiritual is able to protect the poor natural beauty of Leutha ... the idea that beauty was a protection was probably at the root of Blake's decision—so far as it was not decided for him and dictated to him—to adopt the poetic form for his philosophy.'[1]

To continue the story—Oothoon, although married to Theotormon whom she loves, plucks the beautiful flower of desire and is consequently violated by Bromion. Yeats puts this episode into magical symbolism:

'There is no law so terrible as the law of paradox in action. Oothoon has plucked the flower, and thus she was flying through the air, over water, bearing earth on her breast, toward fire. In mystic symbol she was going up the spiritual to the higher or inner.'[2]

Yeats and Ellis go on:

'Oothoon—the eye of desire—is condemned, in fact, to find beauty in nature, whose soul is reason and whose conviction is pain, whose morality is punishment, instead of in pure imagination.'

[1] Yeats and Ellis, *William Blake*, Vol. II, p. 96. [2] *Ibid.*, p. 100.

It is likely—and Middleton Murry feels this too—that both Bromion and Oothoon are parts of Theotormon's psychological make-up as well as characters in their own right. Oothoon may be Theotormon's female counterpart and also a kind of romantic ideal which must be kept unviolated. While Bromion could be his active earthy self, the self which acts in accordance with desire, not the self which like Hamlet desires but acts not. For the rest of the poem is given up to Theotormon's jealous self-torture, since he sees Oothoon's act a crime in the light of Urizen's law. He tries to punish the two culprits by tying them back to back as if they were his own conflicting states of mind which must not see one another. But he remains as miserable as if he himself were guilty. Oothoon pleads with him in vain. She says that there are as many forms of delight as there are flowers, and that she had plucked more than one in her search for beauty did not make her seeking spirit any the less pure. If love was no more than the sensory act, she believes, then men's love is no different from that of the animals. Theotormon cannot see it. He cannot see that every joy is different and so of unique worth if made actual.

Bromion's lines are the finest lines of poetry in the book:

> Thou knowest that the ancient trees seen by thine eyes have fruit.
> But knowest thou that trees and fruit flourish upon the earth
> To gratify senses unknown? trees, beasts, and birds unknown;
> Unknown, not unperceiv'd, spread in the infinite microscope,
> In places yet unvisited by the voyager, and in worlds
> Over another kind of seas, and in atmospheres unknown.
> Ah! are there other wars beside the wars of sword and fire?
> And are there other sorrows beside the sorrows of poverty?
> And are there other joys beside the joys of riches and ease?
> And is there not one law for both the Lion and the Ox?
> And is there not eternal fire and eternal chains
> To bind the phantoms of existence from eternal life?

And Oothoon cries despairingly against the false law of Urizen:

> How can one joy absorb another? Are not different joys
> Holy, eternal, infinite? and each joy is a Love.

Both Bromion and Oothoon see validity in the way they have acted, but yet they remain chained and imprisoned by Theotormon's attitude. Oothoon, because of her love for Theotormon, remains crippled by his jealousy although she can see the joys of freedom.

In modern terms, Theotormon is the orthodoxly religious prude or Puritan who sublimates the sides of himself represented by Oothoon and Bromion. Bromion, left alone, has the nobility of the savage in his natural impulses, but seen by Theotormon's shocked eyes, he is evil. Oothoon, if left alone, becomes not a romantic ideal but an actual woman. True, her search is for spiritual beauty, but the fact that she has plucked the flower does not mean that her spiritual essence has been violated. It is Bromion, the sceptic in Theotormon, who violates her. She is soiled in idea rather than in fact, and she is not reconciled to it, and fights against it, but is beaten and hypnotized by Urizen's false orthodoxy. She has the sensation of being made to feel guilty without having done wrong, because of the warped quality of another's mind. This fable could be called one of the psychology of guilt. Theotormon torments himself with religious doubts, although he desires Oothoon's beauty. He violates this beauty by scepticism and false religion which Bromion becomes when questioned. Oothoon, spiritual beauty that knows it is not guilty in seeking delight, pleads without success since Theotormon does not know enough about his own repressions to see her point without feeling renewed guilt.

The *Marriage of Heaven and Hell* (1793) falls into what we have designated as Blake's second period, where he plays natural imagery and metaphysical thought against each other. The *Songs of Innocence* joined thought and imagery in a child-like vision of surface harmony. The *Songs of Experience* contrasted them, revealing the gap between nature and spirit which the disillusioned child discovers: the surface harmony is broken and conflict reigns. *Thel* shows that both sides were necessary to the whole truth, and, in implying the necessity for choice, reveals the unhappy situation when no choice is made. The *Visions of the Daughters of Albion* pointed out another negative way of choosing, that of making a choice without the courage of a firm persuasion. The *Marriage of Heaven and Hell* again takes up the theme of extreme opposites as halves of the whole truth. The second period is characterized by the theme of innocence giving way to the dilemmas of experience, and up to this final book each poem is a fable of experience, magical in that natural symbols are freely employed in an effort to evoke an intangible truth.

In the *Marriage* we find another apparently magical attempt at synthesis, with the difference that Blake speaks directly of his own choice as the way of the eagle, of energy, of the 'devil's party'. Because of the upside-downness of this book where 'devil' means 'angel', and because of the peculiar emphasis on energy, the choice still seems somewhat ambiguous. The conception of harmony is once again that of viewing apparently irreconcilable opposites as two sides of unity. 'Without contraries is no progression. Attraction and Repulsion, Reason and Energy, Love and Hate, are necessary to Human Existence.' It is an essentially dualistic view which extols energy as the dynamic between opposites. What we call evil appears in this book, not so much as good if only we had the eyes to see it, but as a necessary side of the truth which we do not understand. Separateness, opposites are under-scored, not the transforming vision.

'The roaring of lions, the howling of wolves, the raging of the stormy sea, and the destructive sword, are portions of eternity too great for the eye of man.'

The book portrays not so much a marriage as an inversion. It might have seemed a Christian doctrine had not Blake called black, white, and good, evil: angels become wicked and devils are the upholders of energy and imagination. It succeeds in satirizing conventional orthodoxy and its dangers, but it also succeeds or fails in emphasizing separateness instead of unity. The dilemma is the Promethean one.

Of necessity in this strange book, the world of nature which is the realm of magic seems to predominate. There are enchantments and evocations. Always spiritual and mental states are suggested by natural images: 'The eagle never lost so much time as when he sub-mitted to learn of the crow'; 'the tygers of wrath are wiser than the horses of instruction'. Energy, imaged of course in nature, means spiritual energy too, and is the subject of the poem. Blake cries out against orthodox religion as static and decaying: 'expect poison from standing water.' The orthodox call energy evil and they separate body and soul. But Blake says that 'Energy is Eternal De-light', and that 'Man has no Body distinct from his Soul, for that called the Body is a portion of Soul in this use.' And Blake allies himself with energy and the Devil's Party to fight against the Angels and false orthodoxy. This sort of inversion can be interpreted, without being simple-minded, as much nearer to magic's espousal

of physical beauty than to mysticism with its aura of renunciation. Yeats might have lingered especially over the words about
Milton:

'The reason Milton wrote in fetters when he wrote of Angels and
God, and at liberty when of Devils and Hell, is because he was a
true Poet and of the Devil's party without knowing it.'

In fact, Yeats' and Ellis' paraphrase of this is in more or less occultist
terms:

'Milton did his best work when writing of the expanding forces,
not the contracting or boundary-making forces, and was thus of the
Devil's party without knowing it.'[1]

The first 'Memorable Fancy' opens with a humorous dig at the
people who call Blake mad:

'As I was walking among the fires of Hell, delighted with the
enjoyment of Genius, which to Angels look like torments and
insanity . . .'

Blake's ironic humour in this book is one of the most delightful
things about it, and gives an added sense of energy and freshness,
and a sanity born out of 'firm persuasion'. It is the almost unconscious humour of the true mystic, born out of a naïve precision of
supernatural observation:

'Once I saw a Devil in a flame who arose before an Angel that
sat on a cloud, and the Devil uttered these words: "The worship of
God is honouring his gifts in other men each according to his genius
and loving the greatest men best, those who envy or calumniate
great men hate God, for there is no other God." The Angel hearing
this became almost blue but mastering himself he grew yellow and
at last white, pink and smiling and then replied: "Thou Idolator..."'

Following is a long list of the Proverbs of Hell, all extolling spiritual
energy in terms of natural energy: 'He whose face gives no light
shall never become a star'; 'No bird soars too high if he soars with
his own wings'; 'When thou seest an eagle, thou seest a portion of
genius. Lift up thy head!' and, 'Exuberance is Beauty.'

[1] Yeats and Ellis, *William Blake*, Vol. II, p. 64.

Yeats might very easily interpret the next section of the poem as a championship of ancient magic, magic which only by abstraction became a false religion:

'The ancient Poets animated all sensible objects with Gods or Geniuses, calling them by the names and adorning them with the properties of woods, rivers, mountains, lakes, cities, nations, and whatever their enlarged and numerous senses could perceive.

'And particularly they studied the genius of each city and country, placing it under its mental deity.

'Till a system was formed, which some took advantage of, and enslaved the vulgar by attempting to realize or abstract the mental deities from their objects: thus began Priesthood.'

The next 'Memorable Fancy' reveals much about the nature of Blake's own visions or revelations, which reduce, not to Yeats' hope of ghosts and evoked spirits, but to a 'firm persuasion' that the infinite is everywhere:

'The Prophets Isaiah and Ezekiel dined with me, and I asked them how they dared so roundly to assert that God spake to them; and whether they did not think at the time that they would be misunderstood and so be the cause of imposition.

'Isaiah answered: "I saw no God, nor heard any, in a finite organical perception; but my senses discover'd the infinite in everything, and as I was then persuaded, and remain confirm'd, that the voice of honest indignation is the voice of God, I cared not for consequences, but wrote."

'Then I asked: "does a firm persuasion that a thing is so, make it so?"

'He replied: "All poets believe that it does, and in ages of imagination this firm persuasion removed mountains; but many are not capable of a firm persuasion of anything." '

In significant contrast to this are the words Yeats wrote in his private diary: 'O masters of life give me confidence in something even if it be but in my own reason. I can never believe in anything else.' All of Yeats' complicated systematizing, although giving impetus to much of his work, could not give him what he most longed for—belief, a firm persuasion that a thing is so. Masking himself as magician, this is what he was trying to evoke, a vision that would make him *believe*. But, he said bitterly, 'I see always this one thing, in life the Mask is more than the Face.'[1] And Yeats' interpretation of this important 'Memorable Fancy' in Blake's book is a magical one:

'The next "Memorable Fancy" states the fundamental doctrine of transcendentalism in its positive form—"a firm persuasion that a thing is so, makes it so." This is the root of hypnotic suggestion and all magic. Incidentally, it refutes the negative side of transcendentalism which is apt to deny to nature any objectivity, for it is evident that objectivity can come into existence from its opposite by means of a firm persuasion.'[2]

There is another 'Memorable Fancy' in the *Marriage* which gives Yeats justification for thinking that Blake's work is magical. The episode consists of a series of enchantments which the Angel and the Devil impose upon one another. There is no other explanation of what takes place. For this reason it needs ample quotation.

'An Angel came to me and said: "O pitiable foolish young man! O horrible! O dreadful state! consider the hot burning dungeon thou art preparing for thyself to all eternity, to which thou art going in such a career."

'I said: "Perhaps you will be willing to show me my eternal lot and we will contemplate together upon it and see whether your lot or mine is most desirable."

'So he took me thro' a stable and thro' a church and down into the church vault at the end of which was a mill: thro' the mill we went, and came to a cave: down the winding cavern we groped our tedious way, till a void boundless as a nether sky appeared beneath us, and we held by the roots of trees and hung over this immensity, but I said: "if you please we will commit ourselves to this void, and see whether providence is here also: if you will not, I will:" but he answer'd: "do not presume O young man, but as we here remain, behold thy lot which will soon appear when the darkness passes away."

'So I remain'd with him, sitting in the twisted root of an oak; he was suspended in a fungus, which hung with the head downward into the deep.'

The most noticeable thing is the dream-like quality of the descriptions and conversation. Blake tells of the fiery abyss that they see,

[1] Yeats, Unpublished diary.   [2] Yeats and Ellis, *William Blake*, Vol. II, p. 69.

the immense distances and the corrupt shapes of spiders and other sinister animals revolving around the far-off sun.

'I now asked my companion which was my eternal lot? he said: "between the black and white spiders."'

More horrible sights appear, and the monstrous Leviathan advances towards them 'with all the fury of a spiritual existence.'
Then,

'My friend the Angel climb'd up from his station into the mill: I remain'd alone; and then this appearance was no more, but I found myself sitting on a pleasant bank beside a river by moonlight, hearing a harper, who sung to the harp; and his theme was: "The man who never alters his opinion is like standing water, and breeds reptiles of the mind."
'But I arose and sought for the mill, and there I found my Angel who, surprised, asked me how I escaped?
'I answer'd: "All that we saw was owing to your metaphysics; for when you ran away, I found myself on a bank by moonlight hearing a harper. But now we have seen my eternal lot, shall I shew you yours?" he laughed at my proposal; but I by force suddenly caught him in my arms, and flew westerly thro' the night, till we were elevated above the earth's shadow.'

Blake flies with the Angel into the sun and then sinks to the void between Saturn and the stars:

' "Here," said I, "is your lot, in this space—if space it may be call'd." Soon we saw the stable and the church, and I took him to the altar and open'd the Bible, and lo! it was a deep pit, into which I descended, driving the Angel before me; soon we saw seven houses of brick; one we enter'd; in it were a number of monkeys, baboons, and all of that species, chain'd by the middle, grinning and snatching at one another.'

The smell and ugly sight soon

'terribly annoy'd us both, we went into the mill, and I in my hand brought the skeleton of a body, which in the mill was Aristotle's Analytics.
'So the Angel said: "thy phantasy has imposed upon me, and thou oughtest to be ashamed."'

'I answer'd: "we impose on one another, and it is but lost time to converse with you whose works are only Analytics." '

Dream logic and enchantments, the imposition of dream upon dream is the theme of this episode, and Blake criticizes the tendency of human beings to do this. It is by a kind of magical projection that the orthodoxy of the angel imposes its picture of horrible fate on the unbeliever, the Devil. The Angel distorts truth by magic; he changes what is a happy, moonlit scene into evil. His metaphysics is the rational theory of sorcery. The Devil casts a spell too, but there is no indication that it is a distortion of truth, but rather a symbolic pointing out of the error of a purely analytic philosophy.

Nevertheless, the tone of this section of the poem is magical and it is likely that Yeats saw only this and not the implied criticism of projection. The comments in the Yeats and Ellis book are largely paraphrase, but in Yeats' own small edition of Blake, 1893, he refers to the thought in this Memorable Fancy, and adds:

'It is probable that the reading of The Morning Redness, Mysterium Magnum, and stray fragments of medieval magical philosophy, such as the works of Cornelius Agrippa, then not uncommon in translation, delivered his intellect from the spectral and formal intellect of Swedenborg, and taught him to think about the meaning of his own visions. He may also have met mystics and even students of magic, for there was an important secret body working in London under the three brothers named Falk. The miniature painter, Cosway, too, may have come across him, and Cosway kept a house especially for the invocation of spirits.'[1]

It is characteristic that Yeats could only see the magical tone of Blake's comment on the insidious and tragic human tendency to project and impose one's own vision on another. In much more modern and less allegorical terms it is the theme of Eliot's *The Cocktail Party*. It is what Celia discovers about her lover when she sees him for the first time as an actual and complex person instead of as a romantic ideal. It is what Yeats never discovered about Maud Gonne. Celia asks forgiveness for using Edward as an impossible ideal on to which to project her gift of love. This is perhaps the essence of guilt—the knowledge that you must be forgiven for misjudging and misrepresenting something, but even more the

---

[1] Yeats, 1893, *Blake* edition, intro., p. xxxiii.

knowledge that you must be forgiven for not loving the actual person. This is where Celia and Eliot fall short.

> . . . then I suddenly discovered
> That the dream was not enough; that I wanted something more
> And I waited, and wanted to run to tell you.
> Perhaps the dream was better. It seemed the real reality,
> And if this is reality, it is very like a dream.

and,

> I see you as a person I never saw before.
> The man I saw before, he was only a projection—
> I see that now—of something that I wanted—
> No, not wanted—something I aspired to—
> Something that I desperately wanted to exist.
> It must happen somewhere—but what, and where is it?[1]

Blake knew that we depend too much on our own projected ideals of Utopias, of ideal human beings, of foolproof religions, instead of learning to be worthy of the actual, of the incarnated Christ who is Love. But Blake, perhaps because his vision was so complete, did not see the peculiar poignancy of modern man, forced by the disillusionment of ever more ugly experience to live without the romantic ideal which he has built up in desperation against this very experience, and which fails him just at the moment when the earth shifts beneath him and there seems no 'certain' actuality at all. And the modern must feel guilty at forsaking the ideal:

> But even if I find my way out of the forest
> I shall be left with the inconsolable memory
> Of the treasure I went into the forest to find
> And never found, and which was not there
> And perhaps is not anywhere? But if not anywhere,
> Why do I feel guilty at not having found it? . . .
>   But what or whom I loved,
> Or what in me was loving, I do not know.
> And if that is all meaningless, I want to be cured
> Of a craving for something I cannot find
> And of the shame of never finding it.

[1] T. S. Eliot, The Cocktail Party, p. 55.   [2] Ibid., p. 122.

This digression is to point out more clearly that for both Blake and Eliot the only cure for false romantic projection is to turn to the actuality of Christ, who is not unattainable, but incarnated Love, and whose brotherhood is Utopia upon earth. But this is what Yeats could not see: magic and poetry are so tied up with the romantic love he had for Maud Gonne, that they are almost interchangeable parts of a whole, and the collapse of one would mean the collapse of all. Therefore, the romantic ideal must be guarded at all costs from the breath of the actual: projection and dream are instruments of poetry and magic, and are good. Blake's use of a magical dream-like way of writing to criticize this kind of projected dream of the ideal we impose on one another, passes right over Yeats' head, and he solemnly points the passage out as an instance of Blake's occultism. Yeats is particularly obtuse, as if he just did not understand what Blake is driving at, just at the crucial moments where Blake seems to be seeing clear of the magical aura which no doubt had a strong appeal to him during this second period. Yeats could follow in his master's footsteps no further.

It is fitting to end this chapter with what is undoubtedly Blake's greatest poem, a short lyric which might in its simplicity be termed both 'magical' and 'mystical' for precisely the same reason—namely, that it widens out in a moment of almost unbearable intuition to an infinity of inwardness.

THE SICK ROSE

O Rose, thou art sick!
The invisible worm
That flies in the night,
In the howling storm,

Has found out thy bed
Of crimson joy,
And his dark secret love
Does thy life destroy.

Chapter Five

'THE WORLD IN A GRAIN OF SAND'

~~~~~~

BLAKE'S apparent preoccupation with satanic or magical nature in the period just described is so ambiguous that Yeats can hardly be blamed for pushing the interpretation a little too far, to suit his own theory and inclinations. For without a doubt there is a conflict in this period between two selves in Blake, and in his greatest prophetic book he confesses in terms that are startlingly like Yeats' own: 'Man is born a Spectre or Satan and is altogether an Evil, and requires a New Selfhood continually, and must continually be *changed into his direct contrary*.'[1] It is not hard to deduce from this that Blake himself worked through from his magical or satanic self to the self that 'put on mystical significance.' Yeats, who speaks of Blake as both saint and enchanter without ever giving us concise reasons for doing so, could find a good deal that seemed magical in this second period without overlooking much.

Blake's third period begins with the prophetic book called *America* (1793). Natural imagery tends more and more to turn into abstraction, human beings into superhuman types, even archetypes, psychological insight into mysticism. The tone becomes historical, even universal, rather than individual, general rather than particular. Fable has become mythology. Warfare takes place in heaven and no longer on earth, and there is little of the magician's delight in natural imagery and in the conflict between dream and reality. All this is cast impatiently aside as the mystic rushes straight at eternal truth. We are left to follow as best we may, without much guidance from reassuring earth symbols. And although we feel the urgency and fire of ever-greater vision, we are uneasy because we cannot make so

---

[1] *The Complete Poetry of William Blake*, p. 955.

quickly the jump from nature to eternity that is necessary for understanding. Sometimes in desperation we even laugh at Blake, for he
seems to be talking nonsense at our expense. Nevertheless, whether
or not we take the prophetic books seriously, it must be remembered
that Blake himself felt that in them he had at last reached a vision of
eternal truth.

I will do little more than summarize these later mystical poems, since
the ambiguity of the second period was the important point. The main
thing to notice now is that Blake emerges from his semi-magical
theories and technique, and becomes more and more the mystic or
saint, although this position does not solidify until *Milton* and *Jerusalem*.

A. Edward Newton's description of *America* covers the theme of
this poem briefly:

'To Blake, as to Tom Paine and other liberals of the eighteenth
century, the American Revolution appeared as the dawn of the
millennium. The freedom of universal mankind seemed imminent.
Blake, fitting history to his pattern, took the story of the American
Revolution, incidentally disregarding the details, and endued it with
mystical significance. "He regarded the whole of history, not as a
process of events in time, but as the perpetual re-enactment of a
truth which every man might find written for himself in the con-
ditions of his individual life," remarks Basil de Selincourt. The third
phase of Blake's mythology was revolution, and in his mind the
revolt of the American Colonies became the quintessence of all
revolution. The hero of America is Orc, mankind in revolt; the
villain is the guardian Prince of Albion, or oppression, aided by the
repressive forces of Urizen, the God of Dogma. Washington, Frank-
lin, Paine and Warren, Gates, Hancock and Green are introduced;
the Thirteen Original States are given life; and Orc arises to lead them
against the tyrannical Albion. The battle is furious; thrust back by the
flames of Orc, the plagues hurled upon America recoil and work their
destruction on Albion. The triumphant fires of revolt spread over the
world, consuming all material things, all dogma, all restraint, leaving
only absolute spiritual eternity, the alpha and omega of the universe.'[1]

Mr. Newton goes on to comment on the illustrations:

'When Blake was greatly moved, when his visions had tremendous vigour, his designs became freer and more imaginative. The

[1] *W. Blake, A Descriptive Catalogue*, Philadelphia, 1939, p. 32.

designs for *America* are as full of poetic genius as the text; they are
the live steam of Blake's furious fire. But they do not illustrate the
text. Blake devised a second parable of revolt with the same moral;
the designs form a series showing the passage of man through the
state of experience into the state of revolt, but without reference to
the American Revolution. The eternals Orc, Urizen, Beulah, Los,
Enitharmon, Har, Heva, Oothoon, and Rahab, the flames of Revolution, the dragon of War, Death's door, the sea of Time and Space,
the vulture of Remorse, the tree of Religion, all appear in these
designs. None of the prophetic books except *Jerusalem* displays such
startling contrasts, such breadth of vision.'[1]

I am not trying to suggest that there is no natural imagery in this
book, or in any of the prophetic books. This is not true, but it is
true that there is none of the delicate type of natural symbol used
in the *Songs* and in *Thel*, and even in the *Visions of the Daughters of
Albion* and the *Marriage of Heaven and Hell*. That is to say, there is
little of nature brought in for its own or its magically evocative
beauty. The nature imagery is now only a background to the gigantic
archetypal figures, and is used only to emphasize the cosmic character
and unearthly terror of their warfare. It is essentially evil or heraldic
of evil. It has become the satanic Mundane Shell instead of something to be delighted in as energy. Such passages as the following
from *America* illustrate this point:

> *Solemn heave the Atlantic waves between the gloomy nations,*
> *Swelling, belching from its deep red clouds and raging fires.*
> *Albion is sick! America faints! enrag'd the Zenith grew.*
> *As human blood shooting its veins all round the orbed heaven;*
> *Red rose the clouds from the Atlantic in vast wheels of blood,*
> *And in the red clouds rose a Wonder o'er the Atlantic's sea,*
> *Intense! naked! a Human fire, fierce glowing, as the wedge*
> *Of iron heated in the furnace: his terrible limbs were fire*
> *With myriads of cloudy terrors, banners dark and towers*
> *Surrounded: heat but not light went thro' the murky atmosphere.*
>
> *The King of England looking westward trembles at the vision.*
>
> *Albion's Angel stood beside the stone of night, and saw*
> *The terror like a comet, or more like the planet red*
> *That once enclos'd the terrible wandering comets in its sphere.*

[1] *W. Blake, A Descriptive Catalogue*, Philadelphia, 1939, p.311.

Then, Mars, thou wast our center, and the planets three flew around
Thy crimson disk: so ere the Sun was rent from thy red sphere,
The Spectre glow'd his horrid length straining the temple long
With beams of blood; ...

The two prophetic books, *America* and *Europe*, reveal Blake the revolutionary—symbolized by Orc—more than Blake the prophet. It is as if the secular and political view of reform were a step, coming after the struggle with nature and magic, on the road to true mysticism. Even the prophetic books themselves, full of the tone of mysticism as they are, do not become specifically Christian and undoubtedly mystical until after Blake's dark period and his 'slumber on the banks of the Ocean', that is to say, until *Milton* and *Jerusalem*. In both *Milton* and *Jerusalem* the conflicts of experience and social reform are restated, but disappear at last into the tremendous mystical unity of Christ. Until these final books Blake is still rebelling a little, still launching one side against the other in spiritual warfare, still a little drawn by the tremendous forces of Satan, because he did not yet feel within his own mind a unity powerful enough to transcend such contraries.

In most of the existing copies of *Europe* Blake has omitted the following lines, which he probably felt would be grossly misunderstood. It is a pity, because it is the clearest statement of his theory that the senses are gateways to eternity: he puts the words in the mouth of a mocking Fairy who dictates the rest of the poem:

Five windows light the cavern'd Man: thro' one he breathes the air;
Thro' one hears music of the spheres; thro' one the eternal vine
Flourishes, that he may receive the grapes; thro' one can look
And see small portions of the eternal world that ever groweth.
Thro' one himself pass out what time he please; but he will not
For stolen joys are sweet and bread eaten in secret pleasant.

Earlier he had claimed:

'For man has closed himself up, til he sees all things through narrow chinks of his cavern.'

Writing of the poem *Europe* (1794), Mr. Newton summarizes the interpretation of several critics:

'Blake wrote *Europe* after he had finished *America*: historically it covers the eighteen hundred years of the Christian Era that had already elapsed. After the birth of Christ a misleading peace settles over the world. Enitharmon—Inspiration, the Moon, Space—the typical female, imposes her will on Europe. She is separated from her eternal partner, Los—Poetry, the Sun, Time—the typical male, and separated she lives in error, for, according to Blake, dominant womanhood creates the false doctrines of chastity and the sinfulness of free love. At the millennium Enitharmon and Los will become one again, and perfect poetic inspiration will result. Meanwhile the errors of Enitharmon persist in Europe. A tenet in all Blake's work is, that once error can be seen, it can be destroyed. So when science, represented by Newton, defines Enitharmon's principles they become vulnerable to the attacks of Orc. After eighteen hundred years the French Revolution and Blake's Prophetic Books herald the end of Enitharmon's hold on Europe. Whether Blake purposely confused the story of Europe, or whether he was carried away into confusion by his overcrowded imagination, the result is the same. As noted in several other books, the designs retell the story of the poem without following the text. They depict the origin and cause of revolt.'[1]

The next prophetic poem, the First Book of Urizen (1794), is set, not in historical time and place, but in eternity. It is Blake's first draft of the myth of creation and of the fall into error. It is murky, chaotic, with the uneasy sequence of a cosmic dream, and yet it has a certain power and beauty, with a strong emotional charge.

Urizen, whom Blake equates with the Old Testament Jehovah, is abstract dogmatic reason, and as such is the source of all evil. It is significant that it is Urizen and not Satan who fell from Eternity. Satan is a milder evil associated with nature, and is in fact much like the archetype of the enchanter. Urizen is spiritual corruption. His perverted mind creates a false ethical code. Blake makes this very like the gnostic interpretations by saying that Urizen is exiled into chaos.

'From the primeval mists appear the opposing eternals, Los—the expression of poetic genius, Enitharmon—his emanation, and their child Orc—the spirit of revolt. In his struggle against them Urizen creates about himself a material world. Finally he reduces the giants of eternity and compresses them into physical bodies; so mankind is created. The first chapter of Blake's cosmic epic ends with the enslavement of man in the net of religion, and the establishment of civilization in Egypt. Blake's basic mystical theme is clear enough.

[1] W. Blake, A Descriptive Catalogue, Philadelphia, 1939, p. 38.

Reason alone, by bounding infinity and eternity with moral codes
and a material shell, makes them finite and mortal. Casting out
imagination from himself Jehovah created man, the world and
religion; eventually imagination or poetic genius, the Saviour, will
come, and entering again into Jehovah, become one with him.
When reason is wedded to poetic imagination and subservient to it,
all materialism is destroyed. This will be the millennium.'[1]

Of the magnificent plates Arthur Symons says:

'The colours (are) of fire and of blood, an extralunar gold,
putrescent vegetable colours, and the stains in rocks and sunsets, he
sees everywhere.'[2]

Blake's description of Urizen at the beginning of the book brings
to mind with startling clarity Yeats' image in the *Second Coming*.
Mrs. Yeats, when I asked if the Urizen image could have influenced
W. B. Y.'s poem, said that it almost surely must have been in his
mind when he wrote:

> *Surely some revelation is at hand;*
> *Surely the Second Coming is at hand.*
> *The Second Coming! Hardly are these words out*
> *When a vast image out of Spiritus Mundi*
> *Troubles my sight: somewhere in the sands of the desert*
> *A shape with lion body and the head of a man,*
> *A gaze blank and pitiless as the sun,*
> *Is moving its slow thighs, while all about it*
> *Reel shadows of the indignant desert birds.*
> *The darkness drops again; but now I know*
> *That twenty centuries of stony sleep*
> *Were vexed to nightmare by a rocking cradle,*
> *And what rough beast, its hour come round at last,*
> *Slouches towards Bethlehem to be born?*

Blake's lines are:

> *Lo, a shadow of horror is risen*
> *In Eternity! Unknown, prolific,*
> *Self-clos'd, all-repelling; what Demon*
> *Hath form'd this abominable void,*

---

[1] W. Blake, *A Descriptive Catalogue*, Philadelphia, 1939, p. 41.   [2] *Ibid.*, p. 44.

> *This soul-shudd'ring vacuum? Some said*
> *'It is Urizen.' But unknown, abstracted,*
> *Brooding, secret, the dark power hid. . . .*
> *For he strove in battles dire,*
> *In unseen conflictions with shapes*
> *Bred from his forsaken wilderness*
> *Of beast, bird, fish, serpent and element, . . .*
> *A self-contemplating shadow,*
> *In enormous labours occupied. . . .*
> *Ages on ages he lay clos'd, unknown,*
> *Brooding, shut in the deep. . . .*
> *A void immense, wild, dark and deep,*
> *Where nothing was: Nature's wide womb.*

The likeness is too apparent and startling to labour the point. And this is one of Yeats' fairly late poems, a point to remember, since most critics believe Blake's influence only affected Yeats' early poems.

The natural imagery for which Blake still has a vocabulary cannot be pictured: he is using words that denote nature only for emotional connotations or as background for archetypal states of mind:

> *Ages and ages roll'd over him*
> *In stony sleep ages roll'd over him*
> *Like a dark waste stretching, chang'able,*
> *By earthquakes riven, belching sudden fires:*
> *On ages roll'd ages in ghastly*
> *Sick torment; around him in whirlwinds*
> *Of darkness the eternal Prophet howled.*

It is interesting to note that in the *Second Coming* Yeats uses the exact phrases that Blake uses here to indicate the passing of immense ages: 'stony sleep'.

In Blake himself at this period of his work there is still an acute awareness of the split in man's soul which he now sees in terms of a division into male and female principles that cannot exist by themselves. It is Jung long before Jung, with the added penetration into truth that taking sides with eternity brings. It is the consciousness of a division in what should and must be whole.

> *Eternity shudder'd when they saw*
> *Man begetting his likeness*
> *On his own divided image.*

There is a great deal in Blake's work that is inherited from gnostic thinking: above all the period of dualism and the personal recognition that darkness has its charms and that the division of male and female can be pursued into endless ramifications. The terminology of emanations, and the arrangement of abstract divinities in pairs and also as individual progressions is also gnostic, stemming from Valentine and Basilides. Theories of creation such as that set forth in the *Book of Urizen* have also a strange gnostic flavour. When Blake differs from gnosticism is precisely when he defies dualism by postulating as incarnate God who overcomes the false god, Urizen. Urizen, the false law abstracted from nature, widens the dualism by being as far removed from nature as possible. When Christ instead of Urizen is seen to be at the head of (and the sum of) all the Eternals, matter is redeemed from evil. It is interesting that the name Eternals equals the Æons of the gnostics, although for the gnostics it is usually Sophia or Wisdom that falls rather than Reason.

The *Book of Ahania* (1795) is really the second part of the *Book of Urizen*, a continuation of the same myth.

'Continuing from the establishment of man in Egypt, it symbolizes the history of the flight of the Israelites from Egypt, the imposition of the Mosaic code and their settlement in Asia. The main characters of the poem are Urizen, Fuzon (in later books called Luvah) and Ahania. The revolt of Fuzon—Passion—against Urizen—Reason— is continued from the first part of the epic. Passion blasts Reason in the loins, forcing him to throw out his emanation, Pleasure, called Ahania. Blake here hints that Fuzon will be the saviour of the world. Passion in a moment of supposed triumph is struck by the stone of the Decalogue hurled by Reason, who crucifies his body on the tree of religion. Reason then exiles Pleasure, who, hidden, becomes Sin; and the last part of the book is the plaint of Ahania in exile, written in verses as lovely as that in any of the Prophetic Books.'[1]

The *Song of Los* (1795) is a mythological paraphrase of history from the beginning of civilization to the eighteenth century. Urizen imposes many forms of his false religion in pleasant and various disguises upon mankind through the children of Los. The true religion of imagination fades and tyranny reigns until the revolt of Orc in America begins, spreading to Asia and Europe to bring

[1] *W. Blake, A Descriptive Catalogue*, Philadelphia, 1939, p. 50.

about the Last Judgment. The designs for this book are magnificent, particularly the one called 'The Worshippers of Reason', which shows a Job-like figure kneeling before a huge mottled globe outlined fuzzily in the sky.

The *Book of Los* (1795) is a short poem, but full of confusing symbolism. It is another version of the story of creation set forth in the *Book of Urizen*, only Los, the spirit of poetry, is the central figure instead of Urizen. Los, 'the Eternal Prophet, bound in a chain' is 'compell'd to watch Urizen's shadow' which controls the world by false dogma, 'till impatience could no longer bear the hard bondage', and Los breaks his chains only to fall into the boundless void of error. Los builds an anvil and works until he has forged a globe of fire to which he binds Urizen 'till a Form was completed, a Human Illusion, in darkness and deep clouds involv'd.' This poem is another picture of the battle of the eternals upon the stage of infinite space, and the imagery remains accordingly cosmic.

Mr. Newton makes an important point which he does not carry far enough when he says that 'the battle-field of the eternals will now be moved from infinity to within man, and from man will come the saviour.'[1]

The *Four Zoas* (1795–1804) is the book which marks the turning point in the third period of Blake's work. It has been noted already how Blake moves his drama from the realm of experience in nature to a cosmic plane where great elemental figures wield their respective doctrines against one another. Now there is another and vitally important step in the *Four Zoas* whose very existence Mr. Newton omits to mention. It is a very difficult poem, difficult because it represents a painful transition from the philosophy of experience to a specifically Christian belief that is mystical, and whose dazzling truths spring from the inner world. It is the exact point at which Blake breaks away from any semi-magical expressions of belief and reaches through to the realm of mystical faith. One could say that it is the point at which he stops being the poet and becomes the mystic who may or may not express himself in poetry.

As Mr. Newton said, the struggle is put back within the soul of man, but of man who is now prepared to receive the saviour within himself. It is Blake's own victory at the point of what Yeats would call the enchanter's vision forcing down the saint's. By grace or by choice Blake is treading the mystical way now, and nearing his goal.

[1] *W. Blake, A Descriptive Catalogue*, Philadelphia, 1939, p. 53.

He has passed through the Dark Night and is on the verge of four-fold vision.

The motto and the quotation from Ephesians heading the *Four Zoas* reveal the tremendous importance of this point in the struggle for the saint's vision. 'Rest before labour,' cries Blake, and quotes:

'For our contention is not with the blood and the flesh, but with dominion, with authority, with the blind world-rulers of this life, with the spirit of evil in things heavenly.'

The battle has been with Satan and Urizen, with magic and perverted power which has tried through forbidden knowledge to dominate what should be left to Heaven, rather than with the senses.

For the first time Blake begins speaking more of unity than of battle: the unity of the Eternals before the Fall, the unity of the states of soul which the Eternals represent which is possible within every man, and above all, the ultimate unity of all that is in Christ.

> *Four Mighty Ones are in Every Man; a perfect Unity*
> *Cannot Exist, but from the Universal Brotherhood of Eden*
> *The Universal Man, To Whom be Glory Evermore.*

These four beings are, Los or Imagination; Urizen, or Intellect; Luvah or Passion; and Tharmas (Doubting Tharmas) is Instinct, or perhaps Sensation. In Eternity and before the Fall they lived in harmony together, but once fallen into division, each was divided from his emanation and became a shadow of his former self. Each in turn fights for pre-eminence and becomes evil. This can also happen within a single soul. Albion or Universal Man, when complete, is united to Jerusalem, who is total femininity. But instead of seeking for her, he goes to Vala, Luvah's emanation who has separated from him and become worldly illusions of the senses. That is, fallen man seeks mere passion instead of his fitting bride. This upsets the balance, and life divides immediately into male and female incompleteness. This is what happened at the Fall, and accounts for evil. For when man and his true emanation live apart, each becomes exaggerated into evil proportions and a false self-sufficiency. Each shows a tyrannical side. There are many divisions within divisions, and the rest of the confusing book is concerned with the search of each of these tortured and torturing souls for its true mate. Until this is accomplished there can be no unity or balance where the individual self suppresses its self-seeking in favour of Eternal Oneness.

The problem is only presented in the *Four Zoas*: the fact of separation and the need for unity. The *Four Zoas*, in a degree hitherto only hinted at, shows the separation of all that is by the Fall. *Milton* and especially *Jerusalem* represent Blake's vision of total unity, the unity of all that is. By myth, by a strange parade of symbols dividing and redividing, Blake at the end finds a vision of truth, a vision of nature transformed. And this is why the *Four Zoas* is the point at which Blake breaks through to mysticism, to the vision of the saint.

Imagery too is undergoing a significant change. No longer is there delight in external nature. Nor is there much cosmic imagery as a drop-curtain background to gigantic archetypes. It has turned startlingly inwards, and has to do with nerves, arteries, the brain, with moments of mental apprehension which stretch to eternity, with atoms of space that become 'windows into Eden', with the interior landscape of Beulah where opposites are lit by the same moon and seem equally true.

In gnawing pain drawn out by her lov'd fingers, every nerve
She counted, every vein and lacteal, threading them among
Her woof of terra . . . took a moment of Time
And drew it out to seven thousand years with much care and affliction. . . .
She also took an atom of space and open'd its centre
Into Infinitude and ornamented it with wondrous art.

Those who read Blake in anthologies assume that he was always a mystic and had no difficult road to travel to this goal. This is untrue: the road was long and hard, and the poems achieving this strange interior imagery, the climax of a lifetime. The famous lyric beginning:

> *To see a World in a Grain of Sand*
> *And a Heaven in a Wild Flower,*
> *Hold Infinity in the palm of your hand*
> *And Eternity in an hour.*

is undated, and generally thought by its simplicity of presentation to be an early poem. But it may be because of this unique type of imagery and the thought that this lyric falls into the same period as the *Four Zoas*, *Milton*, and *Jerusalem*. The ability of a natural object to become in the mind's eye of the poet an infinite world is a thing that only happens in Blake's final period, when he has truly solved for himself the dualism of mind and body.

I have called the *Four Zoas* the wall between the magical poet and the true mystic. To determine whether Blake did really 'beat upon the wall, Til Truth obeyed his call', and so was both Enchanter and Saint, we must look at the two final prophetic works, *Milton* and *Jerusalem*.

Jerusalem is Blake's final and in many ways most beautiful book, and is more interesting to examine than *Milton*. The thought of *Milton* (1804–1808) may be briefly sketched in the concise phrases of Mr. Newton:

'The parable recited in eternity is an account of the conflict between Satan and Palamabron. It is an allegory of the struggle of perverted art against true art, of an unappreciative and uncomprehending world, crystallized in Hayley, against Blake.

'The skeleton of the plot appears to be that Milton, "a true Poet, and of the Devil's Party" (that is, he sided with imagination against dogma), came to the realization in eternity that he had failed in his mission as a prophet on earth. "I saw Milton in imagination," Blake later told Crabb Robinson, "and he told me to beware of being misled by his *Paradise Lost*." Milton had been deluded by worldly materialism and Puritan morals. To right these wrongs—after they had been pointed out in the parable told by a heavenly bard—Milton comes down to earth and enters into Blake. As truth in apparent error disappears, so when Milton sees his errors as such, they, personified by Satan, disappear. By self-annihilation, by achieving perfect unity with his sexual emanation—his three wives and three daughters—Milton turns himself into the perfect man, Jesus, the saviour of the world. Human vision is unable to look upon the final union of God and man, and so Blake ends his poem by bringing himself back to his mundane natural surroundings at Felpham. On this framework he has built a long confused poem referring, in recognizable passages, to some of the events in *America*, *Urizen*, and *Vala or The Four Zoas*.'[1]

Satan in this book is almost the archetype of the Enchanter. When the dualism or conflict between nature and spirit is seen as false, Satan or the magician disappears and everything can be gathered

[1] *W. Blake, A Descriptive Catalogue*, Philadelphia, 1939, p. 68.

into a mystical unity. For the magician is the main instigator of a dualism between nature and the mind which desires control. Ever since Blake wrote, 'There is No Natural Religion,'[1] he has preached that there is no dualism of body and soul, nature and spirit. And yet, he did not act or feel accordingly. When he was not siding with Nature, extolling energy and man's imaginative control, he was crying out against it, calling it the illusion or Mundane Shell and muttering disapprovingly over Wordsworth, 'I fear this man loves nature.' In other words, despite his protestations to the contrary, there was still an unresolved dualism in his own mind, making his view akin to the magician's in some respects. It is only in *Milton* that he at last realizes this and pictures what has happened. The errors of Milton, personified in Satan, are the errors of Blake himself, the falsity of acting upon a magical materialism despite a deep yearning for spiritual unity. The confusion occurs (and it is Yeats' main trouble as well as Blake's) because magic is made out of two sides over against one another—mind and nature—and the side of mind seems comparatively spiritual because it deals with the invisible and seeks a mystery. The poet, adopting this side, may be deluded into thinking that his views have become truly mystical. But true mysticism is neither over-againstness nor one-sided. Nature is neither extolled as powerful energy nor cried out against as illusion. Blake admits the mistake in *Milton*:

> The Starry Mills of Satan
> Are built beneath the Earth and Waters of the Mundane Shell . . . .
> 'Every Man's Wisdom is peculiar to his own Individuality.
> O Satan . . . art thou not Prince of the Starry Hosts
> And of the Wheels of Heaven, to turn the Mills day and night?
> Art thou not Newton's Pantocrator, weaving the Woof of Locke?
> To Mortals thy Mills seem everything, and the Harrow of Shaddai
> A scheme of Human Conduct invisible and incomprehensible.
> Get to thy Labours at the Mills and leave me to my wrath.'
> Satan was going to reply, byt Los roll'd his loud thunders.
> 'Anger me not! thou canst not drive the Harrow in pity's paths:
> Thy Work is Eternal Death with Mills and Ovens and Cauldrons.
> Trouble me no more; thou canst not have Eternal Life.'

Remember that in the earlier books both Blake and Milton were on Satan's side—'of the Devil's Party'—even if the values were

---

[1] *The Complete Poetry of William Blake*, p. 619.

topsy-turvy. But now Blake's values are more or less right side up, and he repudiates Satan's scheme of 'conduct invisible and incomprehensible' as eternal death, along with its paraphernalia of Mills, Ovens and Cauldrons. And yet Blake allows Satan his full individuality. Satan is a real force to be contended with and not to be minimized. Was not he himself deceived by Satan's cunning? Over and over during this long book of confession Blake cries: 'Mark well my words! they are of your eternal salvation,' lest others fall into the error of worshipping Satan disguised as an Angel, 'the spirit of evil in things heavenly.'

Too, the Promethean motif, the conviction that evil is somehow woven into man's creative energies, has always had a strong influence. This being so, it was an easy step for Blake to choose mistakenly and defiantly to be 'of the Devil's Party.'

Note how significant here is the symbol of the wheel, which Yeats took for the dominant image of his magical creed, *A Vision*. The wheel is almost the inevitable visual diagram of a magical system.

Blake continues his archetypal confession of how Satan, the Enchanter, by his soft wiles usurped the rightful place of the mystic in his poetry and almost, in fact, convincing Los, the spirit of poetry itself, that he belonged there. The terrible thing is—and here Blake might turn pitying eyes on Yeats' delusion that poetry is magic—that Satan is firmly persuaded that he is right and others wrong. Blake's condemnation has compassion in it:

Then Palamabron reddening like the Moon in an Eclipse
Spoke, saying: 'You know Satan's mildness and his self-imposition
Seeming a brother, being a tyrant, even thinking himself a brother
While he is murdering the just: prophetic I behold
His future course thro' darkness and despair to eternal death
But we must not be tyrants also: he hath assum'd my place
For one whole day under pretence of pity and love to me.
My horses hath he madden'd and my fellow servants injur'd.
How should he, he, know the duties of another? O foolish forbearance!
Would I had told Los all my heart! . . .' Satan's blandishments almost
Persuaded the Prophet of Eternity that Palamabron
Was Satan's enemy.

And Los, the spirit of poetry and prophecy, says that it is his fault, that he 'should have remembered that pity divides the soul.'

There is more of the unique 'inward' imagery characteristic of

Blake's truly mystical work in the famous description of Beulah, and in such beautiful, if difficult, lines as the following:

> But to himself he seem'd a wanderer lost in dreary night. . . .
> The nature of infinity is this: That every thing has its
> Own Vortex, and when once a traveller thro' Eternity
> Has pass'd that Vortex, he perceives it roll backward behind
> His path, into a globe infolding itself like a sun,
> Or like a moon, or like a universe of starry majesty,
> While he keeps onward in his wondrous journey on the earth, . . .
> Also the rising sun and setting moon he views surrounding
> His cornfields and his valleys of five-hundred acres square,
> Thus is the earth one infinite plane, and not as apparent
> To the weak traveller confin'd beneath the moony shade.
> Thus is the heaven a Vortex pass'd already, and the earth
> A Vortex not yet pass'd by the traveller thro' Eternity.

The fluctuating back and forth between the extremely inward view and the wide cosmic comparison (not like *the* sun, but like 'a' sun, *any* sun in the universe!) makes the flight more dizzy, the mystery more mysterious and yet more precise. Blake then describes the worshippers of Satan:

'All the spectres of the Dead, calling themselves Sons of God, in his Synagogues worship Satan under the Unutterable Name.'[1]

How like them is Yeats, trying to break through the wheel of nature to the spirit world of Anima Mundi, crying the 'Ineffable Name.'

Jerusalem (1804–1820) is, of course, Blake's longest poem, even though he did not complete the twelve books he had planned. Fruit of his 'three years' slumber on the banks of the ocean' at Felpham, he began this prophetic book in 1804, but no complete copy was produced until 1820. Mr. Newton comments:

'Reading *Jerusalem*—and rare is the hardy soul who finishes it— one is antagonized and exhausted by the nearly unintelligible parade of eternals who create and are created, who disappear, divide them- selves into characters of the opposite sexes and reunite themselves into sexless wholes. Familiar names seem here and there to offer a refuge in the chaos, but the refuge is a mirage; the names are used symbolically. They bear a significance all Blake's own.

1 *The Complete Poetry of William Blake*, p. 840.

'The epic recounts the contention within man, or Albion, of the forces of reason against those of the imagination, of Satan against Jesus, of emanations against spectres, until all error, all material creation, disappears and man becomes an eternal one with his saviour. . . . The verse of *Jerusalem* is too full of strange symbolism, too far beyond most readers' comprehension. It is poetry by Aristotle's definition . . . the most pregnant with truth and the sincerest, but fails otherwise as poetry because Blake would not translate his vision for the understanding of others. . . . On the other hand the designs to *Jerusalem* are, with the exception of those to the *Book of Job*, the greatest which Blake ever issued in book form.'[1]

The precise reason that in both *Milton* and *Jerusalem* Blake's poetry is 'most pregnant with truth and sincerest' yet 'fails otherwise as poetry' is because Blake has stopped seeing at all with the eye of the enchanter, and has become wholly the mystic, seeing with the eye of the saint who cares nothing for alluring and controlling his material and audience, but only with presenting the highest truth. It is curious that this change of attitude took place while Blake was living at Felpham in the midst of most magical nature. The following quotation from a letter, when he and his wife moved to the cottage in 1800, reveals his great joy and hopes: before he left Felpham he had passed through the perils of the dark night of the soul 'not unlike a champion': . . . 'Felpham is a sweet place for study, because it is more spiritual than London. Heaven opens here on all sides her golden gates; her windows are not obstructed by vapours; voices of celestial inhabitants are most distinctly heard, and their forms more distinctly seen; and my cottage is also a shadow of their houses. My wife and sister are both well, courting Neptune for an embrace.' Later, back in London he writes to Hayley about the three years spent at Felpham: 'You, dear sir, are one who has my particular gratitude, having conducted me through three that would have been the darkest years that ever mortal suffered, which were rendered through your means a mild and pleasant slumber. I speak of spiritual things, not of natural; of things known only to myself and to spirits good and evil, but not known to men on earth.' The old arrogance that had something of the Enchanter in it is gone, and so is the control imposed by playing to an audience. No longer would Blake write as arrogantly as he did at thirty-three—'A new heaven is

[1] *Philadelphia Catalogue*, p. 72.

begun, and it is now thirty-three years since its advent.'[1] We are surprised almost at the humble note now dominant in Blake's writing:

'The Spirit of Jesus is continual forgiveness of Sin: he who waits to be righteous before he enters into the Saviour's Kingdom, the Divine Body, will never enter there. I am perhaps the most sinful of men. I pretend not to holiness: yet I pretend to love, to see, to converse with daily as man to man, and more to have an interest in the Friend of Sinners.'[2]

This new humility and emphasis on Christ's forgiveness of naturally sinful man is the first, and one of the most striking, indications that Blake is seeing with the eyes of the saint.

The underscoring of the unity of all that is in the One of the Saviour is another clear sign, perhaps the most important.

> *I see the Saviour over me. . . .*
> *Awake! awake O sleeper of the land of shadows, wake! expand.*
> *I am in you and you in me, mutual in love divine.*

And again, the great passage of dedication with its humility, its sense of contact with and unity in Christ, and its mysterious in-turning imagery:

Trembling I sit day and night, my friends are astonish'd at me,
Yet they forgive my wanderings. I rest not from my great task!
To open the Eternal Worlds, to open the immortal Eyes
Of Man inwards into the Worlds of Thought, into Eternity
Ever expanding in the Bosom of God, the Human Imagination.
O Saviour pour upon me thy spirit of meekness and love!
Annihilate the Selfhood in me: be thou all my life!
Guide thou my hand, which trembles exceedingly upon the rock of ages.

Blake, by asking that his selfhood be annihilated, is by no means asking to have his personality taken away. Rather, to have it emerge victorious. He would, I believe, agree with Berdaev's distinction:

'Christian ethics is personalistic, but not individualistic. The narrow isolation of personality in modern individualism is the destruction and not the triumph of personality. Hardened selfhood—the

---

[1] Blake, *Marriage of Heaven and Hell.*
[2] *The Complete Poetry of William Blake*, p. 893.

result of original sin—is not personality. It is only when the hardened selfhood melts away and is transcended that personality manifests itself.'

And elsewhere Berdaev says that personality is the impact of spirit upon matter.

The next indication of Blake's triumphant mystical vision is the note of discipline, the will to ascend the four steps of vision which comprise Blake's mystical ladder, despite the fact that Satan's 'starry wheels' are still at work dividing man's soul:

> The Starry Wheels revolv'd heavily over the Furnaces
> Drawing Jerusalem in anguish of maternal love. . . .
> A dark and unknown night, indefinite, immeasurable, without end,
> Abstract Philosophy warring in enmity against Jerusalem
> (Which is the Divine Body of the Lord Jesus, blessed for ever). . . .
> Los heard her lamentations in the deeps afar! his tears fall
> Incessant before the Furnaces, and his emanation divided in pairs
> Eastward towards the Starry Wheels. . . .
> His Spectre driven by the Starry Wheels of Albion's sons.

This division is the work of Satan: 'the abstract voids between the stars are the Satanic Wheels' just as the idiot questioner is a disciple of Satan's:

> . . . the idiot questioner who is always questioning
> But never capable of answering, who sits with a sly grin
> Silent plotting when to question, like a thief in a cave . . .

In 'the furnaces of affliction' 'they take the Two Contraries which are called Qualities with which every substance is clothed: they name them Good and Evil. From them they make an Abstract which is a Negation.'[1] There are many such divisions and much unhappy striving in this prophetic book, and yet there is always the note of discipline, of a difficult Way to be travelled:

> From every One of the Four Regions of Human Majesty
> There is an Outside spread Without and an Outside spread Within
> Beyond the Outline of Identity both ways, which meet in One,
> An orbed Void of doubt, despair, hunger and thirst and sorrow.

[1] The Complete Poetry of William Blake, p. 902.

In the actual story of *Jerusalem*, Albion is separated from Jerusalem, the Bride of the Lamb of God, and is led by his spectre, that part of him which is Satanic, the magical, rational Selfhood:

> *So spoke the Spectre to Albion: he is the great Selfhood,*
> *Satan, worshipp'd as God by the Mighty Ones of the Earth,*
> *Having a white Dot call'd a Center, from which branches out*
> *A Circle in continual gyrations: this becomes a Heart*
> *From which sprang numerous branches varying their motions.*

Albion has forgotten the state of sanctity or innocence before the Fall, and has entered the state of Satan or magical illusion:

The Divine Hand found the Two Limits, Satan and Adam,
In Albion's bosom, for in every Human bosom those Limits stand. . . .
Albion hath enter'd the state Satan! . . . Albion is sick to death.
He hath leagued himself with robbers: he hath studied the arts of unbelief.

But the Saviour follows Albion, no matter how often He is repelled, until at last Albion, who has become almost completely Satanic, cries, like Faust, 'Hope is banished from me.'

> *These were his last words; and the merciful Saviour in his arms*
> *Receiv'd him, in the arms of tender mercy, and repos'd*
> *Upon the Rock of Ages.*

This is an enormously moving moment, led up to, as we have seen, by a conviction against experience that unity is attainable, and the concurrent humility and will to self-discipline which make it certain that Blake has had the vision of the saint. To emphasize this, it is as well to quote one or two more passages. Los or Imagination speaks:

'Fear not, my Sons, this Waking Death; he is become One with me.
Behold him here! We shall not Die! we shall be united in Jesus.
Will you suffer this Satan, this Body of Doubt, that seems but Is Not
To occupy the very threshold of Eternal Life? If Bacon, Newton, Locke
Deny a conscience in Man and the Communion of Saints and Angels,
Contemning the Divine Vision and Fruition, worshipping the Deus
Of the Heathen, the God of this World, and the Goddess Nature,
Mystery, Babylon the Great, the Druid Dragon, and Hidden Harlot,
Is not that signal of the Morning which was told us in the Beginning?'

This is very clear in showing Satan as the archetypal magician. At last, in sharp contrast, is the mystic's triumphant vision of four-fold unity:

And every Man stood Fourfold; each Four Faces had: One to the West,
One towards the East, One to the South, One to the North, the Horses Fourfold.
. . . The Four Living Creatures, Chariots of Humanity, Divine Incom-
    prehensible,
In beautiful Paradise expand. These are the Four Rivers of Paradise
And the Four Faces of Humanity, fronting the Four Cardinal Points
Of Heaven, going forward, forward irresistible from Eternity to Eternity.
And they conversed together in Visionary Forms dramatic which bright
Redounded from their Tongues in thunderous majesty, in Visions
In new Expanses, creating Exemplars of Memory and of Intellect,
Creating Space, Creating Time, according to the Wonders Divine
Of Human Imagination throughout all the three Regions immense. . . .
                    And I heard Jehovah speak
Terrific from his Holy Place, and saw the Words of the Mutual Covenant
    Divine
On Chariots of gold and jewels, with Living Creatures, starry and flaming
With every Colour, Lion, Tyger, Horse, Elephant, Eagle, Dove, Fly,
    Worm,
And all the wondrous Serpent clothed in gems and rich array, Humanize
In the Forgiveness of Sins according to thy Covenant, Jehovah. . . .
All Human Forms identified, even Tree, Metal, Earth and Stone: all
Into the Planetary Lives of Years, Months, Days and Hours: reposing
And then Awaking into his Bosom in the Life of Immortality.
And I heard the Name of their Emanations: they are named Jerusalem.

To return to the body of this prophetic book where there are some passages which relate to Yeats: the introduction to the third chapter of *Jerusalem* contains important points about natural religion which is magic. It is called 'To the Deists.' Blake does not minimize the power of this magical state of mind: it is as real as any other, but it is essentially false. 'The Spiritual States of the Soul are all Eternal. Distinguish between the Man and his present State.' Out of choice man can leave a state of error and enter into a better one, but nevertheless, all the states, good or bad, are eternal. 'Rahab is an Eternal State.' Blake goes on:

'He can never be a Friend to the Human Race who is the Preacher of Natural Morality or Natural Religion; he is a flatterer who means to betray, to perpetuate Tyrant Pride and the Laws of that Babylon which he foresees shall be shortly destroyed, with the spiritual not the Natural Sword. He is in the State named Rahab, which State must be put off before he can be the Friend of Man.

'You, O Deists, profess yourselves the Enemies of Christianity and you are so: you are also the Enemies of the Human Race and of Universal Nature. Man is born a Spectre or Satan and is altogether an Evil, and requires a New Selfhood continually, and must continually be changed into his direct Contrary.

'Man must and will have some Religion: if he has not the Religion of Jesus, he will have the Religion of Satan and will erect the Synagogue of Satan, calling the Prince of this World, God. . . . Every Religion that preaches Vengeance for Sin is the Religion of the Enemy.'

It is very likely, no matter how doctrinally Blake meant them, that these words about the necessity for man to become his direct contrary took hold of Yeats' imagination as he worked on Blake's *Jerusalem*. Very likely they called up something in himself and set seeds for the later theory of self and anti-self. This theory of self and anti-self, in turn, was elaborated into the system of *A Vision* with its Great Wheel of twenty-eight phases, which reveals the human types recurring in history. It is significant that in the same chapter of *Jerusalem* Yeats found this passage:

And all her Twenty-Seven Heavens, now hid and now reveal'd. . . .
And these the names of the Twenty-Seven Heavens and their Churches. . . .
A Male within a Female hid as in an Ark and Curtains. . . .
The Female hid within a Male: thus Rahab is reveal'd,
Mystery, Babylon the Great, the Abomination of Desolation,
Religion hid in War, a Dragon red and hidden Harlot. . . .
Thus are the Heavens form'd by Los within the Mundane Shell
And where Luther ends Adam begins again in Eternal Circle.

The Yeats and Ellis commentary on these lines is also significant:

'The writers of this book may say with the famous Eliphas Levi Zahed: "I have evoked and I have seen," and in the visions produced by the evocation of symbolic magic they have learned what Blake knew so well, that the phantoms often appear in forms not inherent to themselves, but borrowed from the personality of the seer as a clothing for their impalpable essence. The palpable forms would have been classed by Blake as a portion of the "Covering Cherub" or mask of created form in which the uncreated spirit makes itself visible.... The story of the Bible is, according to the Mystics, not merely a history of historic men and women, but of states of human life and stages of man's pilgrimage. Therefore the Bible and the history of religion are themselves types of nature, and of its relation to man upon the one hand and to God upon the other. The Cherub is divided into twenty-seven heavens or Churches, that is to say, into twenty-seven passive states through which man travels, and these heavens or churches are typified by twenty-seven great personages from Adam to Luther, by the initiation, progress, and close of a religious era; and after Luther, who preached "private judgment", Adam, its symbol, is said to begin again "in endless circle", one era closes, another commences. In these twenty-seven great personages, and in their lives as set forth in sacred and profane history, Blake found, wrapped up in obscure symbolism, the whole story of man's life, and of the life of moods, religions, ideas, and nations.'[1]

About thirty years after interpreting Blake's passage, Yeats too put forth in *A Vision* his theory of 'man's life, and of the life of moods, religions, ideas, and nations'. He, too, used the image of the endless circle, the Great Wheel divided into twenty-eight phases. He credited, dramatically at any rate, this 'vision' to 'the Unknown Instructors'. We may or may not agree with the substance of the interpretation of Blake's passage. And we may or may not believe in Yeats' invisible instructors. Nevertheless, in Blake's passage and in Yeats' interpretation of it lie the basic ideas and symbols of *A Vision*. The debt seems to be to Blake whether or not Yeats realized it. Yeats and Ellis continue the interpretation in words that sound surprisingly like Yeats' own later 'system' (twenty-eight phases are substituted for twenty-seven churches) :

'When at last matter or dogma, according to whether we are dealing with nature or its type, religion, becomes wholly unimaginative it is a tendency fulfilled and is "cut off". Then "Adam begins again in endless circle", and the first Church comes once more in some new form. This is purely Blakean. With the finality of the sectary and reformer Swedenborg believed that his new revelation was to last forever and not to be merely a new turn of the old wheel.

[1] Yeats and Ellis, *Works of William Blake*, Vol. I, p. 289.

Blake's mind was infinitely more subtle. Not only did it widen the whole doctrine of the three Churches by tracing its relation to nature, and all bodily and mental growth, but it deepened it by making it part of the inevitable rotation of all things. Blake dared to see that the serpent must always keep its tail in its mouth, and creed follow creed, no matter how final be our longing for finality. Into this ever-revolving circle Christ only can descend and draw men upward out of nature into supernature, out of the "Wheel of birth" into the eternity of the uncreated.'[1]

It must be added that in Yeats' system of the great wheel there is little Blakean emphasis on the entering of Christ into the circle of cause and effect, although there is one phase at which Christ or some other form of supernature may descend and change the cause of events. Yeats, it seems, has worked on those images and ideas which he called 'purely Blakean', assimilated them, and restated them in *A Vision* as they rose out of forgotten depths. He credited them to the Unknown Instructors without realizing or wanting to admit that he first met them in his master, Blake. All this is quite consistent with his desire to have visions such as Blake had. Yeats declared that his system of *A Vision* was complete before he read Spengler and Flinders Petrie,[2] but, obviously, it was not complete before he read Blake!

Another passage in this section of the Yeats and Ellis interpretation gives one more instance of Yeats believing or hoping that Blake had reached through the wheel of nature, via magic manipulation, to the vision of the saint. Remembering the end of *John Sherman* (who is Yeats) where he 'saw standing before his Eden the angel with the flaming sword', we have in the following lines another example of Yeats' conscious or unconscious striving to make himself like Blake:

'When man ascends wholly out of "the wheel of birth" into "the imagination that liveth for ever", a last judgment is said to pass over him. He is done with the opacity of corporeal existence and has attained that state which Blake announced or rather summoned in the *Marriage of Heaven and Hell* with the words "The Cherub with his flaming sword is hereby commanded to leave his guard at the tree of life, and when he does, the whole creation will be consumed and appear infinite and holy, whereas it now appears finite and

---

[1] Yeats and Ellis, *Works of William Blake*, Vol. I, p. 293.   [2] Mrs. Yeats.

corrupt." The interpretation of the flaming sword in this passage is the same as that in the Jewish Kabala. When the Last Judgment has passed over a man he enters that community of saints who "are no longer talking of what is good or evil, or of what is right and wrong, and puzzling themselves in Satan's labyrinth; but are conversing with eternal realities". . . . Men are admitted into heaven not because they have curbed and governed their passions, but because they have cultivated their understandings . . . the fool shall not enter into heaven, let him be ever so holy: holiness is not the price of entrance into heaven.'[1]

Yeats was strongly attracted to the gnostic doctrines of the Kabala, which, concerning the search for complete knowledge of divine causation, is always hovering on the edge of magic.[2] Like the kabalists, he tended to believe that this dangerous process would get him to heaven, and liked to exaggerate Blake's occultist leanings. And he added: 'Nearly all the ancient and medieval mystics have made great use of the zodiacal signs in their system of expression.' But Yeats and Ellis have to admit that:

'It is not possible to find very numerous traces of their use in the mystical books. Blake, however, found a substitute for them by arranging the twenty-seven heavens upon the sun's path.'

Yeats, close behind his master, tried to find his substitute by arranging the twenty-eight states on the moon's path! His phases of the moon, like Blake's Heavens, are states of mind or of existence. Perhaps when writing A Vision he recalled these lines he had written about Blake:

'It must be remembered that all these complex symbols contain the others in miniature within them. All is within all, and every one of the twenty-seven churches contains the whole twenty-sevenfold symbols in miniature . . . we are all passing through it. "These states," Blake writes, "exist now. Man passes on, but states remain forever: he passes through them like a traveller, who may as well suppose that the places he has passed through exist no more. Every thing is eternal." '[3]

---

[1] Yeats and Ellis, Works of William Blake, Vol. I, p. 298.   [2] See Appendix.
[3] Ibid., p. 308.

Chapter Six

'I, THE POET WILLIAM YEATS'

~~~~~~

IN 1889 when Yeats and Ellis were well into their study of Blake, Yeats published the little volume of poems called *Crossways*. A quotation from Blake acts as a kind of motto: 'The stars are threshed, and the souls are threshed from their husks.' This, characteristically, is a misquotation[1] which persists into the most recent editions of Yeats' poems. The correct lines, from Blake's *Vala or the Four Zoas*, are: 'And all Nations were threshed out, and the stars threshed from their husks.'

The book itself, unlike any of Blake's although the Blakean influence is evident, is altogether composed of sorrow and starbeams and other equally unsolid bits of poetic material, and is in style a mixture of the tired and wistful æsthete language prevalent at the end of the century, and of the Yeatsian idea that poetry must consist of and seek

'those wavering, meditative, organic rhythms, which are the embodiment of the imagination, that neither desires nor hates, because it has done with time, and only wishes to gaze on some reality, some beauty . . . a little song made out of a moment of dreamy indolence, or some great epic made out of the dreams of one poet and of a hundred generations whose hands were never weary of the sword.'[2]

Not, perhaps, a theory to lead to great poetry, as may be seen from the following random quotations from Yeats' first volume. Because Yeats was a great poet, he quickly abandoned this theory and technique. There are, of course, single memorable lines such as the first two in the following passage, but they are not generally

[1] Noted by H. M. Margoliouth.   [2] Yeats, *Essays*, p. 201.

137

'wavering, meditative, organic', but carved with a certain precision of line:

> The woods of Arcady are dead,
> And over is their antique joy. . . . seek then,
> No learning from the starry men,
> Who follow with the optic glass
> The whirling ways of stars that pass—
> Seek then, for this is also sooth,
> No word of theirs—the cold star bane
> Has cloven and rent their hearts in twain,
> And dead is all their human truth.
> Go gather by the humming sea
> Some twisted, echo-harbouring shell,
> And to its lips thy story tell,
> And they thy comforter will be. . . .
> I must be gone: there is a grave
> Where daffodil and lily wave,
> And I would please the hapless faun,
> Buried under the sleepy ground. . . .[1]

or, sooth!

> There was a man whom Sorrow named his friend,
> And he, of his high comrade Sorrow dreaming
> Went walking with slow steps along the gleaming
> And humming sands, where windy surges wend.

and,

> 'What do you make so fair and bright?'
> 'I make the cloak of sorrow:
> O lovely to see in all men's sight
> Shall be the cloak of sorrow,
> In all men's sight.'

The dimmer, the more abstractly sorrowful, the paler and dreamier the better it seems, and this technique reaches its climax of the ridiculous in the dialogue poem 'Anashuya and Vijaya' which is set in 'A little Indian temple in the Golden Age':

VIJAYA (entering and throwing a lily at her)
    Hail! hail my Anashuya. . . .

---

[1] The poems quoted are all from Yeats' *Collected Poems* unless otherwise indicated.

ANASHUYA . . . *A sad thought went by me slowly:*
Sigh, O you little stars! O sigh and shake your blue apparel!
The sad thought has gone from me now wholly.

Pensively, in its wavering organic way, the book draws to a close. Despite the insubstantiality of the nature imagery, there is more of it *per se* in this early period than at any later time in Yeats' work. 'The Stolen Child' is famous for pleasant descriptive lines such as these:

> *Where dips the rocky highland*
> *Of Sleuth Wood in the lake,*
> *There lies a leafy island*
> *Where flapping herons wake*
> *The drowsy water-rats;*
> *There we've hid our fairy vats,*
> *Full of berries*
> *And of reddest stolen cherries.*

Nevertheless, despite Yeats' efforts to lure his readers into a trance by dreamy evocative rhythms and shifting outlines of nature, the poems do not strike the reader as truly magical in the strict sense. There is more in their fairy elusiveness that is decadent and weak, perhaps even insincere—the usual imitative offering of the young poet who may or may not find something more powerful to say. However, in his championship of fairies and such magical beings, Yeats undoubtedly felt that he was following in Blake's footsteps, for in his Introduction to the small Blake volume of 1893 Yeats says:

'Blake met all manner of kings and poets and prophets walking in shadowy multitudes on the edge of the sea, majestic shadows, grey but luminous, and superior to the common height of man! Other and more gentle beings likewise. "Did you ever see a fairy's funeral?"'[1]

and here Yeats solemnly recounts the story of Blake's saying this mischievously to a dull woman, forgetting that Blake scorned ghosts and all such shadowy beings as unspiritual. Yeats goes on: 'He has elsewhere described the fairies as "the rulers of the vegetable world". . . . Jacob Boehme is also said to have had a vision of the fairies.'[2] Yeats conveniently forgets that to Blake 'vegetable world' was a term of opprobrium.

It is this sort of enquiry which we must carry over from Yeats'

[1] Yeats, *William Blake*, 1893, p. xli.   [2] *Ibid.*

prose into his poetry to see whether his search for belief is merely background mythology or an integral part of his creative work. The problem of how to believe in the invisible—as magician or as saint—is the main search in Yeats' prose writings, although some critics make the evasive claim that 'history and anthropology predominate clearly over supernaturalism.'

It is important to note at the outset that despite Yeats' claim that as a poet he is the magician, there is, in his work, little of the hallmark of magic—an attempt to control through the hidden powers of nature. In fact, there is little nature imagery to be found at all in his poetry. Yeats' magic manifests itself rather in theory, both in the occult and pantheistic background of Anima Mundi, and in the more geometrical doctrines of *A Vision*. And secondly, Yeats' magic reveals itself in his technique of poetry. As corollaries to the primary concern about the effect of saint and enchanter on Yeats' poetry, we must examine these three things—nature imagery, poetic technique, and background theory.

Four years after his first volume of poetry, the same year that the Blake volumes were published, Yeats brought out another book of verse called *The Rose*. Here there is a tremendous improvement in sureness and sincerity of expression, and at the same time something of a magical control of words, rhythms, and natural symbol:

> *Red Rose, proud Rose, sad Rose of all my days!*
> *Come near me while I sing the ancient ways:*
> *Cuchulain battling with the bitter tide;*
> *The Druid, grey, wood-nurtured, quiet-eyed,*
> *Who cast round Fergus dreams and ruin untold;*
> *And thine own sadness, whereof stars, grown old*
> *In dancing silver-sandalled on the sea,*
> *Sing in their high and lonely melody.*
> *Come near, that no more blinded by man's fate,*
> *I find under the boughs of love and hate*
> *In all poor foolish things that live a day,*
> *Eternal beauty wandering on her way.*

The rose is no longer a bit of natural description to adorn an æsthete's stage set, but has become a concentrated charged symbol, a magical talisman as it were to conjure past associations of beauty and love. Yeats begins to treat nature as the enchanter would, using the rose not as any rose growing on a bush, but as the essence of Roseness, the interior being of all roses by the knowledge of which he can control this one species of nature. Despite the fact that the rhythms are still wavering and meditative, the words have found a new simplicity and sureness, and a hard quality is solidifying such lines as 'Cuchulain battling with the bitter tide'. As Yeats' symbols and technique become more controlled Yeats becomes a better poet than his early theory had allowed him to be. His poems begin to flicker 'with the light of many symbols . . . as a sword-blade may flicker with the light of burning towers.'[1] He has become magical not in the purple-patch nature description of 'The Lake Isle of Innisfree', but more in the apparently simple little love poem based on Ronsard's 'When You are Old'. Here, despite the French basis, Yeats' stars have come under careful control, and the restraint of emotion makes a powerful undertone belying with its simplicity the complexity of past, present, and future. Nature is becoming a tool to externalize a mood, or, if you will, the inner landscape (Mallarme's 'paysage intérieur') becomes a backdrop to personal utterance. Simplicity set against richness:

> When you are old and grey and full of sleep,
> And nodding by the fire, take down this book
> And slowly read, and dream of the soft look
> Your eyes had once, and of their shadows deep;
>
> How many loved your moments of glad grace,
> And loved your beauty with love false or true,
> But one man loved the pilgrim soul in you,
> And loved the sorrows of your changing face;
>
> And bending down beside the glowing bars,
> Murmur, a little sadly, how love fled,
> And paced upon the mountains overhead,
> And hid his face amid a crowd of stars.

There are fine lines in this book of verse, lines that are hard and apparently simple, taut with a complexity clarified through passionate tenderness. Yeats had fallen in love.

> He stood among a crowd at Drumahair;
> His heart hung all upon a silken dress,
> And he had known at last some tenderness,
> Before earth took him to her stoney care;

[1] Yeats, *Essays*, p. 192.

141

But when a man poured fish into a pile,
It seems they raised their little silver heads
And sang what gold morning or evening sheds
Upon a woven world-forgotten isle. . . .

This is fine poetry until the fishes, and yet even the golden enchanted quality of the last four lines is harder and turns the atmosphere into something stately and legendary rather than into the flimsy stuff of faery Celtic twilight. Another memorable sentence is:

There, through the broken branches, go
The ravens of unresting thought.

And finally, the masculine tramping swing of the lines in which Yeats admits that the faery trappings rather hid the bare bones of his poetry:

Know, that I would accounted be
True brother of a company
That sang to sweeten Ireland's wrong,
Ballad and story, rann and song;
Nor be I any less of them
Because the red-rose-bordered hem
Of her, whose history began
Before God made the angelic clan,
Trails all about the written page.

In 1899 came the *Wind Among the Reeds*. In this book Yeats could still say with the proponents of 'Art for Art's sake' that 'the wrong of unshapely things is a wrong too great to be told: I hunger to build them anew and sit on a green knoll apart.' And yet there is a much stronger poem, 'The Unappeasable Host', which all but contradicts the æsthete thinking:

Desolate winds that cry over the wondering sea;
Desolate winds that hover in the flaming west;
Desolate winds that beat the doors of Heaven, beat
The doors of Hell and blow there many a whimpering ghost
O heart the winds have shaken, the unappeasable host
Is comelier than the candles at Mother Mary's feet.

The repetition and control in this poem make it a much more magical poem than the earlier ones. And in quite another way, 'The Song of Wandering Ængus' is magical, not so much because of the trans-

formation that is its subject-matter, but rather because of the monotonous incantation-like rhythm and the subtle echoes within the
poem; because of the restless seeking through time of the timeless
and unattainable; and most of all, because of the force of colourful
natural images—the fire, the hazel wand, the moths, and, wonderful
qualification, 'moth-like stars', the berry, and the silver trout. The
spell which changes the silver trout to the beautiful woman is indicated skilfully, largely by means of the elusive changeable quality
of the adjectives describing each step of the enchantment. The little
trout is 'silver' to begin with, and then 'rustled' while the poet was
blowing 'the fire aflame', and, when he looked again it had become
a 'glimmering girl' who 'faded' through the 'brightening' air. All
of these adjectives, whether describing light or sound or movement,
give the effect of shifting outlines of nature, and yet the words are
hard and precise and therefore loaded with evocative power:

> I went out to the hazel wood,
>   Because a fire was in my head,
> And cut and peeled a hazel wand
>   And hooked a berry to a thread;
> And when white moths were on the wing,
>   And moth-like stars were flickering out,
> I dropped the berry in a stream
>   And caught a little silver trout.
>
> When I had laid it on the floor
>   I went to blow the fire aflame,
> But something rustled on the floor,
>   And someone called me by my name:
> It had become a glimmering girl
>   With apple-blossom in her hair,
> Who called me by my name, and ran
>   And faded through the brightening air.
>
> Though I am old and wandering
>   Through hollow lands and hilly lands,
> I will find out where she has gone,
>   And kiss her lips and take her hands,
> And walk among long dappled grass
>   And pluck till time and times are done
> The silver apples of the moon
>   The golden apples of the sun.

In his essays Yeats remarks:

'some old magical writer, I forget who, says if you wish to be melancholy hold in your left hand an image of the Moon made out of silver, and if you wish to be happy hold in your right hand an image of the sun made out of gold.'[1]

And in his Autobiography, 'Solar ... meant elaborate, full of artifice, rich, all that resembles the work of a goldsmith, whereas "water" meant "lunar", and "lunar" all that is simple, popular, traditional, emotional.'[2] 'The water is sensation, peace, night, silence, indolence; the fire is passion, tension, day, music, energy.'[3] The thought at the end of this poem is one more expression of Yeats' hope that by magic he might reconcile all that is so distressingly antithetical in actual life.

The three stanzas, a magical number, give a pattern to the spell, a certain completeness. Perhaps the new tragic love in Yeats' life adds a solidity to these poems which is altogether lacking in earlier books. The woman is, of course, Maud Gonne, and the 'glimmering girl with apple blossom in her hair' recalls Yeats' description of his first meeting with Maud Gonne:

'Her complexion was luminous like that of the apple blossom through which the light falls, and I remember her standing that first day by a great heap of such blossoms in the window.'[4]

There are short simply-stated love poems in this book, so much more effective than the earlier 'meditative' ones which we suspect had no substance, such as 'He Reproves the Curlew':

> O curlew, cry no more in the air,
> Or only to the water in the West;
> Because your crying brings to my mind
> Passion-dimmed eyes and long heavy hair
> That was shaken out over my breast;
> There is enough evil in the crying of the wind.

And there is that strangely musical poem which Yeats found in a dream, 'The Cap and Bells'. 'The soul in a straight blue garment' and the heart 'in a red and quivering garment' are reminiscent of

---

[1] Yeats, *Essays*, p. 113.
[2] Yeats, *Autobiography*, p. 315.
[3] Yeats, *Letters on Poetry*, p. 95.
[4] Yeats, *Autobiography*, p. 152.

Blake paintings, but the tone of the poem is summed up in the
theme of the troubadours, the bard who is a slave to Eros and pines
for a beautiful unattainable lady. Yeats' attitude to Maud Gonne
has crystallized to that of the medieval troubadour, with perhaps
a little more wishful thinking. The lover has become the third,
most ambiguous figure in the trio of poet-magician, lover, and
saint.

> The jester walked in the garden:
>   The garden had fallen still;
> He bade his soul rise upward
>   And stand on her window-sill.
>
> It rose in a straight blue garment,
>   When owls began to call:
> It had grown wise-tongued by thinking
>   Of a quiet and light footfall.
>
> But the young queen would not listen;
>   She rose in her pale nightgown;
> She drew in the heavy casement
>   And pushed the latches down.
>
> He bade his heart go to her,
>   When the owls called out no more;
> In a red and quivering garment
>   It sang to her through the door.
>
> It had grown sweet-tongued by dreaming
>   Of a flutter of flower-like hair;
> But she took up her fan from the table
>   And waved it off on the air.
>
> 'I have cap and bells,' he pondered,
>   'I will send them to her and die';
> And when the morning whitened
>   He left them where she went by.
>
> She laid them upon her bosom,
>   Under a cloud of her hair;
> And her red lips sang them a love-song
>   Till stars grew out of the air.

She opened her door and her window,
*   And the heart and the soul came through,*
To her right hand came the red one,
*   To her left hand came the blue.*

They set up a noise like crickets,
*   A chattering wise and sweet,*
And her hair was a folded flower
And the quiet of love in her feet.

A poignant poem, a dream significantly full of medieval atmosphere and the conventions of the courts of love. There is magic, slightly evil magic, mixed with this attitude towards love sometimes:

I have drunk ale from the country of the young
*   And weep because I know all things now:*
I have been a hazel tree, and they hung
*   The Pilot Star and the Crooked Plough*
Among my leaves in times out of mind:
*   I became a rush that horses tread:*
I became a man, a hater of the wind,
*   Knowing one, out of all things, alone that his head*
May not lie on the breast nor his lips on the hair
*   Of the woman that he loves, until he dies.*
O beast of the wilderness, bird of the air
*   Must I endure your amorous cries?*

And sometimes the magic is only in the words, the powerful control of words and rhythms that produces seemingly effortless simplicity:

THE FOLLY OF BEING COMFORTED

One that is ever kind said yesterday:
'Your well-beloved's hair has threads of grey,
And little shadows come about her eyes;
Time can but make it easier to be wise,
Though now it seems impossible, and so
All that you need is patience.' Heart cries, 'No,
I have not a crumb of comfort, not a grain.
Time can but make her beauty over again:
Because of that great nobleness of hers
The fire that stirs about her when she stirs,
Burns but more clearly. O she had not these ways
When all the wild summer was in her gaze.'

O heart! O heart! if she'd but turn her head,
You'd know the folly of being comforted.

This poem is in the book of 1904, *In the Seven Woods*, and is the first poem that reveals Yeats' daring new style. Control, power, secret strength, simplicity are the words we must use to describe such work, and they are words which describe the work of a magician. The finest poems of this, Yeats' middle period, are all love poems for Maud Gonne. And the emotions of love are made much clearer and more powerful by the tautness of style that Yeats has achieved. The rhythms are those of speech, the words conversational, the twist of phrase that of a master conversationalist. Hard, simple, with an element of ironic humour, these lines are not unlike many of Donne's in tone. The combination of strong love and equally strong restraint of expression produce poems that cannot even be compared with Yeats' early dreamy, emotionless effusions.

> *Never give all the heart, for love*
> *Will hardly seem worth thinking of*
> *To passionate women if it seem*
> *Certain, and they never dream*
> *That it fades out from kiss to kiss;*
> *For everything that's lovely is*
> *But a brief, dreamy, kind delight.*
> *O never give the heart outright,*
> *For they, for all smooth lips can say,*
> *Have given their hearts up to the play.*
> *And who could play it well enough*
> *If deaf and dumb and blind with love?*
> *He that made this knows all the cost,*
> *For he gave all his heart and lost.*[1]

The longer poem, *Adam's Curse*, must also be quoted in full, not only because it is a magnificent love poem of this new style, but because it contains the famous lines about this new theory of poetry which is such a far cry from the earlier style of dreamy organic rhythms:

> *We sat together at one summer's end,*
> *That beautiful mild woman, your close friend,*
> *And you and I and talked of poetry.*
> *I said, 'A line will take us hours maybe;*
> *Yet if it does not seem a moment's thought,*
> *Our stitching and unstitching has been naught.*

Better go down upon your marrow bones
And scrub a kitchen pavement, or break stones
Like an old pauper, in all kinds of weather;
For to articulate sweet sounds together
Is to work harder than all these, and yet
Be thought an idler by the noisy set
Of bankers, schoolmasters, and clergymen
The martyrs call the world.'
     And thereupon
That beautiful mild woman for whose sake
There's many a one shall find out all heartache
On finding that her voice is sweet and low
Replied, 'To be born woman is to know—
Although they do not talk of it at school—
That we must labour to be beautiful.'

I said, 'It's certain there is no fine thing
Since Adam's fall but needs much labouring.
There have been lovers who thought love should be
So much compounded of high courtesy
That they would sigh and quote with learned looks
Precedents out of beautiful old books;
Yet now it seems an idle trade enough.'

We sat grown quiet at the name of love;
We saw the last embers of daylight die,
And in the trembling blue-green of the sky
A moon, worn as if it had been a shell
Washed by time's waters as they rose and fell
About the stars and broke in days and years.

I had a thought for no one's but your ears:
That you were beautiful, and that I strove
To love you in the old high way of love;
That it had all seemed happy, and yet we'd grown
As weary-hearted as that hollow moon.

Needless to say, despite its surface ease this poem needed a great deal of working out, combining as it does thoughts about love, about poetry, about physical beauty, and about the labour of creating beauty since Adam's fall. Yet it seems almost like a recorded conversation, and indeed notes of this conversation are available.

'Think like a wise man, yet express ourselves like the common people,' Yeats wrote to Dorothy Wellesley in the last years of his life.[1] Yet he had discovered this before 1904, and that 'the true poetic movement of our times is towards some heroic discipline.'[2] Even then he wanted 'speech carried to its highest intensity of sound and meaning,' 'the speech of the common people,' 'the natural words in the natural order,' 'a modern vocabulary with traditional richness.' Of course, this is no new way of thinking: Wordsworth in his *Preface to the Lyrical Ballads* said much the same thing. And yet, after a period of decadence or rationalism, it is a tendency which comes like a refreshing sea wind.

In 1910 came the *Green Helmet and other Poems*, more verse of this new controlled genre, its own beauty 'like a tightened bow'. The lyric 'Words' reveals just how much Yeats' unhappy love for Maud Gonne contributed towards his development in poetry. We suspect that Yeats, like the troubadours, is not too sad that he was not forced to 'have thrown poor words away and been content to live.' And Maud Gonne herself has said that the world should thank her for not marrying Yeats.

> I had this thought a while ago,
>   'My darling cannot understand
> What I have done, or what would do
>   In this blind bitter land.'
>
> And I grew weary of the sun
>   Until my thoughts cleared up again,
> Remembering that the best I've done
>   Was done to make it plain.
>
> That every year I have cried, 'At length
>   My darling understands it all,
> Because I have come into my strength
>   And words obey my call';
>
> That had she done so who can say
>   What might have shaken from the sieve?
> I might have thrown poor words away
>   And been content to live.

---

[1] Yeats, *Letters on Poetry*, p. 64.   [2] *Ibid.*

In Yeats' original version of this poem in his diary, was this heartfelt but somewhat libellous stanza:

> *My dear is angry that of late*
> *I cry all base blood down,*
> *As if she had not taught me hate*
> *By kisses to a clown.*

Yeats tells of the importance of the Mask, even in love. He did, in fact, try to hide his shyness and awkwardness under the mask of Magician which should have appealed to Maud Gonne:

> *'Put off that mask of burning gold*
> *With emerald eyes.'*
> *'O no, my dear, you make so bold*
> *To find if hearts be wild and wise*
> *And yet not cold.'*
>
> *'I would but find what's there to find,*
> *Love or deceit.'*
> *'It was the mask engaged your mind,*
> *And after set your heart to beat,*
> *Not what's behind.'*

However, this poem is largely wishful thinking, and the mask did not engage Madame Gonne's mind, nor her heart. Yeats' inner conflict and misery increased the power of his poems, producing such songs of praise and lament as:

NO SECOND TROY

> *Why should I blame her that she filled my days*
> *With misery, or that she would of late*
> *Have taught to ignorant man most violent ways,*
> *Or hurled the little streets upon the great,*
> *Had they but courage equal to desire?*
> *What could have made her peaceful with a mind*
> *That nobleness made simple as a fire,*
> *With beauty like a tightened bow, a kind*
> *That is not natural in an age like this,*
> *Being high and solitary and most stern?*
> *Why, what could she have done, being what she is?*
> *Was there another Troy for her to burn?*

'My wife said the other night, "AE was the nearest to a saint you or I will ever meet. You are a better poet, but no saint. I suppose one has to choose." '[1] I wonder what Yeats felt as he recorded this comment for Dorothy Wellesley. He had chosen poetry and magic at a point when he might well have chosen religion and the Mystic Way. Love, in the shape of Maud Gonne, was the deciding factor. He chose what might appeal to her earthly active type of beauty, a way of life that came nearer to the man of action than to sainthood. He had chosen and was a better poet because of this choice, but was he not always hoping, consciously or unconsciously, that one day he would see the saint and poet within himself join hands? 'I watch with amusement the emergence of the philosophy of my own poetry, the unconscious becoming conscious. It seems to increase the force of my poetry,' he wrote in one of his later letters,[2] and added, 'Rest is a great instructor, for it brings the soul back to itself. We sink down into our own soil and take root again.'

Nineteen-fourteen showed the publication of *Responsibilities*, with its significant motto of, 'In dreams begins responsibility.' The dreamy, irresponsible land of faery is quite gone, and the opening poem, rough and masculine and galloping, is an apology for past futility:

> *Pardon, old fathers, if you still remain*
> *Somewhere in earshot for the story's end,*
> *Old Dublin merchant, 'free of the ten and four'*
> *Or trading out of Galway into Spain;*
> *Old country scholar, Robert Emmet's friend,*
> *A hundred-year-old memory to the poor;*
> *Merchant and scholar who have left me blood*
> *That has not passed through any huckster's loin,*
> *Soldiers that gave, whatever die was cast:*
> *A Butler or an Armstrong that withstood*
> *Beside the brackish waters of the Boyne*
> *James and his Irish when the Dutchman crossed.*
> *Old merchant skipper that leaped overboard*
> *After a ragged hat in Biscay Bay;*
> *You most of all, silent and fierce old man,*
> *Because the daily spectacle that stirred*
> *My fancy, and set my boyish lips to say,*
> *'Only the wasteful virtues earn the sun';*

[1] Yeats, *Letters on Poetry*, p. 13.   [2] *Ibid.*, p. 169.

Pardon that for a barren passion's sake,
Although I have come close on forty-nine,
I have no child, I have nothing but a book,
Nothing but that to prove your blood and mine.

The style learnt in the love poems is proving highly effective for a wider range of subjects. The colour of past events can be conjured up in the starkly conversational lines, and personal names are used strikingly in an arrogant modern manner, evoking legendary but very human men, and sometimes summing up a whole era and its pageantry:

What need you, being come to sense,
But fumble in a greasy till
And add the halfpence to the pence
And prayer to shivering prayer until
You have dried the marrow from the bone;
For men were born to pray and save:
Romantic Ireland's dead and gone,
It's with O'Leary in the grave.

So begins the powerful poem, 'September 1913', and Yeats cries out against his 'fool-driven land' that he is compelled to love:

Was it for this the wild geese spread
The grey wing upon every tide;
For this that all that blood was shed,
For this Edward Fitzgerald died,
And Robert Emmet and Wolfe Tone,
All the delirium of the brave?
Romantic Ireland's dead and gone,
It's with O'Leary in the grave.

Maud Gonne was able to interest her poet in politics, and the style of the love poems is put to effective use in the political poems. Beneath the bare blunt words, the cool and hard surface tones, there is a wealth of passion and even pathos, though never sentimentality. Yeats has learned to cover his love of mournful 'beauty' with the strength of indignation and daring of homely comment. The vague dreaming and abstraction has solidified into surprisingly concrete lines. His poetry has been carved out of stone because the poet finds himself alarmingly the prey of all the emotion, dreaminess and softness of flesh and blood. For instance, his poem to the beloved Parnell, which might so easily have turned to sentiment, is spiced and saved by a cynical practical humour:

> If you have revisited the town, thin Shade,
> Whether to look upon your monument
> (I wonder if the builder has been paid)
> Or happier-thoughted when the day is spent
> To drink of that salt breath out of the sea
> When grey gulls flit about instead of men,
> And the gaunt houses put on majesty:
> Let these content you and be gone again;
> For they are at their old tricks again. . . .
> Go, unquiet wanderer,
> And gather the Glasnevin coverlet
> About your head until the dust stop your ear,
> The time for you to taste of that salt breath
> And listen at the corners has not come;
> You had enough of sorrow before death—
> Away, away! You are safer in the tomb.

There is a great tenderness in the last seven lines, an understanding and sadness that comes not out of dreaming and fairyland, but out of an acceptance of life and its limitations. There is even a kind of tired affection for the Paudeens and Biddys, a wry smile that they are up to their old tricks again. We remember L. A. G. Strong's letter to Yeats:

'An *interest* in affairs has always been essential to you: indeed, it has been one of the chief strengths of your poetry, for it has kept your mind quick and fierce, and has kept you from acquiescence. . . . Some of your best work has sprung from indignation at public affairs. But you are, and always have been, before everything an artist: pressing everything, patriotism as well, into art's possible service.'[1]

And,

'With the entry of your Muse into contemporary life—i.e. its withdrawal into the wilderness—you stripped your lines bare. Like

[1] Hogarth Press *Letters*, pp. 8, 14, 15.

boughs in winter, they showed the stark perfection of their architecture, the delicate, severe articulation that bound each word to stem and branch and root: the idea bitterly flowing out into the bare, clean boughs. . . . There is, in the poetry of your later period, an intellectual content, an imagination, a passion, and a sure control which is not to be matched in any poet of your generation or of mine. It is contemporary poetry, yet it transcends its time. It is aristocratic, yet has all the vigour coarseness could have given it. It is intellectual, but its blood runs hot. It is full of anger, yet holds perfect equilibrium. It mocks, but keeps its dignity. . . . It is wise without wisdom's chill.'

But Yeats himself says that poets, being human and not wise men, can stoop to trivial misjudgments, as well as the rest of us:

> *We have cried in our despair*
> *That men desert*
> *For some trivial affair*
> *Or noisy insolent sport*
> *Beauty that we have won*
> *From bitterest hours.*
> *Yet we, had we walked within*
> *Those topless towers*
> *Where Helen walked with her boy,*
> *Had given but as the rest*
> *Of the men and women of Troy,*
> *A word and a jest.*

Here is humility mixed with arrogance. And in this and the following poems there is a new acceptance of the role he must play to Maud Gonne's beauty. Like the troubadour, he must be content to worship from afar and record for all time the physical magnificence which must fade, the tempestuous mind that must fail. In three different ways Yeats recreates this theme with the power of simplicity under control.

FALLEN MAJESTY

> *Although crowds gathered once if she but showed her face*
> *And even old men's eyes grew dim, this hand alone,*
> *Like some last courtier at a gipsy camping place*
> *Babbling of fallen majesty, records what's gone.*

These lineaments, a heart that laughter has made sweet,
  These, these remain, but I record what's gone. A crowd
Will gather and not know it walks the very street
  Whereon a thing once walked that seemed a burning cloud.

FRIENDS

Now I must these three praise—
  Three women that have wrought
What joy is in my days:
  One because no thought,
Nor those unpassing cares,
  No, not in these fifteen
Many-times-troubled years,
  Could ever come between
Mind and delighted mind;
  And one because her hand
Had strength that could unbind
  What none could understand,
What none can have and thrive,
  Youth's dreamy load till she
So changed me that I live
  Labouring in ecstasy.
And what of her that took
  All till my youth was gone
With scarce a pitying look?
  How could I praise that one?
When day begins to break
  I count my good and bad,
Being wakeful for her sake,
  Remembering what she had,
What eagle look still shows,
  While up from my heart's root
So great a sweetness flows
  I shake from head to foot.

THAT THE NIGHT COME

She lived in storm and strife,
Her soul had such desire
For what proud death may bring
That it could not endure
The common good of life,

But lived as 'twere a king
That packed his marriage day
With banneret and pennon,
Trumpet and kettledrum,
And the outrageous cannon,
To bundle time away
That the night come.

It is indeed a sure control that can make the ingredients of everyday speech and near cliché phrases like 'storm and strife' or 'the common good of life' into fine poetry, and can dare such deliberate archaisms as ''twere' or such a colourfully vulgar expression as 'to bundle time away'. It is interesting to note that two of these three poems have an atmosphere of being written by a bard at some medieval court. In *Fallen Majesty*, the single phrase 'babbling of fallen majesty' and possibly the last line save the poem from falling into romantic sentimentality and make of it something hard and modern. Although Yeats called himself one of the 'last Romantics' he took a lesson in poem-making from the seventeenth-century poets, leavening the woes of unrequited love with a startlingly hard image, or spicing tradition with ironic humour. Again, in *Friends* the heroic and slightly discordant rhythms combined with the everydayness of speech give great impetus to the ending. The last lines have the concentrated pungency of laconic images—'eagle look', 'heart's root'.

THE MAGI

Now as at all times I can see in the mind's eye,
In their stiff, painted clothes, the pale unsatisfied ones
Appear and disappear in the blue depth of the sky
With all their ancient faces like rain-beaten stones,
And all their helms of silver hovering side by side,
And all their eyes still fixed, hoping to find once more,
Being by Calvary's turbulence unsatisfied,
The uncontrollable mystery on the bestial floor.

This poem is stylistically interesting. It has the simplicity and control of the period of Yeats' work which we have been examining. But it is combined with a complexity of allusion and slight philosophic esotericism that is characteristic of Yeats' next period. Indeed, the poem belongs by rights to the third period although these divisions in Yeats' work are not strictly chronological. Critics argue over what painting of the Nativity Yeats had in mind when he wrote this poem. This does not really matter, since the effect of an archaic painted image is the important point, and comes across very strongly.

The first line, by the simple phrase 'now as at all times', gives an immediate and mysterious importance to the Magi. And the wise men are made infinitely inscrutable and ageless by the next four concrete and vivid lines—mysterious in their restless search for a second epiphany. After this, Yeats can afford to end with an esoteric concept from his own mythology in *A Vision*, namely that the coming of Christ was not enough, and that after two thousand years some monster, the complete opposite of Christ, will come with an equally influential revelation.

At the end of this book is the strange poem called 'The Dolls'. The evil quality that dolls sometimes possess because of their associations with magic and effigies is strongly underscored in this poem as it is in some of Rilke's poems. Yeats is phrasing in an original way the poet's cry of despair at modern values which have become 'something other than human life.'

> *A doll in the doll-maker's house*
> *Looks at the cradle and bawls:*
> *'That is an insult to us.'*
> *But the oldest of the dolls,*
> *Who had seen, being kept for show,*
> *Generations of his sort,*
> *Outscreams the whole shelf: 'Although*
> *There's not a man can record*
> *Evil of this place,*
> *The man and woman bring*
> *Hither, to our disgrace,*
> *A noisy and filthy thing.'*
> *Hearing him groan and stretch*
> *The doll-maker's wife is aware*
> *Her husband has heard the wretch,*
> *And crouched by the arm of his chair,*
> *She murmurs into his ear,*
> *Head upon shoulder leant:*
> *'My dear, my dear, O dear,*
> *It was an accident.'*

The *Wild Swans at Coole* was published in 1919. Yeats expands his new conversational verse into a poem of twelve eight-line stanzas, and maintains it impressively. 'In Memory of Robert Gregory' is something new in English literature.

I

Now that we're almost settled in our house
I'll name the friends that cannot sup with us
Beside a fire of turf in the ancient tower,
And having talked to some late hour
Climb up the narrow winding stair to bed:
Discoverers of forgotten truth
Or mere companions of my youth,
All, all are in my thoughts tonight, being dead ...

III

Lionel Johnson comes first to mind,
That loved his learning better than mankind,
Though courteous to the worst; much falling he
Brooded upon sanctity
Till all his Greek and Latin learning seemed
A long blast upon the horn that brought
A little nearer to his thought
A measureless consummation that he dreamed ...

I am accustomed to their lack of breath,
But not that my dear friend's dear son,
Our Sidney and our perfect man,
Could share in that discourtesy of death ...

We dreamed that a great painter had been born
To cold Clare rock and Galway rock and thorn,
To that stern colour and that delicate line
That are our secret discipline
Wherein the gazing heart doubles her might.
Soldier, scholar, horseman, he,
And yet he had the intensity
To have published all to be a world's delight.

This style, itself like 'cold Clare rock and Galway rock and thorn', is peculiarly fitted to long poems such as this and is very satisfying, and as much so in the short complete lyrics such as 'An Irish Airman foresees his Death':

> I know that I shall meet my fate
> Somewhere among the clouds above;
> Those that I fight I do not hate,
> Those that I guard I do not love;
> My country is Kiltartan's Cross,
> My countrymen Kiltartan's poor,
> No likely end could bring them loss
> Or leave them happier than before.
> Nor law nor duty bade me fight
> Nor public men, nor cheering crowds,
> A lonely impulse of delight
> Drove to this tumult in the clouds;
> I balanced all, brought all to mind,
> The years to come seemed waste of breath,
> A waste of breath the years behind
> In balance with this life, this death.

Subtle repetition, as in a magical incantation, is used daringly in this poem, punctuating its balance. A certain arrogance, or rather, the heroic attitude, is well in evidence, and sometimes, as in 'The Scholars', there is an exaggeratedly humorous sarcasm:

> Bald heads forgetful of their sins,
> Old learned, respectable bald heads
> Edit and annotate the lines
> That young men, tossing on their beds,
> Rhymed out in love's despair
> To flatter beauty's ignorant ear.
>
> All shuffle there; all cough in ink;
> All wear the carpet with their shoes;
> All think what other people think;
> All know the man their neighbour knows.
> Lord, what would they say
> Did their Catullus walk that way?

Yeats seems by now to have complete control over his medium in such poems, and his masterpieces 'seem but a moment's thought.' Yet he can slip back into a very inferior kind of verse such as the lament called 'Shepherd and Goatherd', and think it one of his best poems. For the most part, however, the poems in this book maintain the standard of hard simplicity. *The Fisherman* is an important poem because of the emphasis on the simple, wise countryman against his native landscape as what is good in Ireland, and Yeats' resolve to write for him one poem 'as cold and passionate as the dawn.'

> Although I can see him still,
> The freckled man who goes
> To a grey place on a hill
> In grey Connemara clothes
> At dawn to cast his flies,
> It's long since I began
> To call up to the eyes
> This wise and simple man.
> All day I'd looked in the face
> What I had hoped 'twould be
> To write for my own race
> And the reality;
> The living men that I hate,
> The dead man that I loved,
> The craven man in his seat,
> The insolent unreproved,
> And no man brought to book
> Who has won a drunken cheer,
> The witty man and his joke
> Aimed at the commonest ear,
> The clever man who cries
> The catch-cries of the clown,
> The beating down of the wise
> And great Art beaten down.
>
> Maybe a twelvemonth since
> Suddenly I began,
> In scorn of this audience,
> Imagining a man,
> And his sun-freckled face,
> And grey Connemara cloth,
> Climbing up to a place
> Where stone is dark under froth,
> And the down-turn of his wrist
> When the flies drop in the stream;

> *A man who does not exist,*
> *A man who is but a dream;*
> *And cried, 'Before I am old*
> *I shall have written him one*
> *Poem maybe as cold*
> *And passionate as the dawn.'*

The thrill of the concrete is used very skilfully as a climax, balancing the particular and movingly personal image of 'the downturn of his wrist' against 'a man who does not exist, a man who is but a dream'. Yeats' dreaming is used very sparsely these days, and to very particular effect when it is expressed. His dualism is no longer valid in terms of dream versus reality.

'On Being Asked for a War Poem' is a strange reply to the question for the author of *A Vision*, the master magician who had seen the course of events for thousands of years to come!

> *I think it better that in times like these*
> *A poet's mouth be silent, for in truth*
> *We have no gift to set a statesman right;*
> *He has had enough of meddling who can please*
> *A young girl in the indolence of her youth,*
> *Or an old man upon a winter's night.*

It is the old inferiority complex about not being a man of action which has returned. In 'Meditations in Time of Civil War', Yeats elaborates:

> *I turn away and shut the door, and on the stair*
> *Wonder how many times I could have proved my worth*
> *In something that all others understand or share;*
> *But O! ambitious heart, had such a proof drawn forth*
> *A company of friends, a conscience set at ease,*
> *It had but made us pine the more. The abstract joy,*
> *The half-read wisdom of dæmonic images,*
> *Suffice the ageing man as once the growing boy.*

The two poems, 'Ego Dominus Tuus' and 'The Phases of the Moon', are in this book. Both are dependent on Yeats' theory of self and anti-self, and 'The Phases of the Moon' is almost incomprehensible without some acquaintance with *A Vision*. In these poems Yeats tries to weight his starkly simple style with a richness of esoteric lore which succeeds only in later poems such as the Byzantium ones, or 'Among School Children'.

In 'The Phases of the Moon', Yeats' two characters, the saintly Catholic, Aherne, and Michael Robartes, magician and man of action, speak as two sides of Yeats' inner self, looking at the external figure of the poet in his tower. Robartes speaks:

> '*A rat or water-hen*
> *Splashed, or an otter slid into the stream.*
> *We are on the bridge; that shadow is the tower,*
> *And the light proves that he is reading still.*
> *He has found, after the manner of his kind,*
> *Mere images; chosen this place to live in*
> *Because, it may be, of the candlelight*
> *From the far tower where Milton's Platonist*
> *Sat late, or Shelley's visionary prince:*
> *The lonely light that Samuel Palmer engraved,*
> *An image of mysterious wisdom won by toil;*
> *And now he seeks in book or manuscript*
> *What he shall never find.*'

This is straightforward enough. But then Aherne asks Robartes to sing 'the changes of the moon', and the complicated system of *A Vision* is dragged at some length into the poem. After this mysterious diversion, Aherne says:

> '*Were not our beds far off I'd ring the bell,*
> *Stand under the rough roof-timber of the hall*
> *Beside the castle door, where all is stark*
> *Austerity, a place set out for wisdom*
> *That he will never find; I'd play a part.*
> *He would never know me after all these years*
> *But take me for some drunken country man;*
> *I'd stand and mutter there until he caught*
> *"Hunchback and saint and fool", and that they come*
> *Under the last three crescents of the moon,*
> *And then I'd stagger out. He'd crack his wits*
> *Day after day, yet never find the meaning.*'

It is significant that Yeats makes these two sides of himself talk about his incapacity to find the answer to his search. It calls to mind the passage in Yeats' diary where he pleads with the 'Master of Life' to give him some sort of belief.

The next book, *Michael Robartes and the Dancer*, 1921, contains several more poems in this style, dependent upon a slightly esoteric, too abstract mythology. Suddenly, the book leaps into vitality with the poem, 'Easter, 1916'. The clear, taut style of the love poems, more athletic and sustained, is certainly not esoteric, but neither is it simple in what it expresses:

> *I have met them at close of day*
> *Coming with vivid faces*
> *From counter or desk among grey*
> *Eighteenth century houses.*
> *I have passed with a nod of the head*
> *Or polite meaningless words,*
> *Or have lingered awhile and said*
> *Polite meaningless words,*
> *And thought before I had done*
> *Of a mocking tale or a gibe*
> *To please a companion*
> *Around the fire at the club,*
> *Being certain that they and I*
> *But lived where motley is worn:*
> *All changed, changed utterly:*
> *A terrible beauty is born.*

What simple words to conjure up a grey scene of Dublin, perhaps where Grafton and Nassau Streets join, and the poet walking among the vivid evening crowds to his club in Kildare Street. What simple rhythms made out of singsong and repetition, with a conversational note of discord. Skilfully, Yeats shifts from an undifferentiated street scene to particular people:

> *This other man I had dreamed*
> *A drunken vainglorious lout . . .*
> *Transformed utterly:*
> *A terrible beauty is born.*

And again the scene shifts from people to a symbolic panorama of

Ireland in its changing lights of history, in its restlessness and deep soil roots:

> Hearts with one purpose alone
> Through winter and summer seem
> Enchanted to a stone
> To trouble the living stream.
> The horse that comes from the road,
> The rider, the birds that range
> From cloud to tumbling cloud,
> Minute by minute they change;
> A shadow of cloud on the stream
> Changes minute by minute;
> A horse-hoof slides on the brim,
> And a horse plashes within it;
> The long-legged moor-hens dive,
> And hens to moor-cocks call;
> Minute by minute they live:
> The stone's in the midst of it all.

The stone and the river or stream obviously has some symbolic reference to Anima Mundi, but here a lack of the reference does not spoil our appreciation. It is a thought Yeats often uses. The reference or association probably goes back to the poem in Henry More's *Anthroposophia Theomagica* (p. 28):

> Lord God! This was a stone,
> As hard as any One
> Thy laws in Nature fram'd:
> 'Tis now a springing Well,
> And many Drops can tell,
> Since it by Art was tam'd.
>
> My God! My Heart is so,
> 'Tis all of Flint, and no
> Extract of Teares will yield:
> Dissolve it with thy Fire,
> That something may aspire,
> And grow up in my Field.
>
> Bare Teares Ile not intreat,
> But let thy Spirits seat
> Upon these waters bee,

> *Then I new form'd with Light*
> *Shall move without all Night,*
> *Or Excentricity.*

Yeats' poem is a striking climax to what we have called the style of the second period, stark, conversational, passion made powerful by restraint.

The few esoteric and unsuccessful poems which depend almost entirely on abstraction and private mythology—the style of 'Ego Dominus Tuus' and the Michael Robartes poems—failed as a whole because not held together by a single emotion or tight structure. In the third stylistic period this type of poem occurs with a difference which spells its success. It begins with the *Second Coming*, and the richness and esoteric tone of such poems are perfected by fusion with the conversational style and strong emotional undertones of the second period. Abstraction is made solid, and complicated mythology and characters are replaced by symbols that are complex, but can be understood on the emotional and pictorial levels by everyone, and on the intellectual level by those who have followed Yeats' system. Intensity, vitality, rich emotion underlie the stylistic effects 'as of cold light and tumbling clouds', but suggestive 'esoteric' allusions serve to add warmth instead of murkiness. In my opinion Yeats is at his best and most original in the love poems of the second period and in 'Among School Children', although in as great a poem as 'Leda and the Swan' he comes nearest to achieving the 'inward imagery' that characterized Blake's most mystical work.

THE SECOND COMING

> *Turning and turning in the widening gyre*
> *The falcon cannot hear the falconer;*
> *Things fall apart; the centre cannot hold;*
> *Mere anarchy is loosed upon the world,*
> *The blood-dimmed tide is loosed, and everywhere*
> *The ceremony of innocence is drowned.*
> *The best lack all conviction, while the worst*
> *Are full of passionate intensity.*
>
> *Surely some revelation is at hand.*
> *Surely the Second Coming is at hand.*
> *The Second Coming! Hardly are these words out*
> *When a vast image out of Spiritus Mundi*

Troubles my sight: somewhere in sands of the desert
A shape with lion body and the head of a man,
A gaze blank and pitiless as the sun,
Is moving its slow thighs, while all about it
Reel shadows of the indignant desert birds.
The darkness drops again; but now I know
That twenty centuries of stoney sleep
Were vexed to nightmare by a rocking cradle,
And what rough beast, its hour come round at last,
Slouches towards Bethlehem to be born.

To appreciate this poem it is not necessary to know how the gyres figure in Yeats' system; nor do we need to recall Yeats' theory that a period of anarchy and violence follows a period of innocence and beauty. We do not halt overlong over Spiritus Mundi, nor puzzle over the idea that two thousand years after Christ, some beast of revelation, the complete opposite of Christ, will be born (oddly enough this was a tentative thought of Origen's). We do not need to know all about these things because the emotion and foreboding intensity of the poem are strong enough to carry the idea across intuitively if not intellectually, and because not only the style but the images are immediately comprehensible to the imagination. Instead of stating his philosophy in abstract and unpoetic terms as Yeats tended to do earlier in such lines as:

> *The particular is pounded till it is man.*
> *When had I my own will?*
> *O not since life began.*

Yeats is now able to shift easily into the abstract from a springboard of strong concrete imagery and sinewy lines; from the moving gyres or spirals of the falcon's flight, via the esoteric Yeatsian meaning of gyres into the abstract statement about anarchy. And again, just as we are about to lose sight of the argument, we are given another powerful and tangible image which in turn moves excitingly and easily into abstraction, yet serves to heighten the horrible inevitability of the last two lines. Out of much complexity and what Yeats' detractors call his esoteric, even 'gimcrack' ideas, Yeats has made a poem which stands stark, moving, and apparently simple. This is the tone of the third period.

The next book, *The Tower*, 1928, opens with a very powerful poem of this sort, 'Sailing to Byzantium'. It is followed in a later book by its companion poem, 'Byzantium'. It has been noted many times in reference to these poems that Yeats thought the golden age of Byzantium the perfect time to have lived. In *A Vision* he writes:

'I think if I could be given a month of antiquity and leave to spend it where I chose, I would spend it in Byzantium a little before Justinian opened St. Sophia and closed the Academy of Plato. I think I could find in some little wine shop some philosophical worker in mosaic who could answer all my questions, the supernatural descending nearer to him than to Plotinus even ... I think that in early Byzantium, and maybe never before or since in recorded history, religious, æsthetic and practical life were one, and that architect and artificers—though not, it may be, poets, for language had been the instrument of controversy and must have grown abstract—spoke to the multitude and the few alike. The painter and the mosaic worker, the worker in gold and silver, the illuminator of Sacred Books were almost impersonal, absorbed in their subject matter and that the vision of a whole people. ... The ascetic ... has taken the place of those Greek athletes ... but all about him is an incredible splendour like that which we see pass under our closed eyelids as we lie between sleeping and waking ... even the drilled pupil of the eye, when the drill is in the hand of some Byzantine worker in ivory, undergoes a somnambulistic change, for its deep shadow among the faint lines of the tablet, its mechanical circle, where all else is rhythmical and flowing, give to saint or angel a look of some great bird staring at a miracle. ... To me it seems that He, who among the first Christian communities was little but a ghostly exorcist, had in His assent to a full Divinity made possible this sinking in upon a supernatural splendour, these walls with their little glimmering cubes of blue and green and gold.'[1]

What has not been noted about this passage is its extraordinary juxtaposition, even synthesis, of a religiously ascetic feeling with the worldly splendour of gold and silver and mosaic. It is this relationship that Yeats unconsciously underlines in his description of Byzantium. Byzantium's appeal lies in the fact that the supernatural can descend close to it, yet the enchanter could wish for no more sensuous scenes of beauty. Parallel to this runs the extraordinary idea

---

[1] Yeats, *A Vision*, 1937, p. 279.

that Christ was regarded as a sort of exorcist or enchanter before he consented to the putting on of divinity. Again is the hint that the enchanter's vision precedes the holy vision, and gives concreteness to what else would be an abstraction.

With all this imagery and the many-levelled thought behind it, it is little wonder that the Byzantine poems are so strangely rich and moving, so capable of shifting from their opulent imagery to the austere meanings that form the skeleton. Carrying our thought from the passage above, we begin to wonder whether these poems are Yeats' poetic attempt to break through from the magical vision to the saint's. Let us examine the poems mostly from this point of view, leaving out the many other fascinating aspects that have been dealt with so interestingly by various scholars.

SAILING TO BYZANTIUM

I

That is no country for old men. The young
In one another's arms, birds in the trees,
—Those dying generations—at their song,
The salmon-falls, the mackerel-crowded seas.
Fish, flesh, or fowl, commend all summer long
Whatever is begotten, born, and dies.
Caught in that sensual music all neglect
Monuments of unaging intellect.

II

An aged man is but a paltry thing,
A tattered coat upon a stick, unless
Soul clap its hands and sing, and louder sing
For every tatter in its mortal dress,
Nor is there singing school but studying
Monuments of its own magnificence;
And therefore I have sailed the seas and come
To the holy city of Byzantium.

III

O sages standing in God's holy fire
As in the gold mosaic of a wall,
Come from the holy fire, perne in a gyre
And be the singing masters of my soul.

Consume my heart away; sick with desire
And fastened to a dying animal
It knows not what it is; and gather me
Into the artifice of eternity.

IV

Once out of nature I shall never take
My bodily form from any natural thing,
But such a form as Grecian goldsmiths make
Of hammered gold and gold enamelling
To keep a drowsy emperor awake;
Or set upon a bough to sing
To lords and ladies of Byzantium
Of what is past, or passing, or to come.

The first two stanzas, an expression of Yeats' reasons for going, symbolically, to Byzantium, reveal no religious yearnings at all. Rather they express great regret at leaving the country of the young and of physical love. They are almost, and poignantly, a lecture or reminder to himself that he must grow old gracefully, turn to monuments of spirit and intellect as second best and almost in order to infuse his dying body with spiritual attraction. Here he uses the Blakean image of 'soul clap its hands and sing.'

It is the third stanza which holds our interest. Yeats tells the story of how, looking for new images, he went to a clairvoyant who told him to take down a book which lay in a certain position along a certain shelf and turn to the page named. Doing so, Yeats found a reproduction of one of Blake's paintings on which he based the image of the 'sages standing in God's holy fire as in the gold mosaic of a wall.' Then Yeats commands the sages imperiously, as a magician might, 'to come from the holy fire, perne in a gyre, and be the singing masters of my soul'.

But suddenly the mood changes from arrogance, the fierce old man brushes his eyes and admits that perhaps he does not know after all: 'consume my heart away; sick with desire and fastened to a dying animal it knows not what it is; and gather me into the artifice of eternity.' 'And gather me into the artifice of eternity', this from Yeats the proud magician who would 'beat upon the wall til Truth obeyed his call.' Is this new humility sincere, or is the new note but a graceful substitute for the masterfulness of his youth which is not suitable, perhaps, to an ageing man. How does Yeats reconcile the new wish to be gathered into eternity with his former view that poetry was much more magic than sanctity?

The key to this lies in the odd phrasing of the 'artifice of eternity'. The last stanza of the poem expands this unusual idea of the supernatural being artifice that can sing 'of what is past or passing or to come.' But to turn the key we must look at another later poem in which Yeats indirectly gives himself away:

> *The true faith discovered was*
> *When painted panel, statuary,*
> *Glass-mosaic, window-glass,*
> *Amended what was told awry*
> *By some peasant gospeller;*
> *Swept the sawdust from the floor*
> *Of that working carpenter.*

In other words, Yeats is trying now, more like his master Blake, to equate true religion with art. Revelation was not complete until art refined it, which, incidentally, is *not* Blakean logic, but a Yeatsian interpretation of Blake's statements. This is quite a change, for formerly Yeats took pains to show us that religion and the saint's vision were on the whole incompatible with art, which is closer kin to magic. There is a curious confirmation of this thought in Yeats' introduction to the little Blake book he brought out in 1893:

'He [Blake] is one of those great artificers of God who utter mysterious truths to a little clan. The other spokes to theologians and magicians, and he speaks to poets and artists. The others drew their symbols from theology and alchemy and he from the flowers of spring and the leaves of summer; but the message is the same, and the truth uttered is the truth God spake to the red clay at the beginning of the world.'[1]

In the next poem in this book, 'The Tower', Yeats once more seems chiefly concerned with his dislike of growing old:

> *What shall I do with this absurdity—*
> *O heart, O troubled heart—this caricature,*
> *Decrepit age that has been tied to me*
> *As to a dog's tail?*

[1] Yeats, *William Blake*, 1893, p. xxxv.

> *Never had I more*
> *Excited, passionate, fantastical*
> *Imagination, nor an ear and eye*
> *That more expected the impossible.*

Ruefully, he admits that he must 'bid the Muse go pack' and learn to deal in abstract things 'or be derided by a sort of battered kettle at the heels.' The second section of the poem is concerned with those who have lived in or near Yeats' ancient tower in the past, and Yeats wonders whether these men and women ever 'did in public or in secret rage as I do now against old age?' In the superb final section Yeats in a quieter mood says:

> *It is time that I wrote my will;*
> *I chose upstanding men*
> *That climb the streams until*
> *The fountain leaps and at dawn*
> *Drop their cast at the side*
> *Of dripping stone . . .*

Only to change again into the old man, fierce with creation—Blake or William Morris his model—who cries:

> *And I declare my faith:*
> *I mock Plotinus' thought*
> *And cry in Plato's teeth,*
> *Death and life were not*
> *Till man made up the whole,*
> *Made lock, stock, and barrel*
> *Out of his bitter soul,*
> *Aye, sun and moon and star, all,*
> *And further add to that*
> *That, being dead, we rise,*
> *Dream and so create*
> *Translunar Paradise.*

After the terse triumphant sweep of this, again the mood quietens, shifting to:

> *I have prepared my peace*
> *With learned Italian things*
> *And the proud stones of Greece,*
> *Poet's imaginings*
> *And memories of love . . .*

> Now shall I make my soul,
> Compelling it to study
> In a learned school
> Till the wreck of body,
> Slow decay of blood,
> Testy delirium
> Or dull decrepitude,
> Or what worse evil come—
> The death of friends, or death
> Of every brilliant eye
> That made a catch in the breath—
> Seem but the clouds of the sky
> When the horizon fades;
> Or a bird's sleepy cry
> Among the deepening shades.

There seems no sign at all of religious leanings in this poem. Rather it is the old man wishing for the sensual days of his youth and resigning himself to their absence. Is the note struck in 'Sailing to Byzantium' in that one poem alone, and therefore only perhaps poetic licence? It would be wise to look at its companion-piece, 'Byzantium', to be found in the 1933 book, *The Winding Stair*:

> The unpurged images of day recede;
> The Emperor's drunken soldiery are abed;
> Night resonance recedes, night-walkers' song
> After great cathedral gong;
> A starlit or a moonlit dome disdains
> All that man is,
> All mere complexities,
> The fury and the mire of human veins.
>
> Before me floats an image, man or shade,
> Shade more than man, more image than a shade;
> For Hades' bobbin wound in mummy-cloth
> May unwind the winding path;
> A mouth that has no moisture and no breath
> Breathless mouths may summon;
> I hail the superhuman;
> I call it death-in-life and life-in-death.

Miracle-bird or golden handiwork,
More miracle than bird or handiwork,
Planted on a star-lit golden bough,
Can like the cocks of Hades crow,
Or, by the moon embittered, scorn aloud
In glory of the changeless metal
Common bird or petal
And all complexities of mire or blood.

At midnight on the Emperor's pavement flit
Flames that no faggot feeds, nor steel has lit,
Nor storm disturbs, flames begotten of flame,
Where blood-begotten spirits come
And all complexities of fury leave,
Dying into a dance,
An agony of trance,
An agony of flame that cannot singe a sleeve.

Astraddle on the dolphin's mire and blood,
Spirit after spirit! The smithies break the flood,
The golden smithies of the Emperor!
Marbles of the dancing floor
Break bitter furies of complexity,
Those images that yet
Fresh images beget,
That dolphin-torn, that gong-tormented sea.

The drastic shifting in the first stanza from the sensual images
(curiously, 'of day') to the lunar world of spirit that disdains 'the
fury and the mire of human veins' is indicative. The accent of preference is now on the latter, and not on regrets for the sensual day. In
the next stanza, Yeats elaborates: what he wants from this lunar
world is an image or spirit who, in turn, will summon up supernatural truth, 'for Hades' bobbin bound in mummy-cloth may un-
wind the winding path.' The purpose sounds more magical than
religious. And yet the renunciation of the fury and the mire in
favour of the spirit has something of the ascetic tone. Yeats repeats
this thought more strongly in his hailing of the 'superhuman'—'I
call it death-in-life and life-in-death,' which in this context surely
has a mystical connotation of the death of the senses in life being the

life of the spirit in death. However, this may be wishful thinking on Yeats' part, or a theory born of necessity.

We meet the golden bird again, and are not quite sure what he is doing there. Yeats apparently has already taken this image for granted, carrying over from the earlier poem all its association with the 'artifice of eternity'. For Yeats admits that it is 'more miracle than bird or handiwork'. The next two stanzas, the dominant image in one, water, in the other, flame (combining to the perfect unity of the seal of Solomon), seek also to picture the transformation of complex instincts and fury and mire into the orderly golden artifice of eternity. Yeats, in the first poem, 'Sailing to Byzantium', wishing to become the golden bird, is in fact saying that he wishes to be the singing voice of eternity fashioned by the eternal artificers, as he thought Blake was, being a prophet. To abstract this thin line of thought from the richness of such poems is indeed heretical, but all the same may cast light on a few difficult points.

There is another poem in this book which has a complex relation to a later poem: it is the famous 'Leda and the Swan'.

> *A sudden blow; the great wings beating still*
> *Above the staggering girl, her thighs caressed*
> *By the dark webs, her nape caught in his bill,*
> *He holds her helpless breast upon his breast.*
>
> *How can those terrified vague fingers push*
> *The feathered glory from her loosening thighs?*
> *And how can body, laid in that white rush,*
> *But feel the strange heart beating where it lies?*
>
> *A shudder in the loins engenders there*
> *The broken wall, the burning roof and tower*
> *And Agamemnon dead.*
>   *Being so caught up*
> *So mastered by the brute blood of the air,*
> *Did she put on his knowledge with his power*
> *Before the indifferent beak could let her drop?*

It is significant in relation to his theory of *A Vision* that Yeats first called this poem 'Annunciation'. The following first lines from an early draft of the poem show how much Yeats must have laboured to get the effects, which in the final version seem so effortless:

ANNUNCIATION

Now can the swooping Godhead have his will
Yet hovers though her helpless thighs are pressed
By the webbed toes.

The poem in a later book which is in the relation of contrast to 'Leda and the Swan', is 'The Mother of God', Yeats' effort to deal with the Christian annunciation:

The threefold terror of love: a fallen flare
Through the hollow of an ear;
Wings beating round the room;
The terror of all terrors that I bore
The Heavens in my womb.

Had I not found content among the shows
Every common woman knows,
Chimney corner, garden walk,
Or rocky cistern where we tread the clothes
And gather all the talk?

What is this flesh I purchased with my pains,
This fallen star my milk sustains,
This love that makes my heart's blood stop
Or strikes a sudden chill into my bones
And bids my hair stand up?

How falsely and rather smugly this rings after the intensity of Leda. With the exception of one line, 'Wings beating around the room', and for all Yeats' devices of homely images, there is nothing in this poem to equal the sense of supernatural, the thrilling physical intuition of Leda. And yet it is a very fine poem. Yeats can say nothing about the Incarnation to equal the sense of miracle in

A shudder in the loins engenders there
The broken wall, the burning roof and tower
And Agamemnon dead.

Compare with this the early English poem which does give the sense of inward miracle about the Incarnation:

> There is no rose of such vertu
> As is the rose that bare Jesu.
> Allelulia.
>
> For in this rose contained was
> Heaven and erth in litel space,
> Res miranda.

Yeats, whatever his leanings towards religion and the saint, is more at home in myth than in Christianity. He is uneasy in poems that require true mystical machinery, and cannot bring it off. Whereas, in the pagan sexuality of the Leda myth—not without its own kind of spiritual value, a dreaming of the blood, underscored in modern times by D. H. Lawrence—he is gloriously at home, and his compact, simply stated lyric has a quality that defies the boundaries of inner and outer. Yeats never felt comfortable in Phase 15, although the period of Troy is most important in his Great Wheel. Curiously, 'Leda and the Swan' is the one poem in which Yeats comes close to the 'inward imagery' characterizing Blake's most mystical period.

'Among School Children' is perhaps Yeats' greatest poem. It is complex, even esoteric in the sense that it combines a love poem for Maud Gonne as she was and as she is now, the poet's feelings about old age, the immediate scene of the convent school, with subtle utilizing of myth and philosophy, Christianity and painting to make out of simple words a rich tapestry of images. And yet the dominant emotion is strong enough to carry the poem through in apparently easy unity. The first two sections reveal the type of seemingly effortless transition:

I

> I walk through the long schoolroom questioning;
> A kind old nun in a white hood replies;
> The children learn to cipher and to sing,
> To study reading-books and history,
> To cut and sew, be neat in everything
> In the best modern way—the children's eyes
> In momentary wonder stare upon
> A sixty-year-old smiling public man.

176

II

I dream of a Ledæan body, bent
Above a sinking fire, a tale that she
Told of a harsh reproof, or trivial event
That changed some childish day to tragedy—
Told, and it seemed that our two natures blent
Into a sphere from youthful sympathy,
Or else, to alter Plato's parable,
Into the yoke and white of the one shell.

Here is Yeats at his magical best. He is able to alter at will the texture and evocation of his verse in easy transition. The sweet singsong of the nun's reply turns into the majestic movement of 'I dream of a Ledæan body, bent above a sinking fire.' And again, it shifts to the haunting phrases of

Her present image floats into the mind—
Did Quattrocento finger fashion it
Hollow of cheek as if it drank the wind.

This in turn passes on to the slow-moving and splendidly arrogant statement about old age and philosophical thought:

Plato thought nature but a spume that plays
Upon a ghostly paradigm of things;
Solider Aristotle played the taws
Upon the bottom of a king of kings;
World-famous golden-thighed Pythagoras
Fingered upon a fiddle-stick or strings
What a star sang and careless Muses heard:
Old clothes upon old sticks to scare a bird.

From here it is but one step to the stanza about the images which man worships being 'the self-born mockers of man's enterprise', and to realize that once more Yeats is talking about the unbridgeable gap between appearance and reality, body and spirit. And he asks in the last stanza why this should be so, since in all fine and lovely things spirit and matter seem indivisible:

Labour is blossoming or dancing where
The body is not bruised to pleasure soul,
Nor beauty born out of its own despair,
Nor blear-eyed wisdom out of midnight oil.

O chestnut tree, great-rooted blossomer,
Are you the leaf, the blossom or the bole?
O body swayed to music, O brightening glance,
How can we know the dancer from the dance?

This poem is indeed an achievement with its complexity of image
and thought, and the subtle stylistic improvisation. A great amount
of poetic labour must have been expended to make the poem seem
so comparatively effortless. L. A. G. Strong's enthusiastic letter says
a great deal which needs to be said:

'Your life as a poet has been unusual in that your poetry has become steadily better as you have grown older. Starting with work
that was new and striking and beautiful in one manner, you have
passed on to another manner, and another again: and now you are
writing a poetry that unites the fire of youth, the power of maturity,
and the skill wrung from a lifetime of devotion to that forbidding
end. There is no such poetry elsewhere in the world today. There
is no flame that is engendered from such a heat of conflict: no other
mind melts the ore of so many interests: no other fingers are so
strong and merciless to give the metal form: no other eye so fierce
to seek a flaw when work is cold. . . . Your achievement in poetry
has been precise and definite. You are a magical poet, and by that I
mean something very different from the ordinary use of the word.
Your bias has always been to express the things that lie on the farthest
edge of expression: and it will undoubtedly be said of you in the
future that you enlarged the poetic consciousness of your time. . . .
This was a task for a magician, and you have gone about it as a
practical magician must. . . . The significance of your poetry has
been to evoke by the hardest and most precise of symbols the most
delicate tones of beauty and meaning and in saying this I do not for
an instant overlook its unparalleled music, for music has been a
definite and practical part of the incantation. . . . What is this power, in
which you are pre-eminent, of summoning to our understanding, with
one swift, wrought phrase, a landscape, a sky, a weather, or a history?
. . . No one since Blake has made a few words signify so much.'[1]

Mixed amongst rich poems such as the Byzantium ones and
'Among School Children', are a few of the elaborately simple poems
of Yeats' fourth period. It is the style which of all Yeats' styles rings
least sincerely. These poems are short lyrics, many with refrains,

[1] Hogarth Press *Letters*, p. 9.

'Words for Music Perhaps', and generally put into the mouths of village fools as Crazy Jane, or merely 'a man' or 'a woman'. They are poems for which Yeats does not want to take too personal a responsibility, poems boasting about the physicalness of sex as if the seventy-year-old poet were a schoolboy emancipating himself verbally from parental prudishness. Critics have expressed wonder that Yeats, after his long and laborious search for an entry into the lunar world of spirit, seems, at the end, to be giving up the quest altogether and turning wholly to physical things. And yet, it seems that the opposing force of spirit is holding the choice in tension. In his own way, Yeats is perhaps trying to suggest what Blake stated, that the senses are the gateway to eternity. Some of these poems appear in *The Tower*—'The Fool by the Wayside' and 'A Man Young and Old'—but are still counterbalanced by evocative poems such as 'All Soul's Night' which was, however, written in 1920 as an Epilogue to *A Vision*.

In the *Winding Stair* there are three highly interesting poems which prove that more than ever Yeats is conscious of the conflict and has not yet made his final choice. He continues vacillating between two extremes, which, although now usually in terms of body and spirit, are all based on his old theme of having to choose between holiness and some phase of action. As he said to Mrs. Yeats when he was correcting the proofs of his collected poems: 'I have spent my life saying the same thing in many different ways. I denounced old age before I was twenty and the Swordsman throughout repudiates the Saint—though with vacillation.' The swordsman is, of course, another symbol of the forceful masterful life usually summed up by Yeats in the figure of the magician. The swordsman is superimposed on to the magician symbol in later years, after Yeats had been given an ancient Japanese sword by his friend Sato.

In 'A Dialogue of Self and Soul', the Soul first calls the poet to the mystical ascent, symbolized by the tower stairs winding up to a starlit sky. But the external Self calls him to things 'emblematic of love and war'. Then Soul urges:

> *Think of ancestral night that can,*
> *If but imagination scorn the earth*
> *And intellect its wandering*
> *To this and that and t'other thing,*
> *Deliver from the crime of death and birth.*

179

But again the Self urges that the sword be set up as 'emblems of the day' against the tower, emblematic of the night. The solar day to Yeats always represents sensuality in opposition to night, which is lunar, unearthly. Soul cries in protest:

> . . . . *intellect no longer knows*
> *Is from the Ought, or knower from the known.*
> *That is to say, ascends to Heaven.*

Self justifies itself by saying that after the pain and toil and ignominy of growing up it is pleasant to be able to face the world, and not to reject it for the way of the soul. For, after all, Yeats says, life in the world is not really so bad:

> *I am content to follow it to its source,*
> *Every event in action or in thought;*
> *Measure the lot; forgive myself the lot!*
> *When such as I cast out remorse*
> *So great a sweetness flows into the breast*
> *We must laugh and we must sing,*
> *We are blest by everything,*
> *Everything we look upon is blest.*

The second poem in this group, 'The Choice', states as clearly as one could wish the old battle between perfection of life, or the holiness of the saint, and perfection of the work, which for Yeats postulated the machinery of magic.

> *The intellect of man is forced to choose*
> *Perfection of the life, or of the work,*
> *And if it take the second must refuse*
> *A heavenly mansion, raging in the dark.*
> *When all that story's finished, what's the news?*
> *In luck or out the toil has left its mark:*
> *That old perplexity an empty purse,*
> *Or the clay's vanity, the night's remorse.*

And the third poem, itself called 'Vacillation', begins:

> *Between extremities*
> *Man runs his course;*

while the battle of poet versus saint rages in full force in Sections VII and VIII. The true nature of the conflict that has torn Yeats since his childhood is, for the first time in these late poems, stated plainly and unmistakably. The ancient role of poet, the enchanter who can enchant the very sticks and stones and trees, is the role the heart has accepted. It is significant that it is 'Heart' which has chosen, as consciously or unconsciously it had been because of Maud Gonne. 'Struck dumb in the simplicity of fire' brings to mind 'No Second Troy' and 'Reconciliation', poems from the crucial period when Yeats chose his mask. But Soul still cries out with agonizing appeal:

VII

THE SOUL: *Seek out reality, leave things that seem.*
THE HEART: *What, be a singer born and lack a theme?*
THE SOUL: *Isaiah's coal, what more can man desire?*
THE HEART: *Struck dumb in the simplicity of fire.*
THE SOUL: *Look on that fire, salvation walks within.*
THE HEART: *What theme had Homer but original sin?*

VIII

Must we part, Von Hügel, though much alike, for we
Accept the miracles of the Saints and honour sanctity?
The body of Saint Teresa lies undecayed in the tomb, . . .
I, though heart might find relief
Did I become a Christian man and choose for my belief
What seems most welcome in the tomb—play a predestined part.
Homer is my example and his unchristened heart.
The lion and the honeycomb, what has Scriptures said?
So get you gone, Von Hügel, though with blessings on your head.

After these statements of continued vacillation come the Crazy Jane poems and 'Words for Music Perhaps', the physical tone of which most critics take as Yeats' final choice. But despite their shock tactics, typical of Yeats the magician, they are not at all the conclusive evidence they have been thought to be, proving that Yeats had given up the attempt to break through to the realm of spirit. The old warfare rages, only in different terms and with different emphasis. This is readily seen when we remember that it is usually a Bishop that Crazy Jane talks to in her abandoned way, or the poem is called 'Crazy Jane on the Day of Judgment' or 'Crazy Jane on God'. Both Crazy Jane and the Fool are very useful characters to Yeats, since neither they nor he can be considered wholly responsible for their words and contradictions and, by tradition, the Fool has privileged access to truth. They can be mouthpieces for Yeats' ideas in a way that is both impersonal and blatantly physical, and at the same time more abstract in the working out of theory than Yeats could ever be when he is talking about himself. In a way this lack of overtly personal poetry is the defect of Yeats' final period. It has been said that there is no real warmth or real passion in the physical overstatement of these poems, and that 'we are a little afraid of this fierce old man.' There is a curiously cold tone, perhaps, because Yeats seems to substitute or confuse the abstract statement of physical passion for particular imagery. The fierce old man of an 'Acre of Grass' is far more complex, wanting to be Blake who stated that the senses are good, yes, but also that the senses are the gateways to eternity, and in a very particular way. However, in a way no one can blame Yeats for wanting to put his too personal battle on a different plane—on a stage, as it were, to inspect the problem from the outside and see it in its most elemental form as played out by puppet figures. On the other hand, we cannot take all of it too seriously as poetry, but rather as a digression from the path of highly personalized and complex poetry. In a sense, the problem has returned to the stage at which Yeats left it when he chose, as a young man, the way of magician because of his love for Maud Gonne: and it is in much the same terms of asceticism versus sensuality. And in the end Yeats, following Blake, extols bodily love over against a barren and inverted continence, born out of fear. The most Blakean, and the finest, of these poems is 'Crazy Jane Talks with the Bishop', in which the senses are allied with eternal and spiritual truth. Obviously, with the many echoes of Blake in the poem, this is meant to be similar to Blake's view that the senses are the gateways to eternity. The vision of eternity is still important to Yeats, even though he seems to be concentrating on the gateway:

> I met the Bishop on the road
>   And much said he and I,
> 'Those breasts are flat and fallen now,
>   Those veins must soon be dry;
> Live in a heavenly mansion,
>   Not in some foul sty.'
>
> 'Fair and foul are near of kin,
>   And fair needs foul,' I cried,
> 'My friends are gone, but that's a truth

Nor grace nor bed denied,
Learned in bodily lowliness
And in the heart's pride.

A woman can be proud and stiff
When on love intent.
But love has pitched his mansion in
The place of excrement.
For nothing can be sole or whole
That has not been rent.'

This new vein of expression is continued in *Last Poems* in the songs sung by the lady and her chambermaid. The abstraction and distancing mechanism is carried even further by the formal frame of the ballad style. The poet is disowning his own shock tactics by making them seem traditional in presentation at any rate. Yeats even tried adding a further protective layer of music. Most of Yeats' attempts to wed words and music are most unfortunate. Yeats had no musical ear, was in fact tone deaf, which is thought to be responsible for the peculiarly haunting notes of discord that add charm to his powerful word rhythms, for his sense of rhythm was perfect. Until his later years Yeats distrusted music, was afraid of its effect on the more subtle sounds of poetry.

Consequently, the attempts to join music and poetry strike a little false, and poems such as 'The O'Rahilly' supposed to be sung, with its refrain of 'How goes the weather?', leave themselves wide open to ridicule. One remembers how fascinated Yeats was that 'Blake sang his *Songs of Innocence* in Mrs. William's drawing-room'[1] to music.

And yet in this last book there are poems with all the old terse strength, all the undertones of arrogance and passion and effectiveness of restraint. The blatant extroversion of 'News for the Delphic Oracle' in which Yeats leaves nothing, unhappily, to the imagination, and delights like a mischievous boy in vulgarity, is in sharp contrast to the restraint of 'Beautiful Lofty Things':

Beautiful lofty things: O'Leary's noble head;
My father upon the Abbey stage,. before him a raging crowd:
'This Land of Saints,' and then as the applause died out,
'Of plaster Saints,' his beautiful mischievous head thrown back:

[1] Yeats, *Essays*, p. 18.

183

Standish O'Grady supporting him between the tables
Speaking to a drunken audience high nonsensical words;
Augusta Gregory seated at her great ormulu table,
Her eightieth winter approaching: 'Yesterday he threatened my life.
I told him that nightly from six to seven I sat at this table,
The blinds drawn up'; Maud Gonne at Howth Station waiting a train,
Pallas Athene in that straight back and arrogant head.
All the Olympians; a thing never known again.

This poem, along with 'An Acre of Grass', 'A Bronze Head', 'The Municipal Gallery Revisited', 'The Statutes', 'Are You Content' and one or two more lyrics in this book belong to the old aristocratic Yeats who always towers above the Yeats who is trying to be modern and 'popular'. And the old Yeats who could make the heroic gesture while full of inner doubts and conflicts, never quite dies out. Yeats at the end is rather like the king and queen in his own *Deirdre*, who sat playing chess and awaiting their murderers: 'I never heard a death so out of reach of common hearts, a high and comely end.' The same Yeats, a Romantic to the end, could make the lofty gesture take on personal poignance, as he wrote his own epitaph a year before he died:

Irish poets learn your trade,
Sing whatever is well made,
Scorn the sort now growing up
All out of shape from toe to top,
Their unremembering hearts and heads
Base-born products of base-born beds.
Sing the peasantry, and then
Hard-riding country gentlemen,
The holiness of monks, and after
Porter-drinkers' randy laughter;
Sing the lords and ladies gay
That were beaten into the clay
Through seven heroic centuries;
Cast your mind on other days
That we in coming days may be
Still the indomitable Irishry.

Under bare Ben Bulben's head
In Drumcliffe churchyard Yeats is laid.

An ancestor was rector there
Long years ago, a church stands near,
By the road an ancient cross.
No marble, no conventional phrase;
On limestone quarried near the spot
By his command these words are cut:
        Cast a cold eye
        On life, on death;
        Horseman, pass by.

One cannot help feeling that the shock tactic poems of Yeats' old age are not nearly so important as those poems of vacillation and unmade choice which immediately precede them. They are too extrovertly sexual to have much hidden psychological significance. At most, the Crazy Jane lyrics and others of the same order seem but an attempt to express the old conflict in a simplified and defiant manner without actually choosing one side, although some critics see only the surface and think that the realm of sensuality is Yeats' final choice. After all, Yeats is an old man, feeling himself so close to death, to the Unknown, that he has written his own epitaph. Who among us in this situation, having chosen 'perfection of the work' instead of 'of the life', would not whistle in the dark, defy the plunge into the unknown?

And Yeats himself confessed that his theme has always been vacillation. 'I have spent my life saying the same thing in many different ways. I denounced old age before I was twenty and the Swordsman throughout repudiates the Saint—though with vacillation.'

'Though with vacillation'! This is the secret of Yeats' thought which has such direct bearing upon his poetry, on its variety and richness as well as on its haunting poignancy. It is the theme, as it were, on which all of Yeats' baffling variations are played. 'Between extremities man runs his course.' Not the choosing of one of two extremes—whether in terms of body and spirit or of saint and enchanter—but the conflict itself is Yeats' theme, despite all of his yearnings for a secure belief. Many of Yeats' critics who would like to pin him down at the last, and put him into a neat category, have themselves mistaken Yeats' vacillation for confusion. This is to miss the point completely. Granted that Yeats was no systematic scholar, and was liable to inaccuracies in the poetic sifting and over-emphasis of appealing facts. But he did, for instance, know very well the distinctions between mysticism and magic, although he speaks of them in confusing juxtaposition. In fact he knew quite well that the sensitive man can be torn between such extremes. And his poetry is in large a picture of such a struggle in himself, and shows above all the tragedy of realizing that a choice must be made, and yet the feeling that both sides have equal advantages.

This dilemma of personal choice is the underlying essence of all Yeats' poetry. Yet, characteristically, *A Vision* is concerned little about freedom and its tragic implications, but rather takes sides temporarily with magic and serves as a distancing mechanism which can deal with the problems of personality abstractly.

When all is said and done, Yeats remains essentially a personal poet; not specifically a philosophic or a saintly or a magical poet, but a personal poet. That is not to say that philosophy, religion, and magic were not vital problems for him, but that his actual poetry is an expression, not so much of any one of these points of view, but of their conflict and interaction. His basic doctrine remains, once we have discarded all esoteric embroidery, that every sensitive mind is divided into two, torn between extremes of spirit and matter. To prefer vacillation to choice has a certain poignancy and interest but is undoubtedly a sign of romantic schizophrenia.

However much the pose of magician concerned him, the esoteric Yeatsism it led him into did not satisfy Yeats as a final choice. Monk Gibbons relates:

'Years ago when Yeats was still living in Merrion Square, I dined with him there one night . . . I was on the point of starting a trip to France, and I announced that I had thought of going to Fontainebleau, and perhaps even joining the school of esoteric wisdom being run by Gurdjieff there . . . When I was leaving that night Yeats came with me as far as the top of the stairs. Suddenly he said to me: "Take the advice of an old man. I have seen a lot of the kind of school we have been discussing tonight. My advice to you is to give it all a wide berth." It was said with such kind intention—and Yeats was not a person whose normal conversation breathed benevolence—that it impressed me all the more. From the erstwhile disciple of Madame Blavatsky, from the friend of MacGregor Mathers, and the author of *A Vision*, it meant a lot.'[1]

Although Yeats' particular inner drama generally sorted itself out

[1] *Irish Times*, 24 June, 1950.

into the opposing camps of sanctity and magic, the fact which most concerned him was that both extremes could exist in one man and become alternately dominant. This vacillation to him was the core of the artistic personality: 'out of the quarrel with ourselves we make poetry.'

As we have seen, the quarrel of Yeats with himself after the early rebellion from his father, centred itself around the very personal fact of his love for Maud Gonne. At the time when he wrote most of his love poems for her—perhaps his best and most characteristic poems—he was in the act of choosing between the two ways, that of saint and that of enchanter. This perhaps adds to the intensity of these poems, although the struggle is not directly mentioned in them. For Maud Gonne's sake, he became increasingly interested in politics, occult studies, and the theatre. Of necessity his attitude towards her became that of troubadour, yearning after an unattainable love. Since this has nothing to do with the incarnate love of Christianity he tended more and more to veer towards the symbolic pose of enchanter. Making it a personal myth he could hope to present his beloved with a façade of power, action, and masterfulness, but secretly hoping too, that the efficient technique of the enchanter might, in the end, shake loose for him the vision of the saint. Before and after this period of the love poems when Yeats for a while chose the role of magician, he was always in a state of vacillation—perhaps because the mask of magician had not won him Maud Gonne, but more because by now the struggle was too much a part of him to relinquish. He found it made him 'interesting' to be in a state of conflict, and did not really want to choose by now.

In a way, then, most of Yeats' life was spent in perfection of technique to express a vision that never came. Control of theory, words and music to express a belief never found: 'O masters of life ... I can never believe in anything.' The poignancy of vacillation, of the reversible choice, became more personal and haunting at two points in Yeats' work: first as an undertone of the love poems which represent the saint's repudiation, and again in the poems of vacillation near the end of Yeats' life, when he realizes, an old man near to death, that he has, for the sake of perfecting his work, neglected perfection of the life. This seems, with the above conversation with Monk Gibbons, a repudiation at the last of magic. Was Yeats, having discovered that magical esotericism was no substitute for sanctity, about to make a second choice? Or did the haunting poignance of vacillation still satisfy him and remain his final vision? We are left wondering.

Chapter Seven

SUMMARY

$\sim\sim\sim\sim\sim\sim\sim\sim\sim\sim\sim\sim\sim\sim\sim$

At the last, what is the evidence for Yeats' alleged likeness to his master, Blake? We found at the outset that while Blake firmly identified poetry with prophecy, Yeats, on the other hand, equally categorically equated it with magic. Prose evidence revealed that Yeats was quite aware of departure from his master in this, but that it seemed not such a departure as we might think, for he hoped that, like himself, Blake had passed through a phase of magical vision before reaching the vision of the saint.

Yeats believed that as a poet Blake had found himself torn between an alliance with magic which would help his poetry and an alliance with Christ which would lead him to Truth. For Yeats himself the statement of conflict appeared more than valid, and took the form of vacillation between the extremes of holiness and pagan enchantment. Strongly attracted to both extremes, he hoped that they could be balanced within the soul of a sensitive man, namely, the artist. Blake was the model for this. But since Yeats himself found it easier to work from the side of magical poetic theory, he liked also to think that this might have been Blake's procedure, as if Blake with magical symbols had 'beat upon the wall til Truth obeyed his call.' For if Blake had worked this way, there was every chance that Yeats too might find a symbol powerful enough to shake loose the truth, and 'that invisible gates would open as they opened for Blake.'

Yeats spent a lifetime mastering tools of writing and magical theory in preparation for a vision that never came. His awareness of the reversibility of his choice adds personal poignance to much of his writing. He is afraid that in choosing 'perfection of the work' he has lost his chance of finding ultimate truth. But he will play his chosen role royally to the end:

. . . . though heart might find relief
Did I become a Christian man and choose for my belief
What seems most welcome in the tomb—play a predestined part.

In effect, Yeats substituted vacillation for belief.

The difference, when all is said and done, between Yeats and his master Blake consists of the difference between the beyond-personality nature of belief, and the very personal quality of vacillation, which half fears to give up the poignancy of vacillation, yet longs for the serenity of belief. Such belief as Blake had, postulates inspiration from supernature in the prophetic art of the believer. For Yeats, conflict and the wavering choice imply hard labour in order to achieve art's unity. Blake's situation could be summed up in the diagram of a triangle—two sides of his natural self in conflict, yes, but an escape from warfare in the focus of both on the plane of supernature. Yeats has only the two sides, in endless conflict without escape from the plane of himself, and no outside authority to stop the battle.

This is much the same pattern as that which Soloviev would indicate to show that human love can be other than a dull warfare between the sexes only when it is focused in a third person, namely God—who gives authority and renewal as well as sanctification and a code.

The important likeness between Blake and Yeats is that both are concerned with the drama of the inner life. To an extent this is true of all poets not limiting their subject-matter to externalities of description and narrative. But it is particularly true of those poets who consciously sort out their actors into these two main camps dealt with throughout the ages by theologians more than poets. 'Poets and artists have begun again to carry the burdens that priests and theologians took from them angrily some few hundred years ago,' as Yeats said (*Essays*, p. 78). For Yeats was right in thinking that there are two conflicting selves in Blake, the artist half-drawn to the occult, and the mystic who fights against it. In fact, psychologically speaking, Blake, like the gnostics, stood with one foot on either side of a widening abyss: on one side, Christ and the angels of heaven; on the other side the gigantic evil figures and creeping things that can be given power by that in our nature which is bestial rather than angelic. Two things kept the chasm from widening too much: the fact that Blake was an artist, and that even the minimum of creative labour is both a distancing and a unifying activity. And, more important, the fact that although Blake was aware of the conflict, he was not aware that his choice was reversible.

It often happens that a poet says something verbally long before he sees it emotionally and means it consistently. This is true about Blake's early statement that there is no dualism of body and soul. In actual fact he then proceeds to go through a period of very real dualism that is ultimately that of the gnostics, and gnosticism has recently been underscored as the pathology of mysticism.[1] At the end he comes upon a solution complex enough to have satisfied the gnostics had they hit upon it, yet simple and moving enough to be expressed in the single word, incarnation. The coming together of Albion and Jerusalem in Christ is not only the union of the male and female principles which kept apart become false, but the transfiguration of all that Man is by the very fact that he allows himself to incarnate rather than to separate off his spiritual activities from his more earthy ones.

Jerusalem who is intuitive, physical, earthy, if trying to be self-sufficient, looks for salvation in a kind of overwhelming and murky earthiness and fails. Or, like Thel, she may flee in horror from her own passionate nature and find balm in the inverted and festering passion which is Puritanism and masks as religion, what Blake means by 'pale lecherous virginity'. Albion too can be falsely self-sufficient and then his rational spectre takes over and deceives him into thinking he is being 'spiritual'. He too fails and then sometimes looks for salvation in a form of rational materialism that has nothing to do with true passion. Only when he and Jerusalem discover that the spirit in one desires and needs the bodily passion of the other, and vice versa, is there chance of incarnation and resurrection of both spirit and the senses. In this light the senses are indeed the gateways to eternity. Mystical union is the contact of body with spirit, the *knowing* by the senses of that which the mind cannot contain.

Because Blake takes a stand even when he does not yet comprehend all its implications, the battle is finally won and the opposed extremes converge into the figure of the incarnated Christ. With Yeats the battle throughout remains a personal one and seesaws back and forth as he puts his strength first on one side and then on

[1] Victor White, O.P., *Notes on Gnosticism*, The Guild of Pastoral Psychology.

the other, the participants drawing further and further apart in discord. The figure of himself which is also the plane of battle is not detached or distant enough to focus the warring opposites. Nor do the puppet figures of Crazy Jane and the Fool help much, having no cosmic implication.

A partial likeness between Blake and Yeats exists in the fact that Blake does not always see nature with the mystic's eyes—when God is seen behind every natural thing—but often with the magician's interest in conflict and over-againstness, the war of heaven against recalcitrant nature and vice versa, and its history. Such a gnostic method of inquiry cannot be called 'wrong' but only pitifully complicated in its conjectures on the one hand, and inadequate and unfinished on the other. Blake leaves this method far behind, but there is a residue of confusion and contradiction. For instance, although at the outset Blake equates art and religion, he is nevertheless inconsistent in distinguishing the vision of the artist (Beulah) from that of the Saint (Eden). And Beulah has conflict within it while Eden has passed through conflict to unity. And it has been seen that although Blake claims that there is no dualism between spirit and nature and that the senses are the gateways to eternity, he still cries against nature as illusion, as the Mundane Shell.

Here is the main question stated in a different form. Can the personal conflict which is the artist's subject-matter go hand in hand with the essentially beyond conflict nature of belief and mysticism? For even though the conflict is continued in much more subtle terms, the mystic knows at least the terms of the solution. We must ask, at the last, whether Yeats' vacillation or Blake's conviction is more necessary for a great artist.

It is interesting to note in passing that the mystic, even in the darkest night of the soul, *knows* that everything is possible in Christ. The romantic artist and the modern existentialist makes it his business *not* to know this, and he lapses passively into despair and dividedness, always artistically effective. He mourns the just-missing quality of life and yet refuses to go on in faith lest the missing link be given him and he become boringly integrated. 'Hell is other people', he cries, and never takes stock of himself because it is both dull and discomforting to shed an old self and be fitted for a new one. He weighs great 'summas' of evidence for each side of a choice, yet never takes a stand in personal values. I think it was Tertullian who said that he believed just because it seemed ridiculous to do so. John of the Cross keeps saying that his greatest discoveries came just when the night seemed darkest:

> Y la mās fuerte conquista
> En escuro se hacía.

and,

> El corriente que nace de esta fuente,
> Bien se que estan capaz y omnipotente,
>   Aunque es de noche.

To return to the three questions arising out of this study:

The second problem is that of creative labour versus inspiration in art. Blake, who sets himself firmly on the side of belief, works always from vision towards expression, sacrificing if need be communicability for the sake of recording the truth as it was 'dictated' to him. This is the reverse of Yeats' procedure, and makes a great deal of difference to the amount of creative shaping employed for the sake of artistic unity which is not the same as mystical unity. The more surely Blake trod the mystical path, the less sure he became of his tools of expression, ceasing almost altogether to delight in landmarks of sensuous detail, scorning nature in practice as well as in theory, scorning, in fact, his audience. And finally, in the last prophetic books his work is mainly a kind of passionate belief yearning for expression, dazzling mystical truth for communication.

Thirdly, there is the question out of which these two queries grew and to which they are subsidiary. Speaking in Yeats' terminology, how much of the saint and how much of the magician are in the artist's psychological make-up, or, in wider terms, does the artist's vision depend more on tangible and intangible nature or upon supernature? Can these two opposed visions exist in the same mind? To put the question differently—is the symbolic artist focusing and expressing in his symbols and images energy that may have originated in the realm of spirit, or does this energy necessarily come out of the same subterranean depths from which spring myths and archetypes, folklore, magic, and primitive religions? The symbol that is written or painted or danced out—was its source divine or dæmonic or both, keeping in mind that the dæmonic itself is always ambiguous? This is also to ask whether images and symbols can play any legitimate part in the highest mystical vision. If we can answer this, the problems of poetic labour versus inspiration, and conflict versus unitive vision ought to fall into place.

Of course, this is to eliminate from the discussion entirely that kind of art which is merely representational, empiric and rational. As Bremond says:

'A purely rational or non-mystical philosophy of poetry—be it true or false, a question not here discussed—is an accident, as it were, a comet, in the universal history of æsthetic: Problem sine matre creatam. Such a philosophy contradicts, if not always the theoretic teaching, at all events the experience of poets of all times.'[1]

In discussing these three questions further, it is important to note at the outset that a symbolic artist's work can and is most often completed without any reference to the supernatural at all. Too often the intangibles of nature are confused with supernature. Dream states, the summing up in a concrete image of many elusive emotions, even brilliant intellectual feats, such things are too often called 'mystical'. In this manner we get the confusion and equation of magic and mysticism, which are, in fact, opposites. Many of the steps of an artist's work are invisible and mysterious to the public, and when he distances his art from the actual subject by, for instance, summing up in the image of the rose, traditional and personal emotions concerning love, it gives an effect both mysterious and seductive. It is as if the boundaries of inner and outer were dissolving and we saw strange depths and vistas. But nevertheless, this is not 'mysticism'. We are still in the realm of nature, and are merely watching a technique worthy of a skilful 'enchanter'.

What I must call for lack of a less hackneyed word, 'contemplation', is a natural property of the inner world in which the human mind selects and shapes impressions received from outer nature. It has nothing to do with mystical vision in itself. Yet it is a state of mind which can be open to supernatural events and can be made more so by a discipline or technique of contemplation. But even so, mystical vision is not at all a necessary conclusion.

Such an artist as Yeats would describe this step of contemplation as more like a trance in which the artist's imagination, with its feelers stretching towards both the divine and the dæmonic, dreams upon some natural object until it becomes a powerful symbol capable of evoking more dreams and a knowledge that goes deeper than the surface of things. The seeking of this kind of knowledge has its

---

[1] Henri Bremond, *Prayer and Poetry*, p. 7.

own discipline, but it is not one that leads in itself to supernatural truth.

Nevertheless, such an artist may be painfully conscious of the necessity to choose between the realm of nature with all its fascinating unplumbed depths, and the realm of the supernatural whose attainment seems to him only a possibility not a certainty. His main concern remains, however, like that of the enchanter, the visible and invisible forces of nature, its shifting boundaries of inner and outer, and in particular, that indefinable state which he calls 'beauty'. For him this state is precipitated by the perception of some natural object whose striking quality can survive the many transmutations necessary before it becomes a work of art seen by an audience. He may, although attracted to the beauty of what we call 'spiritual', fear it as too abstract, too tenuous to be translated into the terms of his earthy medium. Poetry particularly, with its capacity of words and music to create simultaneously a trance-like state and an intellectual battering at truth, has an innate resemblance to magic. I cannot quarrel with Yeats who thinks that in itself poetry is more akin to magic, and the unconscious depths magic taps, than to mysticism. It is, essentially, the attitude to images that distinguishes magic and poetry on the one side, from mysticism on the other.

But if, by the gift of grace, the poet is also capable of being a great mystic or saint, must he choose between these two roads? If he tries to keep both poetic magic and sanctity, is his art less beautiful, or the vision of truth dimmed? In other words, can the poet-magician and the saint live together in one sensitive mind, or must the one oust the other? This is, and remains, the central question.

Professor Étienne Gilson favours the theory that one ousts the other, saying that many of the great artists, had they not become artists, might have been saints:

'L'artiste digne de ce nom est si près de la religion dont il emploie souvent le langage, parce que, comme l'âme religieuse, la sienne se sent en présence d'un absolu, que sa transcendance autorise à exiger de ses serviteurs une soumission totale. Il faut prendre au pied de la lettre les passages du Canzoniere où Pétrarque dit que son amour pour Laure le conduit vers Dieu, et non moins littéralement ceux où il nous dit, dans le secretum, que son amour pour Laure l'en detourne, car le spectacle de la beauté sensible peut déchaîner dans l'âme de certains hommes une violent eémotion créatrice à partir de laquelle la création du saint et celle de l'œuvre d'art sont egalement probables. Saint François d'Assise a choisi la première, mais qui ne sent, en lisant Dante et Pétrarque, que la nostalgie de la sainteté sacrifiée à l'art n'a jamais cessé de les hanter, d'autant plus profondément même que leur triomphe sur l'art enfin conquis les laissait désarmés devant le regret de la sainteté perdue?'[1]

Professor Gilson goes on to include both Wagner and Baudelaire in this supposition:

'Baudelaire qui savait fort bien que la fleur du mal aurait pu être sa propre sainteté, si elle n'avait irrésistiblement tendu à fleurir en poèmes; Wagner, enfin, qui écrivait un jour à Mathilde Wesendonck: "Si ce don merveilleux, ce pouvoir si fort de la fantaisie créatrice n'existait pas en moi, je pourrais suivre la claire connaissance et l'élan de mon cœur: je deviendrais un saint." '[2]

Gilson comes to his own conclusion about the relationship of poet and saint:

'*La Divine Comédie, le Canzioniere, Les Fleurs du Mal, Parsifal,* ces grandes œuvres qu'habite la nostalgie d'une spiritualité vraiment religieuse racontent unes eule et même histoire. Peut-être, plus près encore de nous, en pourrait-on citer d'autres exemples. C'est l'éternelle histoire de ces suprêmes artistes qui ont échoué sur le problème que Beato Angelico seul a su résoudre: être un artiste saint, au lieu de n'être des artistes que pour se dispenser d'être des saints. Comment, nous qui ne sommes ni des saints ni des artistes, aurions-nous l'audace de les juger? Nous n'avons vraiment ici voulu que les mieux comprendre. Ce n'est certes pas diminuer l'art que de voir flotter autour de ses œuvres les plus hautes la pâle auréole d'une sainteté manquée. Peut-être même est-ce là qu'il faut chercher le secret de cette résonance quasi sacrée que certaines d'entre elles font entendre et qui nous les rendent si chères, car la poésie pure n'est pas la prière, mais elle jaillit assurément du même fond que le besoin de prier.'[3]

Of course Yeats is a much clearer example than most artists of the poet *aware* of these two tendencies at work in himself. Rilke is another, a poet who hated orthodox religion but was more religious and more concerned with sanctity than any other modern poet, and

[1] Etienne Gilson, *Pétrarque et sa Muse*, pp. 31–33.   [2] *Ibid.*   [3] *Ibid.*

who knew the emptiness and agony of the Dark Night of the soul more than any other poet. Speaking of the lives of the saints, he says, and it calls to mind some of Yeats' self-justifications for not pursuing the way of the saint:

'We no longer make such demands upon ourselves. We suspect that He is too difficult for us, that we must postpone Him in order slowly to perform the long labour that separates us from Him.'[1]

This attitude towards sanctity—a certain envy of the saint's vision combined with a feeling that sanctity is, after all, too arduous and abstract and perhaps, after all, not as interesting as a state of ego-centric sinfulness—is a typical modern one. It stems, I would say, from the romantic and ultimately gnostic dualism that we have been discussing which tends to keep heaven and earth as far apart as they were at the Fall. It leaves out of account altogether the redemptive power implicit in the Incarnation. One cannot help remembering seeing Rilke's words, that humanity has been given a power greater even than the possibility of individual sanctity: it was given to humanity in the form of Our Lady to 'contein heaven and erth in litel space. Res miranda.' Incarnation is within human scope: it can be born in a double sense: it lies at the intersection of the cross.

To return to the visual picture of the process of art. The mystic, working from revelation to expression, has no necessary dealings with the concrete subject-matter of the ordinary artist. There is no guarantee that he will turn from the dazzling supernatural vision which is his initial stimulus to mundane natural imagery, even for help in communication. Even if he is the type of mystic who can see God behind all natural things, his tendency is to try to express the feeling of God, not of nature. For him, the familiar landmarks of nature may serve as a framework to vision, but not necessarily. If he does not use them, he is incoherent to the uninitiated, to those who do not share his vision. If he does, he is always afraid of contaminating the truth he is expressing, and of himself being seduced by concrete 'beauty'.

During contemplation or the preparation for vision, the mystic is very apt to become conscious of nature and its images in all its murky depths as a snare. He is apt to reject it as an evil illusion, the work of Satan. On the other hand, he is conscious that he should see no duality between nature and spirit, that nature is a part of God's

[1] Rilke, *Requiem*, p. 152.

unity. The mystic may reject vacillation, but he cannot do away with paradox.

It seems that if mystical insight is a primal factor in the work of an artist, he is apt to lack concreteness, and vice versa. In Keats, Marvell, and Coleridge there is a strong emphasis on nature, although —differently in each case—there is a strain of something intangible which complicates the analysis (however, it is the intangibility of natural not of spiritual truth). Crashaw, George Herbert, and Emily Brontë tend to sin on the other side, but here too there are un-expected moments of solidity. And what of the greatest—Dante, Goethe, Hopkins, Shakespeare, Donne—each of whom somehow forces nature and spiritual vision to live together in amity, yet with wit, anger, or worldly robustness depreciates his own success? These are the most difficult, the great ones, when the balance is tautest and most difficult to recognize.

And what of that great poet St. John of the Cross, who used his vivid poems, written from intense mystical experience, as the basis for much drier, much more purgative treatises on the mystical way?

Painters have no abstract words as have poets by which they can escape representation and indicate the 'spirit'. It is therefore more significant perhaps to watch the efforts of 'mystical' painters to escape from nature. El Greco, gothic artists such as the one who carved the St. Peter at Boissac, and the Byzantine stylists, today Roualt (rather than more vapid abstractionists)—these artists distort nature almost to the point of transformation to get the desired effect of something very spiritual, of mystical significance. And yet their basis is, and remains, recognizable nature. This, in a way, is the point, nature transformed by the impact of spirit, spirit incarnate instead of a black and white choice or a weak compromise. How-ever, there is always a great fear in the mind of the painter who is concerned with the expression of spiritual truths. He is fascinated by yet fears the seduction, the enchantment of unredeemed nature, with its secret pleasures and lurking demons. This perhaps accounts for the almost repellent quality some people find in the distortions of El Greco or Blake or Roualt. There is a kind of double attraction and repulsion in the mind of the artist which is reflected in that of the beholder, and this may produce effects uncomfortable to look at, not at all like the ordinary comfortable ideas of heaven or of earth!

Some artists, such as Brueghel and Bosch and gothic sculptors, recognized this as a psychological fact, and externalized it: they painted in small diabolic or angelic figures to signify that divine and dæmonic implications accompany every significant act. Alone Blessed Angelico—significantly a brother of the Dominican Order, that order founded in an effort to overcome the Albigensian heresy of dualism between spirit and matter—the only artist who can be said to be also a saint, oddly enough has no sense of strain or repulsion from images and nature in his work. The angels for which he is famous, are happy angels, heralds of the Incarnation, equally at home in heaven or on earth, not, like Plotinus, ashamed that the soul is in body. And that Fra Angelico sometimes conceived of angels taking on earthly images or bodies is certain, for one of his angels at least casts a shadow!

It would almost seem that Yeats is right. The artist, most sensitive of men, is for ever expressing the paradox of all men who have been given the terrible gift of freedom. To partake of two worlds, to vacillate between them and express the poignancy of vacillation, this would seem to be his job. Neither to choose the realm of beast nor that of angel, but to stand between both, unless his choice can bring him the sublime vision of Angelico or the evil flowering of Baudelaire. Blake the artist ended when Blake the mystic began, for the mystic tries to hold in tension more paradox than language can bear: images shatter beneath the weight.

There is, finally, the corollary problem of whether art is primarily inspiration or technique. If we think of it as inspiration, we must accept the possibility of its being incomprehensible and unshaped, and must allow that the artist is not personally responsible for any dangerous ideas his art may embody. If, on the other hand, art is the rational shaping of nature's raw material into the sectional unity of a work of art, no matter how far the representation departs from the original, it is a copy and so must communicate its meaning to an audience. It is subject to the same yard-stick as nature itself is.

These are the same alternatives which troubled the Greeks, and no phrasing of them has been finer. Plato in the *Phaedrus* states definitely that inspired art is infinitely superior to the art of rule and measure which is, after all, but a copy of a copy.

'There is also a third kind of madness, which is a possession of the Muses; this enters into a delicate and virgin soul, and there inspiring frenzy, awakens lyric and all other numbers; with these adorning the myriad actions of ancient heroes for the instruction of posterity.

But he who, not being inspired and having no touch of madness in his soul, comes to the door and thinks he will get into the temple by the help of art—he, I say, and his poetry are not admitted; the sane man is nowhere at all when he enters into rivalry with the madman.'[1]

Here follows the description of the soul as a charioteer controlling two winged horses, one evil, one good. In this myth lies the inner conflict of Plato himself. For at heart he is the inspired poet, yet he must reject poetry and inspiration because intellectually he advocates the 'Greek heresy' which makes reason the only true approach to the higher world. Aristotle goes even further in this, believing that by using his mind to the full, man can find ultimate truth. And in modern times Descartes restated the view that clear and distinct ideas are the only part of the personal vision that can lead to truth.

But Plato, whose own instincts made the problem much less cut and dried than for Aristotle and Descartes, finds he must give all honour to the inspired poets, yet must cast them out of his ideal city as disturbing to law and order, stirrers up of emotion and uncontrollable depths. This is a very moving passage:

'And therefore when any of these clever multiform gentlemen, who can imitate anything, comes to our State, and proposes to exhibit himself and his poetry, we will fall down and worship him as a sweet and holy and wonderful being; but we must also inform him that there is no place for such as he in our State—the law will not allow them. And so when we have anointed him with myrrh, and set a garland of wool upon his head, we shall send him away to another city. For we mean to employ for our soul's health the rougher and severer poet and story-teller, who will imitate the style of the virtuous only, and will follow those models which we prescribed at first when we began to speak of the education of our soldiers.

'That', he said, 'we certainly will do if we have the power.'[2]

'If we have the power'! How simply and ironically Plato states his problem. In the dialogue called *Ion*, Socrates speaks to the rhapsode, again reiterating that art is not creative labour, but inspiration, that even the interpretation of art is inspired:

'This gift which you have of speaking excellently about Homer is not an art, but, as I was just saying, an inspiration; there is a

[1] Plato, *Phaedrus*, 245a.   [2] Plato, *Republic*, III, 398a.

divinity moving you, like that in the stone which Euripides calls a magnet, but which is commonly known as the stone of Heraclea. For that stone not only attracts iron rings but also imparts to them a similar power of attracting other rings; and sometimes you may see a number of pieces of iron and rings suspended from one another so as to form quite a long chain: and all of them derive their power of suspension from the original stone. Now this is like the Muse, who first gives to men inspiration herself; and from these inspired persons a chain of other persons is suspended, who take the inspiration from them. For all good poets, epic as well as lyric, compose their beautiful poems not as works of art, but because they are inspired and possessed ... for the poet is a light and winged and holy thing, and there is no invention in him until he has been inspired and is out of his senses ... for not by art does the poet sing, but by power divine. Had he learned by rules of art, he would have known how to speak not of one theme only, but of all; and therefore God takes away the mind of poets, and uses them as his ministers, as he also uses diviners and holy prophets, in order that we who hear them may know that they speak not of themselves who utter these priceless words in a state of unconsciousness, but that God is the speaker, and that through them he is conversing with us.'[1]

This is Blake's view, with one difference, namely that the inspired artist can be the salvation of society rather than a disturbance. But Blake was not a slave, as were the Greeks, to the tyrant Urizen, and he overcame the dualism that Plotinus, ashamed that his soul was in body, could never quite do. As Henri Bremond puts it:

'That is the problem of poetry (which) made Socrates and Plato so unhappy. They adored the poets and feared in doing so to sin against the light of reason. That divine element which they certainly did not hesitate to recognize, embarrassed them as much as it enchanted them.'[2]

Bremond himself thinks that art and mystic inspiration come from the same source, and are, on different levels, the same thing, the same movement towards the interior. And yet, this does not explain the persistent dualism and complexity of such a poet as Yeats who

[1] Plato, *Ion*, 532.   [2] Bremond, *Prayer and Poetry*, p. 8.

was perfectly willing and eager to be inspired, was not a slave to reason, and yet insisted above all on poetic technique.

> *A line will take us hours maybe;*
> *Yet if it does not seem a moment's thought*
> *Our stitching and unstitching has been naught.*
> *Better go down upon your marrow-bones*
> *And scrub a kitchen pavement, or break stones*
> *Like an old pauper, in all kinds of weather;*
> *For to articulate sweet sounds together*
> *Is to work harder than all these, and yet*
> *Be thought an idler by the noisy set*
> *Of bankers, schoolmasters, and clergymen*
> *The martyrs call the world.*

For Yeats, inspired saint and labouring poet, still remained at opposite poles, although he would have given anything to know how someone like John of the Cross or St. Bernard reconciled the two:

'The profound hesitation of his early years—whether to become a man of letters or to become a saint? Bernard found ways to remain a man of letters and become a saint into the bargain.'[1]

[1] Gilson, *The Mystical Theology of St. Bernard*, p. 7.

Chapter Eight

DISCUSSION: THE POET, THE LOVER, AND THE SAINT

B UT is vacillation and dualism the final answer? Must we end with the uneasy suspicion that the poet and saint would do better each to stick to his own trade instead of both longing for and fighting against the vision of the other? Could a less specific and perhaps wildly irrelevant discussion of related problems perhaps clarify the link between poetry and mysticism that everyone feels exists but cannot define? We have seen that poetry and sanctity *per se* can be completely antithetical, but is it not possible that at some stage of each they coincide, and that their apparent irreconcilability is to state in terms of division what should be whole?

The factor of love, eros, and agape, seems to me to have important bearing on this problem. It was noted in passing how important a part their respective theories of love play in the writing of both Blake and Yeats. And it is interesting to notice that the poets Gilson mentions who might have been saints, are also thought of as great lovers.

Obviously the saints and mystics are great lovers in quite a different sense from the poets. But as de Rougemont points out in his very interesting book, *Passion and Society*, the imagery and terms of the two kinds of love have been reversed and intermingled so much that they are barely distinguishable—without, paradoxically, lessening the conflict between their separate goals. Both St. Francis and St. Teresa speak of their great mystical love in the terms made fashionable in the courts of love by the troubadours. And we recall the monastic parallel of the Knights of St. Mary.

Eros, in its widest sense, is common to both saint and poet. Is this common ground of love a possible basis for discussing the relation between the two? Or is the theme of love—so obviously split itself

202

into eros and agape, profane and sacred love—but one more instance of the dualism that seems to permeate Western culture? Stated not only in terms of the poet and the saint, but in terms of denial of the world over against encounter with the world, this dichotomy is the fundamental problem—I would say heresy—of Western culture.

The perplexity and suffering of man because of his own dual nature is the essence of romanticism, and as such, romanticism has existed always in Western civilization. Man as the intersection of two worlds suffers because he partakes of the nature of animals, and of God. He is both creature and creator. Thinking men in every age have tried to find some way out of the difficulty, almost always trying to shut off half the truth and simplify matters to an either-or. Instead of the cross, the intersection of aspiration and necessity, the spirit and flesh, one would much prefer to be either all spirit or all determined creature. There are religions that deny the creature and would have us all spirit, while those who speak the jargon of the world would do away with spirit and pronounce us all creature, albeit highly complex creature. All heresy is essentially the exaltation of one side of the Incarnation at the expense of the other.

We who have not yet taken in the fact of the Incarnation emphasize the cross as the central fact of Christianity. We confuse our own suffering and wish for death with Christ's death on the cross. This is to ignore Incarnation. This is the problem of Western man: resurrection is not yet possible, and the cross exists for us, without the glory of Incarnation. The romantic, instead of seeking redeemed nature, the organized innocence which lies beyond Incarnation and the cross, looks back with nostalgia at the original vision of innocence, the Garden of Eden, which can never return again. For Adam and Eve, innocence was ignorance. But for sophisticated man, innocence is only found through the simplification of complexity, generally with great pain, if it is the right kind of simplification.[1]

All this, of course, is no more than facing the fact, or tragedy if you will, of free will. At the Fall man was given this ironic gift, when he distinguished good from evil and inherited the earth. To oversimplify, Eastern man prefers on the whole to ignore free will, choosing not to choose, ignoring freedom in order to find tranquillity. The West, and that fraction of the East which migrated in the form of Manichæanism, is all too troubled by choice. It does not know how to solve the dilemma of two plausible alternatives, except

[1] See Appendix.

by alternately denying one in favour of the other. Many, especially the poets who reflect our common predicament most sensitively, come to a kind of glorification of suffering and vacillation for their own sake. Or rather, they provide a picturesque road to the self-awareness of an interesting self. Unfortunately, it is a dead end. It is Orpheus in his journey, pulled between love of death and love of the world, wistfully uncertain:

> *A God can do it. But can man expect*
> *To penetrate the narrow lyre and follow?*
> *His sense is discord. Temples for Apollo*
> *Are not found where two heart-ways intersect.*[1]

Only the Christian mystics, choosing to give the choice back to God, have found a way out. And this way is repugnant to the poets, and to the great mass of humanity, whose experience they sensitively reflect.

There are moments in history as well as in an individual life when an offer is made of a possible choice beyond vacillation. The saint, the poet, and the lover have each claimed at one time or another to be the mouthpiece for this choice.

The twelfth century, with its flowering of poets who were also troubadours of the courts of love, is a particularly interesting time, for it was also an age of great mystics. We see the problem at its most intense and most simple at this time: the concrete, not the theoretical, conflict of eros and agape.

'That all European poetry has come out of the provençal poetry written in the twelfth century by the troubadours of Languedoc is now accepted on every side. This poetry magnified unhappy love.'[2]

Rambaut of Orange writes: 'I interweave words rare, dark, and colourful, pensively pensive,'[3] and de Rougemont comments:

'Love and death, a fatal love—in these phrases is summed up, if not the whole of poetry, at least whatever is popular, whatever is universally moving in European literature, alike as regards the oldest legends and the sweetest songs. Happy love has no history. Romance only comes into existence where love is fatal, frowned upon and doomed by life itself. What stirs lyrical poets to their finest flights is neither the delight of the senses nor the fruitful contentment of the

---

[1] Rilke, *Sonnets to Orpheus*, p. 39.
[2] de Rougemont, *Passion and Society*, p. 84.   [3] *Ibid.*, p. 109.

settled couples; not of the satisfaction of love, but its *passion*. And passion means suffering. There we have the fundamental fact.'[1]

Gilson, in his book on St. Bernard, draws the initial distinction between the eros of the poets and the agape of the saint:

'What is true of animal forms is also true of ideas: you cannot pass indifferently from any one of them to any other. Can we pass from the *raptus* of the mystic to the *ravissements* of the poet, or from the *excessus mentis* of the mystic to the ecstasies of courtly love? This is the whole question . . . there lies the ambiguity; are the poet's rapture or ecstasy really mystical states, or did they not rather cease to be when they passed from mysticism into poetry? Let us not call that a subtlety of merely theological interest.'[2]

This seems to me to put the question in its true light instead of in that flattering shadow where one can say that poetry and mysticism, both being spiritual activities, must have something in common. Are they so alike that poetry can become mysticism? This is the question which concerned Yeats so profoundly, and which Gilson phrases clearly. Can the eros of the poet become agape without losing its own poignancy? Can the poet *dare* to seek the wholeness and grace of surrender to God?

Father D'Arcy in *The Mind and Heart of Love* sums up de Rougemont's lengthy distinction between the poet's romantic passion and the Christian agape:

'In this book de Rougemont dares what Lewis refrains from doing: he tries to explain why the love of the romantics is so different from that of Christian love;—and here the surprise comes— the reason given is that romantic love springs from an unholy and forbidden source, the strange wild Eros, the necromancing and un-baptized witch, who is an implacable foe of Christianity and ever seeks to cast her spells over the true lover. These are the two loves, so de Rougemont holds, which fight for man's soul, Eros and agape, and each has its own definite characteristics which enable us to recognize it. Agape is there for all to see in the Christian teaching; Eros, on the other hand, in a Christian world has to conceal itself and goes disguised under symbols.'[3]

---

[1] de Rougemont, *Passion and Society*, p. 109.
[2] Gilson, *The Mystical Theology of St. Bernard*, p. 189.
[3] D'Arcy, *The Mind and Heart of Love*, p. 28.

The question of these two kinds of love was very much in the air in the twelfth century, for over against the courts of love and the Kathars was St. Bernard writing his mystical theology, Anselm, William of Thierry, and a strong Benedictine and Cistercian strain of mysticism. Abelard, of course, was the colourful figure somewhere in between all this.

'The Eros of cortezia claimed to release men from the life of matter by the way of death; and Christian agape aims at sanctifying life itself.'[1]

It is quite obvious that eros, the magical unbaptized witch of a love followed by the poets, is divided by a long gulf from the mystical love of a St. Bernard. This is not to say that I consider eros unredeemable as de Rougemont tends to think and Nygren certainly does, which is a Kathar conclusion in itself. Eros is saved, *not* by postulating a human unattainable, but through Incarnation. This is my point, but to indicate it more fully, it is necessary to examine further the ambiguous concept of eros, that makes it so attractive to the dualistic romantic. What is significant is the division within eros itself, the romantic schizophrenia which is the hallmark of all such love. Eros is not only divided off from agape, but is also ambiguous in itself. It is a name that covers both erotic love, *and* the unfulfilled yearning for a lover who is out of reach. Carnal love alone denies the spiritual side of incarnation, while a preference for the unattainable denies that perfection can become flesh.

The pattern of all gnostic heresy is such division within a main dualism. It was no new thing to the Greeks, especially to the neo-Platonists: Numenius' dividing of God into two beings, the lower of which (interestingly, the Creator) is himself divided.

'What was there in the very nature of things that condemned nature?' asks Santayana. 'Plato, Plotinus, and the secret force of Christianity drew all their poignance from that question.'[2]

It is such a romantic dualism which rose to the surface during the Middle Ages in Katharism, the dualistic religion which was a background to, and was somehow allied with, the concepts of courtly love. Even Christian mysticism was not left untouched by it. The Kathars or Albigenses, in turn, were descended from the Manichees, a Persian import which took hold of Western thought. It has been suggested

[1] de Rougemont, *Passion and Society*, p. 201.   [2] Santayana, *The Last Puritan*.

that there may even be a line connecting such dualistic religions with the Druid worship of the Celts. It is certainly in line with gnosticism. Katharism was, in short, an upsurgence of that underground dualism which has always existed in Western culture, and has only recently come permanently into the open under the name of romanticism.

The strength of such dualistic belief in Western culture is emphasized by the fact that in the midst of this great age of Christianity, it not only existed in the Kathar religion, but it also allowed the Kathars to be strong enough to support the Albigensian Pope who had headquarters in Yugoslavia. It was for a time a rival religion to Rome, and had its secular parallel. When in the thirteenth century Rome formed a crusade to destroy the Kathars, along with the heresy the troubadour culture of Provence was driven underground. But neither were, as I have suggested, killed.

It is now a generally accepted fact that Katharism was reflected in the theory of courtly love. This religion preached the typical Manichæan doctrine that matter is inherently evil, and that, therefore, soul must dissociate itself from bodily matter. Although in many ways a highly spiritual belief—that of fallen angels striving to soar out of the corporeal prison house—double conclusions are implied in the moral sphere. The Kathars drew both, and went to extremes of asceticism and libertinism because of their belief in the separate goals of body and soul. Like most heresies, Katharism and its secular parallel, courtly love, is not merely a sect that has broken off from the main body of orthodoxy, but a rival belief that is divided in itself—a split within a split, as it were.

The point of bringing up Katharism and the troubadour culture to illustrate the division of the poet's eros and the saint's agape is to emphasize the permeation upon all levels of even a highly Christian age, of the heretical 'romantic' dualism.

Romanticism is still the basis of Western culture, which, without realizing it, has plunged further into the abyss. The problem of the soul that will not incarnate, the body which refuses transformation, exists more than ever today. We no longer have the powerful juxtaposition of holiness and passion which makes the writings of the Middle Ages so moving, for we have forgotten the meaning of incarnation. Instead we make the choice either on the side of the passions, adopting for our credo all that psychology has unearthed, or else we choose the Church and a kind of thin Puritanism which has become the weak protest of uncertain spirit. Rarely do we find the two together these days. Who now could write like that exquisite ancestor of the Provençal poets, Petronius Arbiter?

> Qualis nox fuit, di deaeque,
> quam mollis torus. haesimus calentes
> et transfudimus hinc et hinc laebellis
> errantes animas. valete, curae
> mortales.[1]

I would go so far as to say that the great poetry of the Middle Ages, in fact, most of its art, depended like its religion, on this very powerful juxtaposition of holiness and passion: the rushing together of spirit and flesh as in the Incarnation. With the coming of the troubadours in whom poet and lover are one, however, romantic poetry begins and the powerful tension of body and soul snaps, and they tend to draw wider and wider apart. The poet, mourning a love which is so spiritual that to make it actual is to kill it, finds no paradox in living a libertine life on the level of the actual. He scorns the bonds of marriage, yet sings of a fair unattainable lady who is often unattainable just because she is married. His undying spiritual devotion to her lasts only as long as she says, 'No'. Were she to step from her pedestal and murmur, 'Yes', the rules of the game would be broken and the troubadour probably retire in sulky disgust. It seems to me that always in this kind of love—the worshipping from afar of an ideal woman or man—there is a wish for an intercessor; the beloved is a figure in whom is focused divine power to heal the breach between heaven and earth and the split in the lover's soul. Certainly it is in Dante's Beatrice, Petrarch's Laura, Yeats' Maud Gonne—'I thought her supernatural'. And yet, because possession is not really wanted, the split grows wider. Indeed, were possession possible through the fall of a human ideal who is falsely postulated unattainable, it would be a diabolic interpretation of incarnation. The troubadour takes hedonistic delight in the situation. He prefers the perpetual tension of unfulfilled desire. This ambiguous game of love which is eros has been handed down through the centuries by the poets. It is interesting to note the convention that unreciprocated love is true love exists not only in modern poets such as Yeats and Rilke, but in its decadent form in popular torch songs. 'Look how interesting I am,' cried the poet in the twelfth century, torn between desire and the wish to keep the ideal inviolate. And the cry echoes

[1] Helen Waddell, *Medieval Latin Lyrics*, p. 21.

down the ages, flung from Dante to Petrarch and down to the romantic of all ages. 'We were the last Romantics,' shouted Yeats, proud of it. The hardest thing in the world is to learn how to live without the romantic ideal in order to become worthy of the actual. We who by inclination and tradition prefer this romantic love, this cruel and perverse eros, seem not to care that all eros desires is suffering and conflict. It makes too good reading for a culture very much aware of the conflicts of day and night, passion and otherworldliness, sexual attraction and desire for the untouched. 'The troubadours who feared nothing more than to be granted what they asked!'[1] We fear that in going beyond such suffering and conflict we would become less interesting.

I suggest that the heresy of romantic dualism, so native is it to the Western mind, has become permanently fixed in the very mystical core of Christianity. It exists not only in the poet and the lover, but also in the saint. I would also submit that this dualism is unavoidable if the Western mind is to comprehend fully the meaning of Christianity. The only way out of it is through it. In the danger itself lies the rescuing power as romantic Hölderlin insisted, and Father Victor White quotes in relating gnosticism to the critical stage of analysis. Charles Williams says:

'Of all the heresies it is one of the few most generally and most subtly nourished by our common natures. There is in it always a renewed emotional energy . . . It is due to Manichæanism that there has grown up in Christiandom—in spite of the myth of the Fall in Genesis—the vague suggestion that the body has somehow fallen farther than the soul. It was certainly nourished within the Church by the desert ascetics—especially in their ingenuous repudiation of sex. This is probably the one thing generally known about them—except for the pillar of St. Simon Stylites—and the contempt and hatred they too rashly expressed for it has been heartily reciprocated against them by a later world. It was no more than a part of their general passion for singleness of soul, even when that singleness tended to become a singularity,'[2]

and

'It is an accepted fact that there have, on the whole, been two chief ways of approach to God defined in Christian thought. One, which is most familiar in the records of sanctity, has been known

---

[1] Rilke, *The Notebook of Malte Laurids Brigge*, p. 238.
[2] Charles Williams, *The Descent of the Dove*, pp. 55–56.

as the Way of Rejection. It consists, generally speaking, in the renunciation of all images except the final one of God himself, and
even—sometimes but not always—of the exclusion of that only
Image of all human sense. The great teacher of that Way was
Dionysius the Areopagite. . . . The tangle of affirmation and rejection which is in each of us has to be drawn into some kind of pattern,
and has so been drawn by all men who have ever lived. The records
of Christian sanctity have on the whole stressed the rejection.'[1]

I would go further than Charles Williams, and say that, in postulating two diametrically opposed mystical Ways that exclude one
another, man has carried his personal sense of dualism into the midst
of Christian doctrine. The way out of it is through it, but the trick
is to recognize that one must get out of it! True to an essentially
romantic outlook, he has divided out of his despair what should be
one long, difficult Way into a choice of two possible Ways, each
of which in fact is half a truth. The popular conception of all holiness as extreme asceticism points once more to the strength of underground dualism. Western man cannot get it into his head that the
Word really *did* become flesh. It seems as if each individual must go
through much the same conflict that was valid before the coming
of Christ to reach the conclusion of incarnation, which in turn
implies all unity.

This apparently simple truth is arrived at fully only by the most
persevering of Christians—the mystics and the saints who have
climbed a ladder in which one dualism shifts into a second, and
Eros must be crucified and resurrected. The mystics go *through*
dualism, but the commentators of mysticism rarely see this and
postulate as two separate Ways what the mystic comes to see as one
long and very difficult Way.

This is why St. Bernard had to pass through *four* stages of love
to reach the point where eros and agape walked side by side. It is
why St. Francis had to renounce the world in order to give all he
possessed back to the world transfigured. Because of this, Blake had
four stages of vision, two of which were full of conflict and an implied dualism where God seemed a cruel God, and nature itself evil.
And John of the Cross, the ascetic, warns against the image-loving
nature of his friend St. Teresa, yet remained incorrigibly a poet in
his expression of ultimate love.

[1] C. Williams, *The Figure of Beatrice*, pp. 8, 10.

The first dualism, the poet's dilemma, is a common enough one. Many sensitive people find their physical desires at war with their spiritual beliefs. It is the age-old poetic conflict of body and soul. It is what the troubadours sang. It may manifest itself as romantic schizophrenia in its most Byronic form, or it may be the few doubts remaining in the mind of a poet like Hopkins, who had chosen priesthood yet never got to the second 'mystical' dualism. As in Yeats' case, the choice may never be made at all, and the dualism almost extolled, or we may find a choice such as D. H. Lawrence made, a looking for salvation in the dreaming of the blood, which has to take the place of the supernatural. It is odd how many intellectual men, mistaking their talented intellects for true spirituality, and not finding an answer therein, give up the idea of religion altogether and turn to a kind of 'mystical' materialism.

As I have said, this first dilemma is a frequent one, and although it makes good subject-matter for poetry, it has nothing to do with mysticism. It is only when a choice is truly made on the side of the spirit that there is a possible way out of this reversibility. But the way out is by entering into a second dualism. When one begins to talk about this second dualism which is on the level of mystical experience, one is necessarily presumptuous and groping in the dark since it is a level of experience never vouchsafed to the commentator of mysticism, else he would no longer comment but record! Nevertheless, it is important to try to understand a little better the pattern of what the mystic is trying to express in language too narrow to contain truth. The following interpretations are in no wise meant to have a dogmatic tone.

The figure of Christ stands between these two dualisms, a focus point for the moment. But the natural reaction of one who has chosen to be on the side of Christ and the spirit, is a great shame and sorrow for the worldly life he has hitherto led. He therefore tends to renounce the world as evil, and we get the ascetic outlook. Over and over again the mistake has been made by critics of regarding such asceticism—invaluable when seen in its true light as a purgative phase—as a Way in itself that will lead directly to God, and as somehow having sole copyright to agape, the Christian love or attitude. All sensual images are 'trodden down under the cloud of forgetting' and 'nothing lives in the working mind but a naked intent stretching to God.'[1] The body is scorned as evil, and images and the distorting

[1] *The Cloud of Unknowing*, p. 13.

imagination as inevitable roads to sin. This, as a phase, is apt to correspond to the Dark Night of the Soul, during which the arid soul's extreme sensitivity to the possibility of evil in itself makes it feel unworthy of God's love. Such reasoning is dangerous if it marks more than a very brief phase, since it tends to lead to a permanent dualism, not unlike that of the Kathars, and belittles the meaning of both the Incarnation and the Resurrection—that is, the redemption of eros and images in general.

To consider the self-imposed discipline of the ascetic way a sufficient pulley to heaven is to be a victim of spiritual pride. Asceticism is a tricky business, lending itself to states of arrogant intolerance as well as to complete self-abnegation. Too rarely is true humility achieved, a sense of hopefulness while waiting for divine Grace. Both guilt and humility dissolve into wonder at the end. For it is by Grace, and Grace alone, that the opposite side of this second 'dualism' shifts into its proper place, but if it comes this way it achieves unity rather than conflict. This second side is the vision of affirmation which, like asceticism, is only dangerous and at war with the way of denial when considered a whole truth too easily. Affirmation *is* the final goal of mysticism, but if found through an easy process without an element of withdrawal and asceticism, it is almost meaningless. It has need of a rigorous discipline. It is not to be confused with the mild liking of the world and way-of-least-resistance religion which passes for affirmation among Christians too weak to even consider a period of asceticism. It is not crude eros, but eros transformed.

To make a long story short, only when the two Ways—that of denial and that of affirmation—are set up as rival roads to God are they in conflict, a 'dualism'. Unfortunately, they generally are seen this way by critics. In the life of the true mystic they follow one after the other, although while he is passing through one stage it seems almost a whole Way. Just as he chooses the way of the soul instead of the way of the flesh in the first dilemma, again the mystic will experience a period of asceticism but in the end be shown how to affirm all that is holy. Although the process looks, in fact, like a kind of double dualism, it is actually more like a series of encounters and withdrawals only for the sake of re-encounter.

All mystics who have written of their mystical experience must inevitably have passed through this second dilemma where the ascetic who has renounced the world realizes that union with God implies the affirmation of the world transfigured. Otherwise they could not have overcome their fear of imagination enough to express their vision in communicable and, for the most part, highly imaginative terms. Nor would they have bothered to turn back towards an evil world to communicate a message of hope that would not be understood, but rather pressed on towards an image-less and abstract union. The fact that all the saints and mystics *do* bring themselves to do these very things seems, once more, to show that imageless asceticism is not a 'Way' in itself, but only part of a single Way which must end in affirmation, else leave within the core of Christianity a dualism as pernicious as that persecuted in Katharism.

Obviously, asceticism is the crux of the matter, involving as it does the denial of imagination, of human love or eros, and of the beauty and value of nature. Critical theology in the West is to blame for the misinterpretation, insisting as it does that asceticism is *one* of *two* possible Ways, equally effective, that are open to union with God. And because of the paradox involved, it explains, rather naïvely, that the difference in the two ways is to allow for tempera-mental differences in mystics. That is, those whose temperamental preference is for corporeal images (on the level of the psyche) will walk the way of affirmation, while those who have the higher capacity for abstraction will plunge into asceticism and denial. The realm of the psyche is accounted lower because it lets in imagination, and what is more, images of human love which get confused with union to God. As a modern novelist remarked, if Christ had made a single joke about sex the whole course of Western culture would have been changed, and the ascetics not done their ugly work. Bold as this sounds, it holds true for corporeal images in general.[1]

Of these two supposed Ways, the popular mind sees only the spectacular one, asceticism. In this manner mysticism has become synonymous with asceticism. The poet, feeling that sometimes his work touches upon the same source that the mystic has tapped, must nevertheless, due to popular misconception, cry out against what seems an arid way of looking for mystery, a way that seems to deny the very substance of his own vision.

If asceticism is the crux of the matter, its key point is the attitude to images, including sexual images. In fact, the attitude to images is the key point in almost any version of the basic dualism between spirit and matter that one could discuss. It is this above all that

[1] See Appendix.

213

distinguishes the poet-magician who uses and wields—almost bows down to—images to induce a powerful state of enchantment, from the mystic who distrusts images with all his heart until they have been proven to be of divine origin—begging, as St. Teresa did of her spiritual directors, to be reassured that they were not diabolic and as such a quick non-stop slipping sliding road to hell from the very gates of heaven. For the poet's images used magically are nearly always dæmonic, and as such are ambiguous: the same kind of images crowd the psyche on the lowest rung of the mystical ladder. How to distinguish such personal and ambiguous symbols that tap the source of all archetypal Selfhood—and as such can be either dangerous or good according to the attitude of the imaginer—from a vision that comes not from the self but from God? There is perhaps some ultimate point of vision where these two insights might fuse, but the mystic knows that it is dangerous to assume this at the start.

I have discussed at length how the romantic poet's attitude to the image of sexual desire is ambiguous—both full of carnal desire and paradoxically a hymn to the inviolate ideal. This ambiguity is true of most poetic images in some way and degree, and such ambiguity is what the mystic is aware of and on guard against. He realizes that with luck such an image—as in Dante's Beatrice—may lead the poet nearer to spiritual truths than he might otherwise have gone, but he realizes also that this is a very rare occurrence. Imagination remains, paradoxically, both the vehicle of all creativity, and the root source of all evil.

It is interesting to note that many ecclesiastical controversies such as the iconoclast episode, and, indeed, the Reformation itself, were largely centred around the attitude to images. The Protestants felt that the Church of Rome's attitude to images was magical and superstitious, and chose for its own partial truth that distorted interpretation of asceticism which is puritanism.

This is not at all to say that asceticism as a stage has not a very real and positive function. As a period of preparation, of gathering force through restraint, even as an oversimplified breathing space from the chaos of the world—it is invaluable. It is negative to call it no more than a stepping-stone or a half-truth. It is a strengthening stage which must be seen by the soul for its duration as the whole truth, lest it fall back via memory or fear or nostalgic imagination into the abyss of romantic dualism. The ascetic feels himself lifted out of the abyss of himself as if by a great hand. And on the brink of the chasm he can rest and learn of redirection, and turn inwards to the still centre through which he will go beyond himself. Had he fled, shaking and disintegrated, from the abyss to cling to God, without this time of strenuous rest, he would have been worthy of help, but not of truth. To listen to truth he must come to God in the dignity of the whole individual, serenely. Asceticism, in its positive sense as the next to last stage of a long and difficult way, is a withdrawal for the sake of encounter, a letting go of the threads of events in order to be redirected, a turning inwards in order to see the outside world with new eyes. It has a lesson to teach to any significant relationship in secular life, with its self-renewing rhythm of encounter and withdrawal for the sake of further engagement. In particular for modern generations who have plunged along with the whole of Western culture into the abyss of romanticism, a kind of secular asceticism may help in the problem of how to live without the romantic ideal while learning to become worthy of the actual.

When, in the life of the mystic, the danger that the soul may fall back into the initial dichotomy has passed, the soul may cautiously and with all its love directed heavenwards, look once more at corporeal images. It will see with detachment, quietly, without desire: it will see with new eyes. And when final union with God is granted, the mystic finds all nature transfigured with glory. He is no longer at war with imagination and images. But this seems so ridiculously obvious to him that he forgets to mention this armistice and thereby confuses his commentators. Instead, he acts upon it, and records his mystical experience in symbolic form as imaginative as the finest poem. He speaks of it as the climbing of a ladder, or the following of a narrow path, or traversing the rooms of a castle in an image as complexly beautiful as that of St. Teresa, inspired, one cannot help thinking, by such a view as El Greco had of her own city, Toledo, set like a fortressed castle on the hillside:

'There the external thing itself—tower, mountain, bridge— already possessed the stupendous, unsurpassable intensity of those inner equivalents by means of which it might have been represented. Everywhere appearance and vision came, as it were, together in the object, in every one of them a whole inner world was exhibited, as though an angel, in whom space was included, were blind and looking into himself.'[1]

[1] Rilke, *Duino Elegies*, p. 18.

The imagery in which the mystic expresses his final affirmation of God's creation is a highly interesting and baffling question. Of necessity such an image is a mere hieroglyphic, a shorthand note rather than a simile to describe the indescribable. And such an image can never be particular, for a particular image would shatter and disintegrate, be smashed beneath the load of what it must try to contain. It is a shorthand notation that stands for an infinite list of other images that are equally translatable into an expression of the transfiguration of nature in God. Yet, while possessing a certain radiance and mystery of its own, this image must be understood to contain nothing of the power it is standing for. This is in direct opposition to the magician's attitude. The images of the poet-magician are particular, charged with concentrated power and precision, and must hold at least within the range of suggestion the truth they are trying to indicate.

Precisely because particular images cannot bear the weight of mystical vision, Blake in his later poetry never achieved the Minute Particularity he thought so important. This is a primary reason for the failure of the final Prophetic Books as poetry. His images belong rather to the heroically impersonal (yet at the same time unbearably personal) realm of archetypal patterns when the relationship of one gigantic figure to another is the important concern. One could say that such imagery lies between abstraction and the particularity of the concrete in much the same way that geometry lies between pure mathematics and the ordinary addition of apples and eggs. It is a difficult realm, an uneasy realm perhaps to many, yet it has its own validity and beauty.

All this we try to understand when we hear about the mystic's denial of images, only to find his ultimate vision expressed in some strangely moving yet elusive image. The mystic's final statement is not a philosophic one and cannot be examined as such: in fact, it maddens the rational philosopher because it presupposes a direct knowledge and love of something that can only be arrived at by him in a spirit of doubt, of 'let's see', and mental gymnastics that can only end in exhaustion. The philosopher cannot allow himself to love and believe something that he cannot prove, and the mystic cannot find his truth without love. The mystic's statement is a hieroglyphic standing for something that cannot be known in the philosopher's sense—that is, contained in the mind by a process of deduction—but that can be *seen*. And what can only be seen can only be expressed in terms of images, no matter how inadequate.

It is significant to note that the Russian Orthodox Church, in the unique position of being Christian yet non-European, should take a subtly different view of asceticism on the whole, and the role of imagination is particular. Although their common practices of fasting and discipline are much more severe than in Western Christianity, there is little or no sense of conflict and suffering in their asceticism, and the question of renouncing images does not seem now to occur. In short, the kind of dualism we have been discussing has no stronghold in Russian Orthodoxy, because it is a way of thinking more native to the Western mind. Mr. Gombrich comments on the interesting question of images and icons:

'This question of the proper purpose of art in churches proved of immense importance for the whole history of Europe. For it was one of the principal issues on which the Eastern Greek-speaking parts of the Roman Empire, whose capital was Byzantium or Constantinople, refused to accept the lead of the Latin Pope. One party there was against all images of a religious nature. They were called iconoclasts or image-smashers. In 745 they gained the upper hand and all religious art was forbidden in the Eastern Church. But their opponents were even less in agreement with Pope Gregory's ideas. To them images were not just useful, they were holy.[1] The arguments with which they tried to justify this point of view were as subtle as those used by the other party: "If God in His mercy could decide to reveal Himself to mortal eyes in the human nature of Christ," they argued, " why should He not also be willing to manifest Himself in visible images? We do not worship these images themselves as the pagans did, we worship God and the Saints through or across their images." Whatever we may think of the logic of this plea, its importance for the history of art was tremendous. For when this party had returned to power after a century of repression the paintings in a church could no longer be regarded as mere illustrations for the use of those who could not read. They were looked upon as mysterious reflections of the supernatural world. The Eastern Church, therefore, could no longer allow the artist to follow his fancy in these works. Surely it was not any beautiful painting of a mother with her child that could be accepted as the true image or "icon" of the Mother of God, but only types hallowed by an age-old tradition . . . Images such as these, looking

[1] Stemming back no doubt to such thinkers as Cyril of Alexandria.

down on us from the golden, glimmering walls, seemed to be such perfect symbols of the Holy Truth that there appeared to be no need ever to depart from them. Thus they continued to hold their sway in all countries ruled by the Eastern Church. The holy images or "icons" of the Russians still reflect these great creations of Byzantine artists.'[1]

It is interesting to note in addition that while we in the West dwell upon the cross and the purgative Way as the central fact of Christianity, the Russians emphasize the Resurrection. They go *through* the cross to resurrection, through suffering and sacrifice to affirmation, just as they go through the icons to what they represent. We, on the other hand, linger over the suffering itself, and confuse our own conflict with that on the cross. We have a very real tendency towards this confusion and towards the dualism of conflict, but we are all the same too ready to accuse others of it: as de Rougemont says of some Arabian poets:

'The symbolism employed by the poets caused them accordingly to be accused of holding disguised Manichæanism, and the charge cost al Hallaj and Suhrawardi their lives. There is something poignant in the discovery that the grounds of the controversy are those which reappear in the case of the troubadours, and later on— as we shall see—in the case of two great western mystics, Master Eckhart and John of the Cross.'[2]

There is always ground for those who wish to accuse poets or mystics of dualistic heresy. And there is also danger of the necessary dualism in the mystic way becoming static and therefore heretical.

To emphasize the similarity of final mystic affirmation to the vision of great poets (who perhaps have also passed through, intuitively or in telescoped form, similar spiritual stages), it would be well to quote both mystics and poets. St. Teresa speaks of the value of conflict:

'Our Lord leads by another way those who have not offended him so deeply, but I would always choose the way of suffering, if only to imitate our Lord Jesus Christ, and it had no other advantages; but especially when there are so many others. Oh, then if we speak of interior trials! Could we succeed in describing them, others would appear insignificant, but it is impossible to give any idea of

[1] Gombrich, *The Story of Art*, p. 97.   [2] de Rougemont, *Passion and Society*.

them. . . . They feel great envy of those who live and have lived in desert places; on the other hand, they would plunge into the midst of the world, if they could thereby in any way induce some soul to praise God more.'[1]

Poets such as Wordsworth and Blake reached through poetry a conclusion not unlike this. The word 'Romantic' is totally inadequate to describe either of these two poets. Wordsworth, like Blake, puts great emphasis on imagination—the dynamic usage of images —as an essential factor in healing the split in the human soul.

> *Imagination—here the power so-called*
> *Through sad incompetence of human speech,*
> *That awful Power, rose from the mind's abyss.*

and

> *This Spiritual love acts not nor can exist*
> *Without Imagination. . . .*
> *For they are each in each, and cannot stand*
> *Dividually.*

Rilke's view of outer nature transformed in the inner world is very poignant, and nearer to mystical affirmation than any other modern poetry, despite his anti-Christian bias and his romantic theory about love. Such a poem as 'Wendung', combining as it does a kind of wistful romanticism with the seer's vision of nature transfigured, is poetically irresistible. But in such passages of the *Duino Elegies* as the following one, there is the militant note of triumphant praise:

> *Angel,*
> *I'll show it to you as well—there! In your gaze*
> *It shall stand redeemed at last, in a final uprightness—*
> *Pillars, pylons, the sphinx, all the striving thrust,*
> *Grey, from fading or foreign town, of the spire!*
> *Was it not miracle? Angel, gaze, for it's we—*
> *O mightiness, tell them that we are capable of it—my breath's*
> *Too short for this celebration. So, after all, we have not*
> *Failed to make use of the spaces, these generous spaces, these*
> *Our spaces. (How terribly big they must be,*
> *When, with thousands of years of our feeling, they're not over-crowded.)*

---

[1] St. Teresa, *The Interior Castle*, pp. 60, 80.

But a tower was great, was it not? Oh Angel, it was, though—
Even compared with you? Chartres was great—and music
Towered still higher and passed beyond us. Why, even
A girl in love, alone, at her window, at night—
Did she not reach to your knee?[1]

Or the lovely lyric which tells us precisely of affirmation:

O tell us, Poet, what do you do? I praise.
But the dark, the deadly, the desperate ways,
How do you endure them—how bear them? I praise.
But the nameless, anonymous—which no word portrays—
What do you call that, Poet, nevertheless?—I praise.
From whence is your right your assumed role essays
To be sincere in each mask?—I praise.
And you know the stillness, and the passionate blaze
As of star, and of storm?—Because I praise.[2]

And St. Teresa's description of the sixth mansion has much in it like Wordsworth's 'light that never was', not to speak of Vaughan's descriptions; it brings to mind Blake's knowledge of eternity gained in one pulsation of the artery, and his clear visions of saints and prophets:

'It seems to her that she has been, body and soul, in a very different region from that in which we live, where a light shines quite other than the light of this world, and many other things are seen, which if she spent all her life in trying to depict them, it would be impossible to do so. At the same time she learns so many things at once, that in many years of labour, with her imagination and thought she could not sort them out, nor even one thousandth part of them. This is not an intellectual, but an imaginative vision, and it is seen with the eyes of the soul much more clearly than we here can see with the eyes of the body; some things are also explained without words. For instance, if Saints are seen, they are known as well as if much conversation had been held with them.'[3]

This is also an admonition to such mystics who, by temperament primarily ascetic, wish to banish imagination as evil. She adds:

'I think I have made it clear that however spiritual we may be, it is wise not to banish corporeal images to such a degree that we come

---

[1] Rilke, *Duino Elegies*, trans. J. B. Leishman.   [2] Rilke, *Rodin*, intro., p. xiii.
[3] St. Teresa, *The Interior Castle*, p. 77.

to regard even the most sacred Humanity as a source of danger,' and, we may add, the Incarnation as a doubtful resort of the God-head.[1]

Why all this fuss about reaching the simple fact that the mystic's affirmation is not incompatible with poetry? If so, why must every mystic reach it by a path of double dualism, with such conflict, suffering and renunciation? Could he not, like Mr. Eliot, fastidious yet wishing to remain a poet, tread the orderly short-cut to mystical vision, secure in the knowledge that he has arranged a fine welcome in heaven, and avoided the long and muddy-emotioned highway?

I would say no. The hardest thing in the world for the intellectual to learn is that he cannot do everything by means of his great talents and gifts. He must submit to Grace. And Grace, like the words of a great teacher, is given only at the moment the receiver is ready for it, neither sooner nor later. And Grace is almost inevitably accom-panied by strange new emotions, particularly the fear that further Grace will be withheld. The poorer in talent are better in accepting hardships. For how is Mr. Eliot, picking his way delicately along the pleasant short-cut, to endure the flying stones and spattering mud as the chariot of the Great Lover rushes to greet him? Yeats, in his Introduction to the *Oxford Book of Modern Verse*, speaks wisely about Eliot:

'Not until *The Hollow Men* and *Ash Wednesday*, where he is helped by the short lines, and the dramatic poems where his remark-able sense of actor, chanter, scene, sweep him away, is there rhyth-mical animation. Two or three of my friends attribute the change to an emotional enrichment from religion, but his religion, com-pared to that of John Gray, Francis Thompson, Lionel Johnson in the *Dark Angel* lacks all strong emotion; a New England Pro-testant by descent, there is little self-surrender in his personal rela-tion to God and the soul. *Murder in the Cathedral* is a powerful stage play because the actor, the monkish habit, certain repeated words, symbolize what we know, not what the author knows. . . . Speaking through Becket's mouth, Eliot confronts a world growing always more terrible with a religion like that of some great statesman, a pity not less poignant because it tempers the prayer book with the results of mathematical philosophy.'[2]

---

[1] St. Teresa, *The Interior Castle*, p. 87.
[2] *Oxford Book of Modern Verse*, p. xxii.

Like the ascetic, the modern Puritan must beware of thinking a partial truth the whole truth. For there are those, today as always, for whom it is harder *not* to become ascetics than it would be for most of us to become ascetics. It is sheer courage for these people to stay in the world and face its animality and ugliness.

The point of the 'double dualism' that must occur in the way of true mysticism is to provide a test for every kind of temperament. To have to go through complete reversals of his attitude to the world is necessary for the ascetic as well as for him who loves the world too much. It is easy to split this one long and difficult Way into two separate Ways between which the mystic can choose. But neither asceticism nor affirmation alone is a 'Way', but rather, a part of the single Way where partial truths become whole truths, and extreme states of soul are united with their opposites. In short, the conflict and apparent chaos of the mystical path are as essential as is the final vision of unity for the instruction of the soul.

Blake knew this, and illustrated it very clearly by postulating four stages of vision. An even more precise representation of this mystical process is given in the myth of the four Zoas who divide off from their true mates and so become evil if regarded as whole truths. They can only become good again by reuniting, through conflict and imaginative struggle and forgiving love, with their true mates, and so stand in harmony with each of the other Zoas. The final coming together of Jerusalem and Albion is, in effect, the coming together of intellectual discipline and intuitive imaginative understanding, along with all the warring opposites than can be ranged under these two headings. This is why the terms of mysticism shift and slide and jostle one another, and why they seem to the layman so misty and vague. In actual fact the terms of the true mystic are quite precise, although in an effort to embrace and telescope too much, they often seem very abstract and abstruse, while the commentaries on the mystical process are even cloudier.

I have made no attempt to answer Yeats' headache about the relation of magic to the saint's vision—whether they can, as it were, exist side by side in the same sensitive mind. I will not go any further than to suggest once more in this as in related questions the attitude to images and to seeing in the key point. In my opinion, the attitude of the magician cannot exist simultaneously with the attitude of the saint, although it can conceivably be of help in shaking loose the greater vision.

I would suggest that the attitude of the magician must disappear in the face of the greater insight of the saint, although it may have served its purpose. The horizontal dynamics of evocation which is the magician's job must come to rest in the final evocation—as one might be permitted to call the vision of the saint without forgetting the vertical dynamics of Grace. Images remain, albeit thin and hieroglyphic, for the sake of communication, but the magician's attitude to images is transformed into something else.

Conflict, over-againstness, shock tactics which must be the equipment of the working magician belong to the period of dualism and can very well go hand in hand with poetry, but not with the vision of nature transformed. Magic which is naturalistic must die its natural death. There is no need for its kind of forced knowledge in the Nature that is resurrected into unity.

There is, however, a curious and illuminating parallel in the experience of depth psychology. I would call this problem of the relation of psychological technique to religious experience the more living terms in which Yeats' problem of magic and sanctity can be seen. It is true that the psychologist is not exactly a magician, but he does nevertheless have the attitude of a highly skilled magician to images which he uses as evocative instruments to probe the hidden depths of the patient's mind. He makes use of dream states and induced trance and shock tactics. And it is true that the vision of himself that the patient must see before he can be healed has nothing to do with mystical vision; it is also true that psychologically it tells of 'his fall into division and resurrection into unity'.

Breakdown is very close to despair. Psychology, or, if you will, skilled magic, can probe until it finds the hidden reasons for despair, the sickness unto death, but it cannot give of itself that faith that things can come right which is the vision necessary for healing. To make the patient *see* where things went wrong is the trick, and no man wants to be made to look at the chaos within himself unless a way out of it is offered simultaneously. Faith is often very close to healing because it gives the necessary courage to accept the wrongness of the *status quo*. This sudden *seeing* of the patient seems to be a gift from the unknown coming without warning and without apparent physical causation. Some scientists believe that when more research has been done, this effect will be found to have a naturalistic cause. However, it seems quite clear to me that this missing link between what the technique of psychology unearths and the seeing that makes healing possible must always be of the nature of faith, and that the positivist will reluctantly have to admit that it is a faith or belief in the resurrecting power of something outside himself—be it only some magical pill!—that is the cause for this particular effect in the patient. As behaviour is their prime concern, it seems only logical that this outside power to be believed in will impose order on the interior chaos, i.e. offer some workable ethic. This effect may be produced by the patient's faith in his physician, but this cannot be a permanent relation of spoon feeding with its tendency to permanent transference, even obsession.

This seems to me where the value of the priest who is also a psychiatrist is to be seen. He offers a belief more than the rabbit out of the hat that lopes around so clumsily after the first thrill of its magical entrance. He is important not only because he can incorporate into religion much of the valuable and rich human material it lost with the exclusion of myth, folklore, superstititions and magical rites, but because over and above his power to unearth the horrific archetypal patterns of mental illness, he also has the power to absolve from sin and guilt which always accompanies these discoveries and distinguish true from false guilt. He offers, too, a set of values to impose order on chaos, and a firm persuasion that if these values are accepted things will come right. He offers control for the unknown forces discovered in the self. He is intercessor in a double capacity. He has more than usual strength and an unpossessive love necessary to set the patient free as soon as he can stand on his own feet. Finally, what he offers in the way of belief remains after the intercessor himself has withdrawn. This seems to me the true place where a certain kind of skilled magical technique and sanctity *must* almost exist side by side in the healer if there are to be results. The priest-psychologist or just the psychologist who himself has faith and recognizes the role of faith in healing may be neither a saint nor a magician, but he will be getting into their proper relation these two kinds of vision that Yeats very rightly felt should not exclude one another. Blake enfolded the psychological attitude within Christianity.

Blake knew all about despair and writes his annals of despair, 'his fall into division', in the *Four Zoas*. But in this chaotic book he has also glimpsed what is needed for 'resurrection into unity' and tells movingly how powerless is psychological probing and examination *alone* to cure this despair at the sense of sin and nothingness:

> *Why wilt thou Examine every little fibre of my soul,*
> *Spreading them out before the sun like stalks of flax to dry?*
> *The infant joy is beautiful, but its anatomy*
> *Horrible, Ghast and Deadly; nought shalt thou find in it*
> *But Death, Despair and Everlasting brooding Melancholy.*
> *Thou wilt go mad with horror if thou dost Examine thus*
> *Every moment of my secret hours. Yea, I know*
> *That I have sinn'd, and that my Emanations have become harlots.*
> *I am already distracted at their deeds, and if I look*
> *Upon them more, Despair will bring self-murder on my soul . . .*
> > *I am like an atom,*
> *A Nothing, left in darkness; yet I am an identity:*
> *I wish and feel and weep and groan. Ah, terrible! terrible!*

It is no accident that romanticism echoes very startlingly the myths of dualistic gnosticism (as the emphasis on an earth weary and in chains because it is somehow guilty of a great discrepancy between the Creator's plan and the actuality) and that these same myths recur in the modern psychotic. It is no accident that the most sensitive minds of the eighteenth century heralded our own age of breakdown. The fall into division the gnostics and subsequent sects tried to solve by being impossibly spiritual and without success for they denied one side of the Incarnation yet acted with depravity. The romantic glories in the split and his own cosmic suffering. Today when breakdown is a mass product and everyone talks the jargon of psychology we are in danger of finding our solution as inadequate as the earlier dualists found theirs, for we are denying the spiritual ethical side of the Incarnation and depending on a relative materialism for the revelation of healing. It will not come from science or psychology itself, but only when it is doing its work almost in order to shake loose a vision which it humbly acknowledges as greater than itself.

The Middle Ages seems to be the only time that the Incarnation was really understood. The attitude of the great 'Summa's' reached into every recess of ordinary life. Things spiritual and physical rushed together and were understood as together in a curiously hodge-podge form. There was no need to specify what was the province of magic or literature or understanding of people or of religion. The Reformation perhaps helped to exclude from religion all that area of human activity found in magic, folklore, etc., and to exclude the spirit of this was a bad thing, although technically magic and myth are at war with religion. We have lost much of understanding shown by medieval people who would rush to get a priest to exorcise a devil from a sick friend. They knew that the friend was no longer himself, that he had a devil inside him, and that it was weak of him to let it happen. This reveals a profound understanding of what is mental sickness and what the self is responsible for in terms of good and evil. Religion, magic, psychology, and a highly dramatic sense of artistic presentation are part and parcel of such an ordinary medieval occurrence, and they did not have to scratch their heads to wonder whether it would be best to call a doctor, a priest, or a sorcerer—they understood that elements of all three were implicit in the situation and they rallied to the drama of it.

A brief summary of my main points is perhaps necessary here lest this commentary seem too cloudy. I hoped to show that dualism is a way of thought native to the Western mind, so native that it appears in the core of mystical Christianity itself. I suggest that this way of thinking lying at the core of Christian belief is always in danger of becoming heretical, but that in the danger itself lies the hope of recovery—that is, that this dichotomy can be overcome by going through two consecutive dualisms, the second a healing one. This is the essence of the mystical Way and this is what the critic of mysticism rarely sees. It also makes clear the link with poetry.

For the mystic's first dualism is no more than the age-old division between body and soul that troubles the romantic poet of every age. But where the poet may be waylaid by delight in the poignance of schizophrenia itself, or definitely choose to be on the side of sensual beauty, he who is to be a mystic, focuses for a moment his own division and suffering in the figure of Christ: he sees the meaning of Incarnation where body and spirit rush together instead of straining apart, even against his pre-knowledge of the cross. The mystic resolves to become worthy of this great Actuality.

It is here that he enters into the second dualism, what the critics think is a choice depending on his temperament as to whether he takes the road of affirmation or of denial. But I would like to suggest that denial or asceticism is and must be only a stage that comes before affirmation; that there is, in fact, no dualism at all although it looks and feels like one to all concerned. Most dangerous of all, it *could* always turn into some form of schizophrenia such as gnosticism, and that gnosticism has very aptly been called the pathological phase of mysticism I have already noted. This can happen quite easily if the meaning of the Incarnation is not kept firmly in mind.

The stage of asceticism or denial is in fact the crucial point, the testing ground and the psychological event that stands between poetry and mysticism. The ascetic must renounce all images, particularly the images of erotic love, and it seems to him in his heightened state of awareness induced by bodily and spiritual discipline that he has reached nothingness, that he has been deserted by God and has no glimpses of Him through the senses that he has tried to subjugate in an effort to achieve death-in-life. The romantic poet longs for death: the ascetic longs for death of the senses, death-in-life. But suddenly and purely through grace—possibly, but not always in proportion to his denial of Selfhood,—the enjoyment of his senses is restored to the mystic and he is completely overcome by the sweetness of the vision vouchsafed to him of all nature transformed and resurrected in Christ. There is no question once this vision has been granted of his wishing to focus his love and desire on some earthly creature as there might have been earlier. And yet, so inadequate is language that he must express what he has seen in terms of the least corrupted earthly images he can find, such as light or a garden or a clear fountain of water, and like as not he will express his union with God in terms of human love—the image of the bride and bridegroom. The poet and the lover are sometimes resurrected in the saint but only because they were willing to die, as Christ was willing to die.

It is fairly clear that the ascetic stage must neither be seen as the whole truth nor left out of the picture. Blake sought to avoid it by equating religion and imagination and postulating the senses as direct gateways to eternity. This was a striving towards a doctrine of redemption built on the vision of incarnation. Yet there was something missing—a certain humility perhaps and the realization that personal incarnation is achieved not by will but by grace—until he was forced in actual fact to go through that dark night of the soul he called his sleep on the banks of the ocean. It involved, I am sure, a certain letting go of his human love for his wife which was at that time making her so unhappy because of its almost perverted intensity

—until he came to see that their human love was at the same time union with Christ. Then truly the senses became the gateways to eternity.

All this is to suggest the likenesses and differences between poetry and mysticism, and that the mystic in his final stage can at the same time be a poet, while the 'romantic' poet need never have anything to do with mystical vision, remaining as he does in the initial dualism which merely recognizes the disease without wishing or attempting to be cured of it. And yet he may be a very good poet.

Yeats was the latter. It would be nice to feel that out of all Yeats' strange and difficult 'mystical' machinery he had salvaged something of this essentially simple principle of the mystical Way. Certainly, for all he would have us believe, he never came anywhere near to mystical vision. He came nearest to understanding the mystic in the question he wrote quite simply in his diary: 'Why does a struggle to come at truth take away our poetry and the struggle to overcome our passions restore it again?' But unfortunately the published comments on his own mystical proficiency right up to the end show little more than an excessive pride in having created a 'mystical' symbolism as complicated as the most esoteric:

'Some, perhaps all, of those readers I most value, those who have read me many years, will be repelled by what must seem an arbitrary, harsh, difficult symbolism. Yet such has almost always accompanied expression that unites the sleeping and the waking mind. One remembers the six wings of Daniel's angels, the Pythagorean numbers, a venerated book of the Cabala where the beard of God winds in and out among the stars, its hairs all numbered, those complicated mathematic tables that Kelly saw in Dr. Dee's black scrying-stone, the diagrams in Law's *Boehme*, where one lifts a flap of paper to discover both the human entrails and the starry heavens. William Blake thought these diagrams worthy of Michelangelo but remains himself almost incomprehensible because he never drew the like. We can (those hard symbolic bones under the skin) substitute for a treatise on logic the *Divine Comedy*, or some little song about a rose, or be content to live our thought.'[1]

Alas, Yeats' ambition in mysticism remained that of finding a symbol as esoteric as 'the beard of God' winding in and out among the stars, 'its hairs all numbered.'

[1] Yeats, *A Vision*, p. 23.

Speaking of the hero of his story *The Tables of the Law*, Yeats in his unpublished diary is, in effect, speaking of himself:

'I see now what is wrong. . . . He is not the mask but the face. He realizes himself. He cannot obtain vision in the ordinary sense. He is himself its centre. Perhaps he dreams he is speaking. He is not spoken to. He puts himself in place of Christ.'[1]

When all is said and done, Yeats knew he was not like his master, Blake, and knew exactly why: he has had no supernatural vision because he is too much interested in himself and the division in himself to be open to grace. This, somehow, is much more likable, because sincere, than all the elaborate justification of *A Vision*. It took courage for Yeats to admit that he did not attain what he longed for most in life.

[1] Unpublished diary, Yeats.

APPENDIX

Page 64

A marginal note in the Yeats and Ellis Blake (Vol. I, p. 2) on Blake's 'Irish extraction', says: 'My authority for Blake's Irish extraction was Dr. Carter Blake, who claims to be descended from a branch of the family that settled in Mullingan and entered the wine trade there. W. B. Y.'

The following letter from Dr. Carter Blake's daughter shows that she had not heard of the claim to be related to the poet. Nevertheless, Yeats went on publishing his theory that Blake was Irish, an O'Neill.

'Barkley, Gwelo, S. Rhodesia.
         22. iv: 06.

Dear Sir,

I am in receipt of your letter of March 5th and also of the little book, for which many thanks.

I am the daughter of Dr. Charles Carter Blake, but I am afraid that I can give you little help as to the confirmation of the tradition you mention in your book.

My father had an ancestor, I believe, one John O'Neill, a native of the Co. Tyrone; but I never heard him, or his mother, my grandmother, mention any connection with the family of William Blake, the poet.

I am in possession of papers of my father's which show that my grandfather, Charles Blake, lived near Valparaiso. The only dates I could give you are those of my grandfather's marriage and death.

Yours sincerely,

J. J. M. Blake.'

Page 136

Yet Yeats was aware of the danger in the gnostic glorification of reason. In his unpublished diary, August, 1910, he writes: 'I know that reason is almost a blasphemous thing, a claim to an infinity of being while we are limited social creatures half artificial. No, a hundred times, if I had acted upon impulse and against reason, I should have created a finer world of rights and wrongs, a more personal and passionate life than impersonal reason could give. Reason is the stopping of the pendulum, a kind of death. . . . The passionate man must believe he obeys his reason.'

Page 203

Reinhold Niebuhr seems to me to sum up what Blake would have called 'Organized Innocence' in the following words:

'Spiritual health in both individuals and societies is an achievement of maturity in which some excellency of childhood is consciously reclaimed, after being lost in the complexities of life. It is an inner integrity not on this but the other side of inner conflict; it is sincerity not on this but the other side of a contrite recognition of the deceitfulness of the human heart; it is trust in the goodness of life not on this but the other side of disillusionment and despair; it is naïveté and serenity not on this, but the other side of sophistication.'

Dr. Niebuhr speaks also of the delightful sense of humour of the saints who have attained this maturity:

'This sense of humour is based upon a curious quality of disillusionment which has not resulted in either bitterness or despair. . . . This quality of mirthful serenity is unlike the innocency of childhood which knows no evil. It has looked into the abyss of evil and is no longer affrighted by it.'

Beyond Tragedy, pp. 150–51.

Page 213

It is interesting to note that if, as Freud suggests, the sexual impulse is a desire to escape the pain of tension rather than a search for pleasure—then an asceticism of the senses becomes the individual wish to *endure* pain and tension as purification rather than a condemnation *per se* of whatever is pleasurable.

This would seem to me to be much closer to the fierce and almost masochistic spirit of the desert fathers than the modern interpretation or perversion of asceticism—the puritan conscience—would allow, with its wholesale and guilt-ridden condemnation of anything that is touched by earth or joy.

It is perhaps as well to add that the ascetic wish to endure such tension *in general* (for the sake of purgation in preparation for mystical union) has little to do with the secular question of love for a particular person, whether dualistic and unfulfilled as in the troubadour ideal or incarnate as in the coming together of Albion and Jerusalem (William and Catherine). In the latter case, particular union widens out into union in and with Christ.

It is not, in short, a question of asceticism because painful being superior and less guilty than the state of marriage and family life. It is rather a case for clear-cut individual choice, without condemnation of or escapism from the other side. Both ways are capable of highest sanctity or of profoundest error.

BIBLIOGRAPHY

BLAKE: PRIMARY SOURCES

The Works of William Blake, Poetic, Symbolic and Critical. Edited with lithographs of the illustrated Prophetic Books and a memoir and interpretation by E. J. Ellis and W. B. Yeats. 3 vols. London, 1893.

The Poems of W. Blake, ed. by W. B. Yeats, London, 1893.

Poems of William Blake, ed. by W. B. Yeats (The Muses Library), London, 1906.

The Poetical Works of William Blake, ed. and annotated by Edwin J. Ellis. 2 vols. London, 1906.

    All of the illustrated original Blake books and pictures owned by the Bodleian, the British Museum, the Tate Gallery, the Metropolitan Museum of New York, the Morgan Library, the Washington Museum of Art, and the New York Public Library. Also the private collection of Mr. George Goyder, Rotherfield Greys, Oxon.

The Complete Poetry of William Blake, The Modern Library, New York, 1946.

Blair, *The Grave*, designs by William Blake, London.

Blake, *Songs of Innocence and Experience*, Albion Facsimiles, London, 1947.

Blake, *The Letters of William Blake*, together with his life, by F. Tatham, ed. by A. G. B. Russell, London, 1906.

——, *The Marriage of Heaven and Hell*, facsimile, London, 1927.

——, *The Book of Thel*, facsimile, London, 1928.

Catalogue of an Exhibit of original works by William Blake from the Graham Robertson Collection, 1948.

BLAKE: SECONDARY SOURCES

Berger, Pierre, *William Blake—Mysticisme et Poésie*, Paris, 1907.

Blunt, Anthony, 'Blake's Pictorial Imagination', *Journal of the Warburg and Courtauld Inst.*, vol. 6, 1943.

Chesterton, G. K., *William Blake*, London, 1911.

Coutts, Francis, *The Heresy of Job*, London, 1907.

Damon, Foster, *William Blake*, New York, 1924.

Davies, J. D., *The Theology of William Blake*, Oxford, 1948.

de Selincourt, B., *William Blake*, London, 1909.

Ellis, Edwin J., *The Real Blake*, London, 1907.

Frye, Northrop, *Fearful Symmetry: A Study of William Blake*, Princeton, 1947.

Garnett, Richard, *William Blake: The Portfolio*, London, 1895.

Gilchrist, Alexander, *The Life of William Blake*, London, 1907.

MacDonald, G., *The Sanity of William Blake: A Critical Essay*, London, 1906.

Preston, Kerrison, *Blake and Rossetti*, London, 1944.

Saurat, Denis, *Blake and Modern Thought*, London, 1929.

Swainson, W. P., *William Blake: Poet, Seer and Artist*, London, 1908.

Swinburne, A. C., *William Blake: A Critical Essay*, London, 1906.

Wicksteed, Joseph H., *Blake's Vision of the Book of Job*, London, 1910.

Witcutt, W. P., *Blake, a Psychological Study*, London, 1946.

W. B. YEATS: PRIMARY SOURCES

The Collected Plays of W. B. Yeats, London, 1934.

The Collected Poems of W. B. Yeats, London and New York, 1943.

Last Poems and Plays, London and New York, 1940.

Autobiography, London and New York, 1938.

Four Plays for Dancers, London, 1921.

The Player Queen, London, 1922.

Plays and Controversies, London, 1923.

Essays—Ideas of Good and Evil; The Cutting of an Agate; Per Amica Silentia Lunae, London, 1924.

A Vision, London, 1925.

A Vision, London, 1937.

Estrangement, Dublin, 1926.

Stories of Michael Robartes and His Friends, Dublin, 1931.

Letters to the New Island.

The Words upon the Window Pane, Dublin, 1934.

Wheels and Butterflies, London, 1934.

The Celtic Twilight, London, 1893.

The King of the Great Clock Tower, Dublin, 1934.

A Full Moon in March, London, 1935.

Essays '31–'36, Dublin, 1937.

The Herne's Egg, a play, London, 1938.

On the Boiler, Dublin, 1938.

'If I Were Four and Twenty', Swedenborg, Mediums and Desolate Places, Dublin, 1940.

Pages from a Diary Written in 1930, Dublin, 1944.

Ideas of Good and Evil, London, 1903.

Letters on Poetry to Dorothy Wellesley, London and New York, 1940.

BIBLIOGRAPHY

Per Amica Silentia Lunae, London, 1918.
The Oxford Book of Modern Verse, chosen by W. B. Yeats, Oxford, 1947.
Florence Farr, 'Bernard Shaw, W. B. Yeats,' *Letters*, London, 1946.
Unpublished material in the possession of Mrs. Yeats.

W. B. YEATS: SECONDARY SOURCES

Scattering Branches—tributes to the memory of W. B. Yeats, London, 1940.
The Arrow, Summer, 1939. W. B. Yeats Commemoration Number, Dublin, 1939.
The Permanence of Yeats. Selected Criticism, edited by James Hall and Martin Steinmann, New York, 1950.
Colum, Mary, *Life and the Dream*, London, 1947.
Ellman, Richard, *Yeats: The Man and the Masks*, London and New York, 1948.
Henn, T. R., *The Lonely Tower*, London, 1950.
Hone, J. M., *W. B. Yeats*, London, 1942.
Jeffares, A. N., *W. B. Yeats: Man and Poet*, London, 1949.
MacNeice, F. L., *The Poetry of W. B. Yeats*, London, 1941.
Masefield, J., *Some Memories of W. B. Yeats*, London, 1940.
Menon, N., *The Development of W. B. Yeats*, London, 1942.
O'Donnell, J. P., *Sailing to Byzantium*, Harvard, 1939.
Ure, Peter, *Towards a Mythology*, London, 1946.
Yeats, J. B., *Letters to his Son W. B. Yeats and Others*, London and New York, 1946.

MISCELLANEOUS

Berdyaev, Nicholas, *Freedom and the Spirit*, London, 1938.
——, *Solitude and Society*, London, 1938.
Boehme, Jacob, *Mysterium Magnum*, trans. Berdyaev, Paris, 1945.
Bullett, Gerald, *The English Mystics*, London, 1950.
Butler, Dom Cuthbert, *Western Mysticism*, London, 1951.
D'Arcy, Martin C., *The Mind and Heart of Love*, London, 1945.
Eglinton, J., *Irish Literary Portraits*.
Eliot, T. S., *The Cocktail Party*, London, 1950.
Gilson, Étienne, *La Théologie Mystique de St. Bernard*, Paris, 1934.
——, *Pétrarque et sa Muse*, London, 1946. Deneke Lecture.
Gogarty, O. St. J., *As I was Going Down Sackville Street*, London.
Heath Stubbs, John, *The Darkling Plain*, London, 1950.
Hough, Graham, *The Last Romantics*, London, 1949.
St. John of the Cross, *The Dark Night of the Soul*, London, 1916.
Julian of Norwich, *Revelations of Divine Love*, London, 1949.
Lewis, C. S., *The Allegory of Love*, Oxford, 1936.
Lucas, F. L., *The Decline and Fall of the Romantic Ideal*, Cambridge, 1948.

BIBLIOGRAPHY

Maritain, J., *Art and Poetry*, London, 1945.

Moore, George, *Hail and Farewell*, 2 vols., London.

Niebuhr, R., *Beyond Tragedy*, London, 1947.

Peers, Allison, *Spirit of Flame*, London, 1943.

Rilke, R. M., *Rodin*, London, 1946.

——, *Sonnets to Orpheus*, trans. J. B. Leishman, London, 1949.

——, *Requiem and Other Poems*, trans. J. B. Leishman, London, 1949.

——, *Duino Elegies*, trans. J. B. Leishman, London, 1948.

——, *The Notebook of Malte Laurids Brigge*, trans. John Linton, London, 1930.

Steiner, Rudolf, *Jacob Boehme*, London, 1942.

St. Teresa, *The Interior Castle*, London, 1945.

Todd, Ruthven, *Tracks in the Snow*, London, 1946.

Underhill, Evelyn, intro. *The Cloud of Unknowing*, London, 1946.

Waddell, Helen, *The Desert Fathers*, London, 1936.

——, *Medieval Latin Lyrics*, London, 1948.

——, *Lyrics from the Chinese*, London, 1947.

Williams, Charles *The Figure of Beatrice*, London, 1943.

——, *The Descent of the Dove*, London, 1939.

Wilson, Edmund, *Axel's Castle*, London.

INDEX

INDEX